THE
VALUE-ADDED
TAX

The Value-Added Tax

Key to Deficit Reduction?

Charles E. McLure, Jr.

with Commentary by
Mark A. Bloomfield

American Enterprise Institute for Public Policy Research
Washington, D.C.

Charles E. McLure, Jr., is a senior fellow at the Hoover Institution. From 1980 to 1985 he was deputy assistant secretary for tax policy at the U.S. Treasury. Mark A. Bloomfield is president of the American Council for Capital Formation.

Distributed by arrangement with

UPA, Inc.
4720 Boston Way
Lanham, MD 20706
3 Henrietta Street
London WC2E 8LU, England

Library of Congress Cataloging-in-Publication Data

McLure, Charles E.
  The value-added tax.

  (AEI studies ; 450)
  Includes index.
  1. Value-added tax—United States. 2. Budget
deficits—United States. I. Bloomfield, Mark A.
II. Title. III. Series.
HJ5715.U6M364 1987   339.5′25′0973   86-28905
ISBN 0-8447-3613-9 (alk. paper)
ISBN 0-8447-3614-7 (pbk. : alk paper)

1 3 5 7 9 10 8 6 4 2

AEI Studies 450

Printed in the United States of America

To Dick, John, and Carl,
who taught me
about these things

Contents

LIST OF TABLES

FIGURE

COMMENTARY TABLES

Foreword

The value-added tax is a revenue measure indistinguishable in the eyes of taxpayers from a national sales tax. It is widely employed in Europe as a supplement to the income tax. Various forms of a value-added tax are at this time (early 1987) being considered in Canada and Japan. The value-added tax raises many important issues of public policy, among them its relation to state and local sales taxes, its effect on international competitiveness, and the relative burdens it places on taxpayers with different incomes.

In this volume Charles McLure expands and updates his earlier discussion of the value-added tax, published by the American Enterprise Institute in 1972. He pays special attention to the business transfer tax, a version of the value-added tax discussed extensively during deliberations on tax reform that is also under serious consideration by Canada. We are pleased to include in this volume a second discussion of the value-added tax by Mark A. Bloomfield, president of the American Council for Capital Formation.

We at AEI believe that a full airing of the value-added tax is especially appropriate at this time. With budget deficits hovering at 5 percent of GNP and federal spending approximately five percentage points above its postwar norm as a share of GNP, the United States faces some important decisions. Either spending by the federal government will have to be curtailed, or revenue will have to be enhanced. In a country having one of the lowest rates of saving in the industrial world, a tax on consumption such as the value-added tax can be expected to receive careful consideration as a revenue source regardless of choices about expenditures.

JOHN H. MAKIN
Director, Fiscal Policy Studies
American Enterprise Institute

Summary

Interest in the value-added tax (VAT), a form of sales tax on consumption, will increase as the Gramm-Rudman-Hollings targets for deficit reduction become increasingly difficult to achieve through budget cuts. This monograph describes the implementation and economic effects of the VAT.

The VAT would clearly be superior to various alternative sources of revenue that have recently been proposed (such as taxes on energy and increased excise taxes), especially if a substantial amount of additional revenue is needed. It would be preferable to the simpler and more familiar retail sales tax if the combined federal, state, and local sales tax rate were to exceed about 10 percent; at lower rates the retail tax might be preferable. The choice is complicated by the need to coordinate state and federal actions in the sales tax area, since such coordination might imply substantial loss of state fiscal sovereignty.

Several recent proposals for a VAT—most notably the business transfer tax (BTT) proposed by Senator William Roth (Republican, Delaware)—are based on a highly defective means of implementing the VAT, rather than the method employed in virtually all VAT countries. If the VAT were chosen, it should employ the standard method used in Europe, rather than that of the BTT.

For administrative and political reasons, the VAT would probably not apply to more than about 80 percent of consumption. Thus the tax base at 1988 levels would be about $2,500 billion, at most. More liberal exemptions (for example, for food) could reduce the tax base to less than 50 percent of consumption, or $1,500 billion.

The VAT would interfere relatively little with economic decision making and would not discriminate against saving; in both these

The author wishes to thank Yolanda Henderson, Jonathan Kesselman, John Makin, Eugene Steuerle, and especially Carl Shoup for comments on earlier drafts of this monograph. In addition, discussions with Satya Poddar and other members of the staff of the Finance Ministry of Canada have been invaluable in stimulating thought about the attributes of the variants of the subtraction method of imposing the value-added tax.

respects it is superior to the income tax. It would probably cause a one-time increase in prices but not an acceleration of inflation. Contrary to widespread expectations, introduction of a VAT would not, per se, significantly improve the competitive position of the United States, although substituting it for part of the corporate income tax might do so. The proposition that adoption of a VAT would lead to an increase in government spending has recently been questioned.

As a tax on consumption, the VAT would be regressive (taking a higher fraction of low incomes than of high incomes). Regressivity would be reduced by the existing indexation of many transfer payments, but burdens on some low-income households would remain. Exemption of food and other necessities is a blunt and inefficient means of reducing regressivity; it is almost universally condemned by experts on the VAT. Much more effective techniques for reducing burdens on low-income households would be a system of low-income allowances or a novel VAT system that included personal exemptions.

1
Introduction

For at least twenty years certain segments of the American business community have shown sporadic interest in proposals for an American tax on value added, a form of sales tax that is levied as goods and services move through the production-distribution process rather than only at the retail stage, as under state sales taxes.[1] Initial interest in the value-added tax (VAT) during the 1960s can be traced largely to a belief that substituting a VAT for part of the corporate income tax would improve the U.S. balance of payments. A second wave of interest was created by President Richard M. Nixon's 1972 speculations that revenues from a federal VAT might be employed to lighten the burden of local property taxes used to finance public education.[2] A third round of interest in the VAT, during 1979 and 1980, was cut short by the defeat of one of its advocates, Representative Al Ullman, then chairman of the House Ways and Means Committee.[3]

Interest in the VAT has recently revived. Even before passage of the Gramm-Rudman-Hollings legislation mandating elimination of the federal budget deficit, some business groups saw the VAT as a means of reducing the budget deficit and thereby increasing capital formation and stemming the capital inflows stimulated by high interest rates, inducing a drop in the value of the dollar, and improving the competitive position of the U.S. economy in world markets.[4] The passage of Gramm-Rudman-Hollings increases the likelihood that a significant new source of revenue will be sought within the next few years to deal with the problem of budget deficits.[5]

While President Ronald Reagan continues to say that he will not accept any new taxes, even to meet the targets for deficit reduction in Gramm-Rudman-Hollings, the view that taxes will soon need to be raised is increasingly widely held. Although many observers believe that the VAT is the best vehicle for increasing federal revenues, various other sources of additional revenue have recently been proposed during congressional consideration of income tax reform. These include a tax on imported oil, a tax on all oil, a tax on all consumption of energy, a tax on gasoline, and an increase in excise

3

taxes and tariffs. Although these alternatives are no longer being actively discussed, they may reappear if concern for the need to reduce the federal deficit grows.

Although the major European countries have had almost twenty years of experience with a comprehensive VAT that extends to the retail stage, the tax is virtually unknown in the United States, except to a handful of tax experts and to business people who have operated under it in Europe or elsewhere.[6] As a result, neither the mechanics of the VAT nor its likely economic effects are well known in the United States. Even worse, the potential administrative pitfalls and adverse economic effects of a carelessly designed VAT are not well understood or appreciated.

Many observers believe, for example, that the mere imposition of a VAT would cause a structural improvement in the U.S. balance of trade, although virtually all economists who have considered the issue dismiss this possibility as extremely unlikely.[7] Others suggest that the regressivity of the VAT could be offset by differential rates on necessities, ordinary products, and luxury items, disregarding the virtually unanimous opinion based on European experience that imposing a highly differentiated rate structure is a serious mistake.[8] Finally, many economists who understand the concept of value added seem to presume that the subtraction method would be employed to implement an American VAT; almost no one really understands the economic, administrative, and political significance of the differences between the credit and the subtraction methods or why virtually no other country has opted to employ the latter.[9]

This monograph is an attempt to clarify these and other issues in the debate over value-added taxation. It is divided into two major sections. The first, consisting of chapters 2 to 5, is a general discussion of the nature and the pros and cons of the VAT. It expands on this introduction to discuss in somewhat greater detail the need for increased federal revenues (chapter 2); indicates the nature, operation, and likely base of a VAT (chapter 3); describes the likely economic effects of a VAT and summarizes European experience with the VAT and its relevance for the United States (chapter 4); and compares the advantages and disadvantages of a VAT with those of several alternative sources of revenue (chapter 5). Although political judgments are made at various points, for the most part political issues receive little attention—certainly less than in the essay by Mark Bloomfield in this volume.[10]

The second major section, consisting of chapters 6 to 9, deals with more technical issues in the design and functioning of a VAT and with

4

important policy issues that require for their comprehension an understanding of those technical issues. The technical design issues discussed in chapter 6 include the relative merits of the credit and subtraction methods of implementing a VAT, the difference between zero rating and exemptions, and the implications of differential rates. (The addition method is discussed only in the appendix to chapter 6.) The chapter notes that the subtraction method is appropriate only if the VAT is to be applied universally and at a single rate; exemptions and multiple rates cause substantial difficulties that render the method unworkable. The business transfer tax (BTT) and the Hall-Rabushka proposal for a flat-rate tax with personal exemptions clearly belong to the subtraction category. Because of the likelihood that, for both political and administrative reasons, the BTT would not be levied at a uniform rate on a comprehensive base, the subtraction method underlying it should be rejected.

Chapter 7 compares the VAT with other forms of general sales tax, especially the retail sales tax. Chapter 8 discusses possible ways of dealing with particular industries—for example, financial services and life insurance, nonprofit institutions, housing, farming, and small business—that cannot readily be taxed under normal VAT procedures or that are sometimes accorded special treatment, whether for political or for administrative reasons. Although it emphasizes how these problems are or can be handled under the credit method, it also notes problems that would be especially troublesome under the subtraction method, including Senator Roth's proposal for an extraordinarily large exemption for "small business."

Chapter 9 briefly considers issues of intergovernmental relations posed by the possibility of federal adoption of the VAT or other form of sales tax. These include preemption of the sales tax base, the need to harmonize sales taxes levied by the federal, state, and local governments, and the possibility of piggybacking state sales taxes (either retail sales taxes or VATs) on a federal VAT or retail sales tax.

Chapter 10 presents a brief summary and the conclusions of the study. Several of these conclusions deserve special attention. There is much to be said for a VAT, if it is agreed that additional federal revenue is needed. But the subtraction method that underlies the proposal for a BTT is distinctly inferior to the credit method used elsewhere and should be rejected. Finally, the problems of intergovernmental relations that would be raised by federal entry into the sales tax area are serious; indeed, they may determine whether the United States should adopt a national sales tax and, if so, whether a VAT or a retail sales tax would be more appropriate.

5

The proposals for a federal VAT that have received the most publicity are those by Senator William V. Roth, Jr. (Republican, Delaware).[11] Under Roth's latest proposal a BTT would be levied on the difference between receipts from domestic sales and purchases of inputs, such as raw materials and capital. The BTT would differ from the VATs employed elsewhere, especially in the European Economic Community (EEC), in three fundamental respects.

First, it would be based on the subtraction method, rather than the invoice or credit method (these technical terms are explained in chapter 3) that is mandatory in the EEC and used almost universally elsewhere. The subtraction method was presumably chosen to make the true nature of the BTT somewhat less obvious and thereby to increase its political attraction. Roth may also think that a subtraction-method tax would be simpler than a credit-method tax, to the extent that it builds on the concepts and administrative machinery of the income tax, rather than requiring a new and different administrative mechanism, and that it could therefore be introduced more quickly.[12]

Second, the Roth proposal would allow liability for the BTT to be credited against the payroll taxes used to finance social security (the FICA taxes), presumably to enhance the likelihood that the international competitiveness of U.S. industry would be improved. Third, the Roth proposal would exempt from the BTT any business with gross receipts of less than $10 million.

The proposals to use the subtraction method, to allow the FICA offset, and to provide such a large exemption for small business are all unwise. The subtraction method would almost certainly create severe administrative difficulties and economic distortions unless implemented in such a way as to make the tax virtually indistinguishable from a flat-rate VAT using the commonplace credit method. This is particularly troublesome since the subtraction method creates strong incentives for political efforts to achieve differential treatment, incentives that are largely absent under the credit method.

With differential taxation of various activities, it would also be impossible to compensate exactly for the BTT for goods moving in international trade. (These assertions are explained in chapter 6.) Moreover, it is quite unlikely that border tax adjustments for the BTT would even be allowable under the General Agreement on Tariffs and Trade (GATT) unless the offset against FICA taxes were eliminated. (Chapter 6 explains why the BTT with the FICA offset would not be legal under the GATT.)

Finally, exemptions from the tax base are much more troublesome under a subtraction-method tax than under the credit-method taxes employed in Europe. (This is explained in chapters 6 and 8.) Even so, the small-business exemption proposed by Roth is much larger than those allowed in Europe.

A subtraction-method VAT is also implicit in a proposal for income tax reform by Robert Hall and Alvin Rabushka of the Hoover Institution.[13] Seen from the perspective of a VAT, this tax is novel in at least two additional ways. It is constructed in such a way that personal exemptions can be allowed for workers, and it is levied on the origin principle, rather than the commonly employed destination principle (two more terms to be explained in chapter 3). The "personal exemption VAT" deserves consideration in the debate because it offers a promising way to deal with the potential regressivity of the VAT.[14]

Notes

1. The first round of business interest in an American value-added tax is conveniently dated with the publication of Committee for Economic Development, *A Better Balance in Federal Taxes on Business* (New York: CED, 1966).

2. See Advisory Commission on Intergovernmental Relations, *The Value-added Tax and Alternative Sources of Federal Revenue*, M-78 (Washington, D.C., 1973). The American fascination with the VAT through mid-1973 is discussed in Charles E. McLure, Jr., "A Federal Tax on Value Added: U.S. View," in *Proceedings of the 1973 Conference on Taxation of the National Tax Association–Tax Institute of America* (Toronto, 1973), pp. 96–103. Interest in an American VAT has been relatively dormant since then, except for the 1979–1980 proposal by Ullman mentioned below. But see the papers in Charls E. Walker and Mark A. Bloomfield, eds., *New Directions in Federal Tax Policy for the 1980s* (Cambridge, Mass.: Ballinger, 1983).

3. For an appraisal of the Ullman proposal, see Charles E. McLure, Jr., "The Tax Restructuring Act of 1979: Time for an American Value Added Tax?" *Public Policy*, vol. 28 (Summer 1980), pp. 301–22.

4. These postulated macroeconomic effects on international competitiveness are separate from, and additional to, any structural effect that would occur, because border tax adjustments (to be defined below) can be made for VAT but not for the corporate income tax. Any reduction in the deficit should have similar macroeconomic effects.

5. It is estimated that the Tax Reform Act of 1986 will increase fiscal 1987 revenues by $11 billion, compared with current law, and thus help meet the Gramm-Rudman-Hollings targets in that year. But the reductions in revenues

in fiscal 1988 and 1989 of $15–17 billion will exacerbate the already considerable difficulties of meeting the target for deficit reduction in those years and increase the likelihood that a new source of federal revenue will be required.

6. Although France had the VAT as early as 1954, its tax did not extend to the retail level until 1968. The experience under the Michigan VAT since 1976 is of little relevance for this discussion, since the Michigan tax uses the addition method, rather than either the subtraction method proposed by Roth or the more commonly used credit method. For a description of the operation and defects of an addition-method VAT, see the appendix to chapter 6 and Charles E. McLure, Jr., "State and Local Implications of a Federal Value Added Tax" (Prepared for the Academy for State and Local Government, Washington, D.C., 1986). Virtually no one advocates enactment of a federal VAT based on the addition method.

7. For further development of this point, see chapters 3 and 4. This is not to deny that using a VAT to reduce the federal budget deficit would have a salutary effect on U.S. competitiveness by causing the dollar to weaken or that replacing part of the corporate income tax with a VAT would stimulate exports and retard imports.

8. See chapter 6; Henry J. Aaron, ed., *The Value Added Tax: Lessons from Europe* (Washington, D.C.: Brookings Institution, 1981), esp. p. 9; Sijbren Cnossen, "What Rate Structure for a Value Added Tax?" *National Tax Journal,* vol. 35 (June 1982), pp. 205–14; and Cedric Sandford and Michael Godwin, "Administrative and Compliance Problems Unique to VAT: The Rebate System, Invoicing Issues, and Related Problems" (Paper presented at World Bank Conference on Value Added Taxation in Developing Countries, Washington, D.C., April 21–23, 1986).

9. These issues are discussed in chapter 6.

10. Political considerations are taken into account in several places: the probability of differential treatment of various activities, which would doom the subtraction-method BTT; the likelihood that a low-rate VAT to finance the Superfund might grow to become a high-rate levy; the need to consider special treatment for selected industries; and the politically sensitive issues of intergovernmental relations.

11. See William V. T. Roth, "The Roth Reforms" (Speech to the National Press Club, Washington, D.C., February 20, 1986). Roth proposed using revenues from the business transfer tax to make possible (1) income tax rates lower than those proposed by President Reagan or included in H.R. 3838, the tax reform bill passed by the House of Representatives in December 1985, (2) super saving accounts that would resemble expanded individual retirement accounts (IRAs), and (3) substantially more rapid depreciation allowances than contained in either the president's proposals or H.R. 3838. Since events have overtaken these proposals for income tax reform, I concentrate on those for the BTT.

12. Some observers may also think that the incidence (burden distribution) of a subtraction-method VAT would differ from that of a credit-method VAT. Such a belief has little basis if the two taxes have roughly equal coverage.

Mark Bloomfield's essay in this volume discusses the political considerations that may determine the packaging of this and other VAT proposals.

13. See Robert E. Hall and Alvin Rabushka, *Low Tax, Simple Tax, Flat Tax* (New York: McGraw-Hill, 1983); and Hall and Rabushka, *The Flat Tax* (Stanford, Calif.: Hoover Institution Press, 1985).

14. The term "personal exemption VAT" is used to describe the Hall-Rabushka tax in U.S. Department of the Treasury, *Tax Reform for Fairness, Simplicity, and Economic Growth* (1984), vol. 1, chap. 10, and vol. 3.

2

The Need for a Value-added Tax

Many Americans concerned about fiscal affairs seem to be increasingly convinced that a new source of federal revenue must be found. Although this perception appears to be shared across the political spectrum, a variety of very different reasons probably underlie the common perception.

Many observers, of all political persuasions, believe that the federal budget deficit must be substantially reduced, if not eliminated.[1] Again, concern about the budget deficit has a variety of roots. At one level is the simple intuitive belief that the federal government must pay its own way over the long haul, just as households must, and that continued deficit finance will eventually become inflationary and lead to a need for difficult adjustments to eliminate inflation.

A more sophisticated version of this view is based on the realization that the federal government is not merely borrowing from its own citizens. Rather, because the private saving rate has not risen since the federal government began to run massive budget deficits in 1982, the nation (on combined public and private account) has been borrowing substantial amounts abroad. During 1985 the United States resumed the status of a net debtor—a position more appropriate to a developing country. Thus it can no longer be said sanguinely of the national debt that "we owe it to ourselves." The reduction in net international balances of the United States seems anomalous to many observers. Why, they ask, should the richest nation in the world not be able to pay its own way? Some observers find it unconscionable that the United States should be absorbing so much of the world's scarce supply of net saving, when countries of the third world need capital so badly.

A somewhat different concern has focused on the implications of budget deficits for international trade. The higher real interest rates resulting from the budget deficit have stimulated capital inflows. Borrowing abroad has led to an overvalued dollar, which has made it extremely difficult for American business, whether in farming, mining, or manufacturing, to compete in world markets. A substantial reduction of the deficit has been seen as essential to permanent success in the effort to bring the value of the dollar to a more realistic level.

Of course, there is no reason that the present federal taxes could not be used to raise additional revenue. But following that course would necessitate one of two things: income tax rates substantially above those in the recently enacted tax reform; or further base broadening, such as taxation of fringe benefits and repeal or substantial limitation of the itemized deductions for state and local income and property taxes and for mortgage interest.[2]

Many analysts believe that the reduction of the top marginal tax rate to below 30 percent is important for incentive reasons and that a top marginal rate below 30 percent is essential if capital gains are to be taxed as ordinary income.[3] Not only do lower marginal tax rates entail fewer disincentives; they also provide less reward for the uneconomical behavior that has caused so much concern about the tax system and spurred interest in tax reform.[4] Perhaps more important, it is hard to imagine the Congress and the president doing an about-face on rates so soon after cutting them with so much fanfare.

Concern that excessive reliance on the income tax creates too great a bias against saving and in favor of present consumption provides further impetus for interest in a value-added tax. Many observers, including many prominent economists, would like to see a shift from income taxation toward greater reliance on taxes on consumption.[5] Consumption-based taxation could be levied on the personal expenditures of households—for example, through a cash-flow-based tax on consumption—or it could be implemented through indirect taxes on transactions, such as a VAT or other form of general sales tax.[6]

The more liberal members of Congress would use revenues from an alternative source for yet another reason. They would avoid budget cuts such as those mandated by Gramm-Rudman-Hollings. In their more optimistic dreams they would use additional revenues to expand government provision of goods and services.

Chapter 5 argues that if a substantial amount of additional revenue is to be raised, it should be through the VAT or some other form of broad-based federal sales tax, rather than through one of the more narrowly based taxes on consumption recently being discussed. The possibility of a broad-based federal sales tax poses a dilemma for both liberals and conservatives. Although many liberals would like to see an important new source of federal revenue introduced to reduce the deficit without sacrificing federal programs, they are concerned about the potential distributional effects of the VAT: because the base of the tax is consumption, the VAT is regressive unless explicit steps are taken to avoid regressivity. Many conservatives would welcome a reduction of the deficit and a shift in the relative emphasis of taxation from income to saving, but they are worried about handing the Congress a new and, they fear, relatively painless source of federal revenues that could be used to expand the scope of government.[7]

The last view is perhaps best epitomized by President Reagan's continued refusal to tolerate proposals for new taxes. He appears to see the threat of continued deficits as the only way to force the Congress to be fiscally responsible. According to this line of reasoning, Congress will exercise fiscal responsibility by reducing expenditures rather than by raising taxes only if no new source of revenue is available. Moreover, if further growth of government is to be avoided, a "money machine" such as a VAT must be kept out of the hands of Congress.

I believe that the federal budget deficit is a major problem and that the American people do not want to see the deficit reduced entirely by cutting federal spending.[8] While I share the concern that revenues from a federal sales tax might lead to greater federal spending than is optimal, I have come to view the continuation of large deficits as a greater threat than the money machine. The regressivity of the VAT or other form of sales tax can probably be dealt with satisfactorily (see chapter 4). Problems of intergovernmental relations strike me as being somewhat more serious (see chapter 9). Thus I believe that it is time to start seriously discussing the VAT, one type of federal sales tax that might be employed to reduce the deficit to an acceptable level.

Whether the United States should adopt a VAT is not, however, the primary topic of this volume, most of which describes how a VAT is implemented, likely problem areas, and economic effects. Greater understanding of the implementation and economic effects of the VAT would help us consider whether it should be used to reduce the deficit or to replace part of the existing revenue system. Moreover, the more that is widely known about alternative ways to implement a VAT, the less likely we are to choose an inferior form of sales tax, such as the business transfer tax.

Notes

1. Some have argued that, for a variety of reasons, reducing the budget deficit to zero would be neither required nor wise. See, for example, Michael J.

Boskin, "Federal Government Deficits: Some Myths and Realities," *American Economic Review*, vol. 72 (May 1982), pp. 296–303; and *The Real Federal Budget* (Cambridge, Mass.: Harvard University Press, forthcoming 1987).

2. *The President's Tax Proposals to the Congress for Fairness, Growth, and Simplicity* (Washington, D.C., 1985); U.S. Congress, *Tax Reform Act of 1985*, Report of the Committee on Ways and Means, House of Representatives, on H.R. 3838 (Washington, D.C., 1985); U.S. Congress, *Tax Reform Act of 1986*, Report of the Committee on Finance of the Senate (Washington, D.C., 1986); and U.S. Congress, *Tax Reform Act of 1986*, Conference Report to accompany H.R. 3838 (Washington, D.C., 1986).

3. Under the recently enacted tax reform the top marginal tax rate is really 33 percent, rather than 28 percent, on the range of income over which the advantage of the 15 percent rate is phased out ($71,900 to $149,250 for a couple filing a joint return) and over the range of phase-out of personal exemptions (from $149,250 until the benefits are gone). Beyond that, it reverts to 28 percent.

4. On the general case for tax reform, see, for example, U.S. Department of the Treasury, *Tax Reform for Fairness, Simplicity, and Economic Growth* (Washington, D.C., 1984), esp. vol. 1, chaps. 1, 2; Henry J. Aaron and Harvey Galper, *Assessing Tax Reform* (Washington, D.C.: Brookings Institution, 1985); and Charles E. McLure, Jr., "Reflections on Recent Proposals to Rationalize the U.S. Income Tax," in *Proceedings of the 41st Congress of the International Institute of Public Finance, Madrid*, August 26–30, 1985.

5. Claudia Scott, in "VAT and Tax Reform" (Paper presented at World Bank Conference on Value Added Taxation in Developing Countries, Washington, D.C., April 21–23, 1986), suggests that the primary motive for introducing a VAT in New Zealand (in October 1986) was to shift the tax burden from income toward consumption. She also expresses some misgivings about that decision. See also Jonathan R. Kesselman, "Role of the Tax Mix in Tax Reform," in John G. Head, ed., *Changing the Tax Mix* (Sydney: Australian Tax Research Foundation, 1986), on the issue of the combination of taxes.

6. For a survey of issues in this field, see the papers in Joseph A. Pechman, *What Should Be Taxed: Income or Expenditure?* (Washington, D.C.: Brookings Institution, 1980); and John H. Makin, ed., *Real Tax Reform: Replacing the Income Tax* (Washington, D.C.: American Enterprise Institute, 1985). U.S. Department of the Treasury, *Blueprints for Basic Tax Reform* (Washington, D.C., 1977), presents a now classic argument for a tax system based on cash flow. David F. Bradford, *Untangling the Income Tax* (Cambridge, Mass.: Harvard University Press, 1986), reemphasizes the benefits of a personal consumption tax.

7. I have expressed this concern in my previous work on the VAT; see, for example, Charles E. McLure, Jr., "The Tax Restructuring Act of 1979: Time for an American Value Added Tax?" *Public Policy*, vol. 28 (Summer 1980), pp. 301–22; and "Value Added Tax: Has the Time Come?" in Charls E. Walker and Mark A. Bloomfield, eds., *New Directions in Federal Tax Policy for the 1980s* (Cambridge, Mass.: Ballinger, 1983), pp. 185–213. J. A. Stockfisch, "Value-

added Taxes and the Size of Government: Some Evidence," *National Tax Journal*, vol. 38 (December 1985), pp. 547–52, has challenged the view that availability of revenues from a VAT would lead to a larger federal budget. See also U.S. Department of the Treasury, *Tax Reform*, vol. 3, pp. 23–26.

It may be useful to clarify my role in the preparation of volume 3 of the Treasury Department tax reform report to President Reagan, which deals with the VAT. Although the report was prepared under my supervision, the volume on the VAT was almost entirely the work of other experts, primarily George Carlson and John Due, with assistance from members of the staff of the Office of Tax Analysis of the Treasury Department. Thus when I cite the Treasury Department report on the VAT as support for views expressed here, I am not simply citing my own views in disguise.

8. It appears that most Americans want to reduce federal spending but that there are few programs on which it is possible to reach agreement that cuts should be made.

3
The Nature and Base of the Value-added Tax

Value-added taxation can best be seen as a particular means of collecting a general sales tax on consumer goods and services.[1] Tax is collected as goods and services pass through the sequential stages of the production-distribution process, rather than entirely on the final sale to consumers, as under a retail sales tax.

A simple example will help to make this clear. Assume that production involves three stages, A, B, and C (which for most purposes can be identified as manufacturing, wholesaling, and retailing) and that in a given taxable period production and transactions are as shown in table 1.[2] Goods move in a direct line from stage A to stage B to stage C and then to consumers.

Under a 10 percent retail sales tax, $100 in revenue would be obtained on the $1,000 of sales made to consumers at stage C, as indicated in line 5. The same amount of revenue would be collected under the value-added tax, but in an administratively different way. If there were no exclusions from the tax base, each firm would pay tax at the 10 percent rate on its contribution to the value of the final product, or its value added.

TABLE 1
THREE-STAGE EXAMPLE OF 10 PERCENT VALUE-ADDED TAX
(dollars)

| | Stage of Production | | | |
	A	B	C	Total
1. Sales	300	700	1,000	2,000
2. Purchased inputs	—	300	700	1,000
3. Value added (1 − 2)	300	400	300	1,000
4. Tax on value added (10% of 3)	30	40	30	100
5. Retail sales tax (10% of C1)	—	—	100	100

15

Value added can be calculated as the difference between sales and purchases of inputs. Thus, for example, firms at stage B have value added of $400, calculated by deducting purchases of $300 from sales of $700. Firms at the three stages in the example would pay VAT of $30, $40, and $30, respectively, on their value added of $300, $400, and $300. Since sales at one stage of the production-distribution process are deductible purchases at the next stage, the aggregate tax base is exactly equal to sales to final consumers.[3] Thus the total of VAT payments at the three stages would equal the $100 collected directly on sales to consumers under the retail sales tax. The advantages and disadvantages of collecting the tax in this way, rather than simply at the retail stage, are discussed in chapter 7, after further explanation and discussion of the operational details of the VAT, especially in chapter 6. (See appendix to this chapter for illustration of the mechanics of a VAT.)

Calculating Tax Liabilities

Under the subtraction method of calculating liability for VAT, the statutory tax rate is applied directly to the firm's value added, which is calculated by subtracting purchased inputs from sales. This is the method illustrated in table 1. The business transfer tax (BTT) proposed by Senator William Roth, the low-rate tax proposed as a source of revenue for the Superfund, and the personal-exemption VAT proposed by Hall and Rabushka are all based on the subtraction method, rather than on the credit method commonly used in Europe and elsewhere.[4] Although the subtraction method might appear to be the most straightforward way of calculating tax liabilities under the VAT, it is not much used in other countries. (A quite different and less satisfactory approach, the addition method, is of little relevance and is discussed only in the appendix to chapter 6.)

Under the credit method the firm calculates its gross tax liability by applying the statutory rate to its total sales. To calculate its net liability, it deducts from its gross liability the amount of tax it has paid on its purchases. This method of calculating the VAT is illustrated in table 2 for the same situation assumed in table 1. As before, tax liability is the same as under a retail sales tax.[5] This method of calculating tax liability is called the credit method, because credit is allowed for the taxes previously paid on purchased inputs. It is also sometimes called the invoice method, since credit can be taken only for taxes paid on purchases that are shown on invoices.

One of the primary themes of this monograph is that the subtrac-

TABLE 2
ILLUSTRATION OF CREDIT-METHOD VALUE-ADDED TAX
(dollars)

| | Stage of Production | | | |
	A	B	C	Total
1. Sales	300	700	1,000	2,000
2. Purchases	—	300	700	1,000
3. Tax on purchases (10% of 2)	0	30	70	100
4. Gross tax liability on sales (10% of 1)	30	70	100	200
5. Credit for tax on purchases (line 3 from invoices)	0	30	70	100
6. Net tax liability (4 − 5)	30	40	30	100

tion method is vastly inferior to the credit method, unless the subtraction-method VAT is imposed in such a way as to make it virtually equivalent to a single-rate credit-method tax levied on all consumption, with no exceptions.[6] This argument is presented in detail in chapter 6. The rest of this chapter is therefore couched in terms of the more familiar and more satisfactory credit method, but warnings of the implications of adopting what I call a "naive" subtraction-method VAT are provided at appropriate points.

Border Tax Adjustments

The best-known aspect of the administration of the VAT (whether rightly or wrongly) is probably the border tax adjustments (BTAs) allowed on international trade. VAT collected before the export stage is rebated on exports, and VAT is collected on imports. Some observers liken the BTAs to export subsidies and import duties and claim that nations that use the VAT gain an unfair competitive advantage. This section describes and evaluates this important administrative feature of the VAT. How the VAT would affect—or, more accurately, not affect—international trade is discussed in chapter 4. But it must be emphasized at the outset that the export rebates and taxation of imports that occur under the VAT do not produce a competitive advantage for nations using this form of sales tax; indeed, a nation using a VAT without these features would be at a competitive disadvantage. A VAT with BTAs is neutral toward international trade, providing neither an advantage nor a disadvantage to producers in the taxing nation.

Commodity taxes on products entering international trade can be levied on either of two bases. If the product is taxed where produced and not where consumed, the tax is said to be an origin-principle tax, or a tax on production. If the product is taxed where it is consumed but not where it is produced, it is a destination-principle tax, or a tax on consumption.

A retail sales tax is a good example of a destination-principle tax.[7] Goods (and ideally services) are taxed at their point of sale to ultimate consumers, whether they are produced domestically or imported, and exports are not taxed. Thus the tax is levied only on consumption, or at the point of destination.

This distinction can be illustrated by the example of table 1. Suppose that the production at stages A and B took place in one country and the production at stage C took place after importation into another country. Value added of $700 would occur in the first country and value added of $300 in the second. Each nation would levy its own tax on the production (as measured by value added) occurring within its borders if it followed the origin principle.[8]

Suppose we wished to tax commodities under the VAT where consumed, however, and only there. We would need to exempt exports from tax and rebate any tax already paid at prior stages of production, so that exports would enter world trade unencumbered by taxes levied in their nation of origin. If the country of destination of U.S. exports followed the same system, the goods would be taxed there when imported; the export rebate would prevent international double taxation. Similarly, we would need to levy a tax on imports to equalize tax burdens vis-à-vis domestically produced goods. The elimination and rebate of taxes on exports and the compensating import duty levied to convert an otherwise origin-principle VAT to a destination-principle levy are commonly called BTAs.

An example based on tables 1 and 2 will help to clarify the function and operation of BTAs. Assume as before that stages A and B occur in one country and stage C in another. Then we would want the goods to leave the first country free of tax and to be taxed on entry into the second, so that taxation would be based on the country of destination. Since tax has already been paid at stage A, simply failing to levy the tax on exports at stage B would not suffice. It would be necessary also to rebate the tax paid at stage A. This is easily achieved under the credit method. Export sales would simply be "zero rated."[9] That is, the exporter would pay no tax on exports but would be allowed to claim credit for any taxes paid on inputs, including those used to produce exports, against its liability for taxes on domestic sales. If the exporter's total credit for taxes paid on inputs exceeded its gross tax liability on domestic sales, it would receive a refund of the excess credit from the treasury. Since the exporter would pay no tax on exports and would be allowed credit (and a refund, if appropriate) for taxes paid on purchases, exports would be tax free.

In principle, the subtraction method could operate in a similar way, provided coverage were universal and only one rate of tax were employed. Purchases of inputs would be subtracted from domestic sales and the VAT paid on the difference. If that figure were negative, as it would typically be for those specializing in exporting, a refund would be due. If, however, coverage of the VAT were not complete or multiple rates were enacted, precise BTAs would be impossible, since the tax content of exports would depend on the exact breakdown of value added among "slices" taxed at different rates. This important defect, which is inherent in the subtraction method, is explained further in chapter 6.

Equalizing the tax burden between imports and domestically produced goods can be achieved by taxing the goods at the point of importation as well as at subsequent sales. But under the credit method it is not even necessary to tax imports directly, except when they are made by ultimate consumers. As long as the goods passed through at least one taxed transaction after being imported, the value added before importation, as well as that added afterward, would be taxed.[10] Since there would be no credit for previously paid taxes, the firm making the first taxed sale after importation would be liable for the tax on the entire value of the goods.[11] In fact, any understatement of value at the time of import would be corrected on subsequent sale under the credit method, since the credit for taxes paid on purchases would be correspondingly lower. If, for example, imports were artificially valued at $50 instead of $70, only $5 of VAT would be collected at the point of importation and available as a credit against tax on sales. Theoretically the same result could be effected under the subtraction method, but only if the VAT were levied at a uniform rate and the sophisticated version of the method were used.

It is worth repeating that the retail sales tax, at least in its pure form—a tax applied only on sales to households for consumption—automatically achieves destination-principle taxation of internationally traded goods.[12] Exports are tax free, since all sales except domestic sales to ultimate consumers are exempt. Similarly, imports and domestically produced goods are treated identically, since the tax is applied at a given rate to all sales to consumers, regardless of the nation of origin of the taxed commodity.

That this is true is especially important since the existence of BTAs under the VAT has drawn so much attention. Those adjustments are necessary solely to provide under the VAT the destination-principle taxation that occurs naturally under the retail sales tax. In their pure forms the two taxes are economically equivalent in their effects on international trade. A VAT with BTAs would therefore constitute no more of a trade advantage than a retail sales tax.

The Likely Base of a Value-added Tax

The U.S. Treasury Department has estimated that in 1988 total personal consumption will be approximately $3,127 billion.[13] If a VAT could be imposed on this base, it would yield $31 billion per percentage point; thus a rate of 5 percent would raise more than $150 billion, more than enough to deal satisfactorily with projected budget deficits. In fact, however, likely exclusions from the tax base would reduce the revenue from a VAT to no more than 75 to 80 percent of this figure ($23–25 billion per percentage point), and liberal exclusions could easily reduce it to less than 60 or even 50 percent ($19 billion, or even $16 billion per percentage point).[14]

Table 3 presents two estimates of the base of a federal VAT.[15] The first reflects only exclusions from the base that are virtually inevitable for administrative reasons or for political reasons that are so strong as to be relatively uncontroversial—for example, for religious organizations. The second reflects a much more liberal policy toward exclusions from the tax base; for example, food for home preparation and all medical care are excluded. Most of the remainder of this section explains the two sets of assumed exclusions from the tax base. Chapter 8 examines further why various items might not be taxed and whether exclusion is likely to, or should, take the form of exemption or of zero rating.

The two estimates in table 3 are intended to bracket the revenue from a politically realistic VAT. Almost 80 percent of total consumption would be covered by the VAT with limited exclusions, but less than 50 percent might be taxed if exclusions were liberal.[16]

Limited-Exclusion VAT. Several items of consumption would probably be excluded from the base of a VAT for administrative reasons. These include food produced and consumed on farms, food provided by employers, domestic services, and expenditures abroad by Americans.[17] (Consumption expenditures of foreign travelers in the United States are reflected in the calculations of the tax base in table 3; in fact, some such expenditures would probably escape tax, since VAT would almost certainly be refunded on many purchases by tourists.)

More important than any of these are the services of financial

TABLE 3

ESTIMATED BASE OF CONSUMPTION-BASED VALUE-ADDED TAX WITH
LIMITED AND LIBERAL EXCLUSIONS, AT 1984 LEVELS OF CONSUMPTION
(billions of dollars)

| | Personal Consumption Expenditures | Estimated Tax Base | |
		Limited exclusions	Liberal exclusions
Food and tobacco	474.4	466.6[a]	155.6[b]
Clothing, accessories, and jewelry	165.5	165.4[c]	165.4[c]
Personal care	29.6	29.6	29.6
Housing	397.9	149.9[d]	—
Household operation	318.2	310.1[e]	189.2[f]
Medical care expenses	258.3	188.8[g]	—
Personal business	139.5	57.0[h]	57.0[h]
Transportation	319.5	319.5	314.2[i]
Recreation	157.1	157.1	153.4[j]
Private education and research	35.4	—	—
Religious and welfare activities	35.2	—	—
Foreign travel and other, net	11.2	12.6[k]	12.6[k]
Total personal consumption	2,341.8	1,856.6	1,077.0
Percentage of personal consumption	100.0	79.3	46.0

a. Excludes food furnished to government and commercial employees and food produced and consumed on farms.
b. Includes only purchased meals, beverages, and tobacco products.
c. Excludes standard clothing issued to military personnel.
d. Includes only purchases of new houses.
e. Excludes domestic services.
f. Excludes domestic services and household utilities except telephone.
g. Excludes physicians' services.
h. Excludes services furnished without payment by financial intermediaries except life insurance companies and expenses of handling life insurance.
i. Excludes bridge, tunnel, ferry, and road tolls; transit systems; and commutation railway expenses.
j. Excludes clubs and fraternal organizations, except insurance.
k. Excludes foreign travel and expenditures abroad by U.S. residents but includes expenditures in United States by foreigners.
SOURCE: U.S. Department of Commerce, *Survey of Current Business* (July 1985), pp. 19, 23.

institutions provided without explicit charge to customers and the services of life insurance companies; for reasons explained in chapter 8, the financial and insurance services of such institutions would probably be exempt (*not* zero rated). Other services of the same institutions for which explicit fees are charged (for example, safe deposit boxes and trust services) might be subject to tax. The estimates of table 3 exclude the full value of the first kind of services from the tax base but include the full value of the second.

Even a VAT with limited exclusions would probably allow for the zero rating of physicians' services and activities of religious and welfare organizations; the same treatment might also be extended to educational and research activities, although exemption would be somewhat more likely.[18] The limited-exclusion option reflects zero rating for education and research organizations, as well as for religious and welfare organizations.

For both administrative and political reasons, the full rental value of housing is unlikely to be subject to the VAT. Although sales of new homes may be unlikely, for political reasons, to be taxed, chapter 8 argues that they should be. The estimate of the limited-exclusion VAT is based on the assumption that they would be taxed.

Liberal-Exclusion VAT. The exclusion of food for home consumption and of water and sanitation services (if implemented through zero rating) would reduce the base for a VAT by 14 percent of total consumption expenditures. Additional exclusions might well be enacted for other household utilities, other expenditures on medical care, such transportation-related expenditures as tolls, urban transit, and railway commuting, and expenditures on clubs and fraternal organizations. Whether these would take the form of exemption or zero rating is uncertain, but the estimates of table 3 reflect zero rating. Finally, the liberal-exclusion estimates assume that sales of new houses are zero rated.[19]

These estimates may understate the base of a VAT (especially of a liberal-exclusion VAT) for several reasons. First, some preferential treatment might take the form of exemption rather than zero rating. Moreover, some exclusions (such as for financial services, farmers, and small business) may take the form of exemptions of sales to businesses that break the chain of credits and result in multiple taxation of value added at the exempt stage. An additional factor is the assumption that the construction of housing would be totally tax free.

These estimates can usefully be compared with the analogous estimates of the Treasury Department. The base-line Treasury estimate that the tax base would be 77 percent of 1988 consumption reflects a base that differs from the limited exclusion estimate of the table primarily by excluding all medical care (not just physicians' services) and including all rental housing. Zero-rating food would reduce the tax base to 66 percent of total consumption, and extending zero rating to sales of new housing, prescription drugs, and household expenditures on electricity, gas, and fuel oil would reduce it to 55 percent.[20]

Tax Rates. It is sometimes suggested that the United States might levy a VAT at a rate of no more than 1 or 2 percent. The extreme case would be the proposal to use a subtraction-method manufacturing-stage VAT at a rate of 0.08 percent to finance the Superfund. The consensus among experts is that this would be a mistake. Because of administrative and compliance costs, it probably would not make sense to introduce a VAT with a rate of less than about 5 percent.[21]

The Treasury Department estimates that 20,000 additional Internal Revenue Service employees and an annual expenditure of $700 million would be needed to administer the VAT.[22] With a tax rate of 5 percent levied on the tax base with limited exclusions, administrative costs of this magnitude would constitute somewhat less than 1 percent of revenues; with liberal exclusions, almost 1½ percent. At a rate of 2 percent, these costs would approach 2 or 3 percent of revenues. By comparison, costs of collecting the income tax amount to less than 1 percent of revenues.[23]

Appendix

Figure 1 may help to clarify the concept of value added and the mechanics of a VAT. It shows the increase in the value of an item (that is, value added) as the item moves through the three-stage production process. (Value and VAT are measured on the left-hand axis. Total VAT is given below value in parentheses.) Sales are noted by the letter S, subscripted to show the stage at which sales are made, and P indicates purchases by firms at the stage shown in the subscript. By definition, in this simple example S_A (sales by stage A) must equal P_B (purchases at stage B), and S_B must equal P_C. P_A is assumed to be zero. V_A indicates value added in the stage shown in the subscript; it is the difference between purchases and sales at that stage. Thus VA_A (value added at stage A) equals S_A minus P_A, or, in this example, $300 minus 0 = $300. Application of a 10 percent rate of tax yields tax liability at stage A: VAT_A = $30. Analogous calculations give VA and VAT at stages B and C. These are written algebraically at the bottom of the figure.

The right-hand column summarizes the information contained in the three-stage example. Value added in the three stages totals $1,000, the value of sales to households at stage C, and total VAT is $100, the same amount that would be collected by application of a 10 percent retail sales tax on sales to final consumers.

The credit method is also illustrated in figure 1. T, properly

23

FIGURE 1
THREE-STAGE ILLUSTRATION OF INCREASE IN VALUE AND CALCULATION OF VALUE ADDED AND VAT

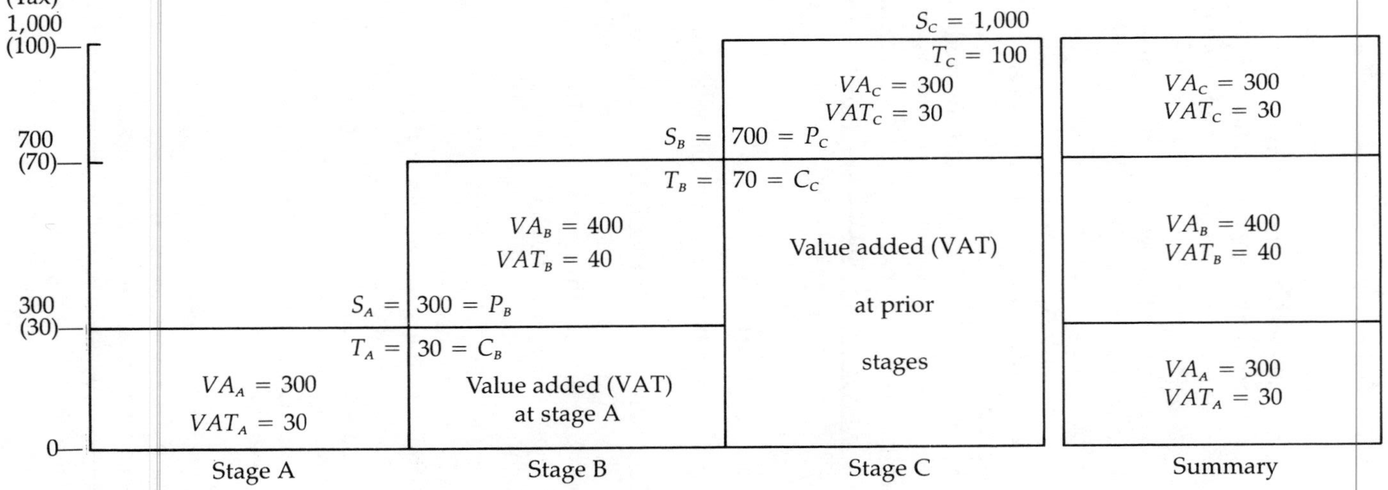

Value
(Tax)
1,000
(100)—

700
(70)—

300
(30)—

0—

$S_C = 1,000$
$T_C = 100$

$S_B = 700 = P_C$
$T_B = 70 = C_C$

$S_A = 300 = P_B$
$T_A = 30 = C_B$

Stage A

$VA_A = 300$
$VAT_A = 30$

Stage B

$VA_B = 400$
$VAT_B = 40$

Value added (VAT)
at stage A

Stage C

$VA_C = 300$
$VAT_C = 30$

Value added (VAT) at prior stages

Summary

$VA_C = 300$
$VAT_C = 30$

$VA_B = 400$
$VAT_B = 40$

$VA_A = 300$
$VAT_A = 30$

Formulas:

$$VA_A = S_A - P_A$$
$$= 300 - 0$$
$$= 300$$

$$VAT_A = T_A - C_A$$
$$= 30 - 0$$
$$= 30$$

$$VA_B = S_B - P_B$$
$$= 700 - 300$$
$$= 400$$

$$VAT_B = T_B - C_B$$
$$= 70 - 30$$
$$= 40$$

$$VA_C = S_C - P_C$$
$$= 1,000 - 700$$
$$= 300$$

$$VAT_C = T_C - C_C$$
$$= 100 - 70$$
$$= 30$$

$$VA = VA_A + VA_B + VA_C$$
$$= 300 + 400 + 300$$
$$= 1,000$$

$$VAT = VAT_A + VAT_B + VAT_C$$
$$= 30 + 40 + 30$$
$$= 100$$

subscripted, represents gross tax liability, and C shows the credit for tax paid on purchases by firms operating at the stage shown in the subscript. At any stage VAT under the credit method is calculated as the difference between T and C. Thus $VAT_A = \$30 - 0$, $VAT_B = \$70 - \$30 = \$40$, and $VAT_C = \$100 - \$70 = \$30$; these calculations are described at the bottom of the figure and summarized in the right-hand column. Of course, given the facts assumed, VAT collected at each stage and total VAT (\$100) are the same as under the subtraction method.

Notes

1. Strictly speaking, this description is accurate only for what is called the consumption-based VAT. Since that is the type of VAT levied in Europe and almost certainly the only type that would receive serious consideration in the United States, it is the only one considered in the text. Under the consumption-based VAT, immediate deduction is allowed for purchases of capital goods, as well as for both intermediate products and other (nonlabor) business inputs; under the income variety deduction for capital goods is allowed only as the assets depreciate. See the appendix to chapter 6 for further discussion of differences between the income and consumption bases for value-added taxation and reasons for preferring the consumption variety.

2. In the extremely simple production-distribution process described in the text, firms at stage A are assumed to have no purchased inputs and to sell only to firms at stage B. Firms at stage B buy inputs only from those at stage A and sell their outputs only to firms at stage C, which buy no other inputs and sell only to ultimate consumers. This simplifying assumption places no limits on the generality of the results, which would hold in more complicated processes. For example, firms at all stages might buy from firms at all other stages, and firms at all stages might make some sales to consumers. For a simple but more general mathematical exposition of the functioning of a VAT, see Jean-Pierre Balladur and Antoine Coutière, "France," in Henry J. Aaron, ed., *The Value Added Tax: Lessons from Europe* (Washington, D.C.: Brookings Institution, 1981), pp. 19–30.

3. This simple identity can be written algebraically as follows:

$$V_i = S_i - P_i$$

where V_i is value added at stage i and S_i and P_i are sales and purchases at that stage. Of course, the purchases of one stage are the sales of the previous stage; thus $P_i = S_{i-1}$. Aggregate value added is given by

$$\sum_{i=1}^{3} V_i = S_3 - P_1$$

Since the first stage, by definition, has no purchases in this simple example, aggregate value added is identically equal to sales to consumers.

4. The Superfund tax uses the mechanism of a tax credit. But since the credit is calculated by multiplying purchases by the tax rate, it is really a subtraction-method tax.

5. This can be demonstrated using the notation of note 3 by noting that $T_i = tS_i - C_i$, where T_i is VAT due at stage i, C_i is credit for tax paid on purchases at stage i, and t is the tax rate. Since credit at stage i equals tax on sales at the previous stage, aggregate tax liability can be written as

$$\sum_{i=1}^{3} T_i = t(S_3 - P_1) = tS_3$$

6. The subtraction method is sometimes called the accounts method to indicate that it would be based on firms' accounts rather than on invoices. Chapter 6 discusses "naive" and "sophisticated" versions of the subtraction method and their advantages and disadvantages. It argues that the only form of subtraction-method tax that makes any sense is a single-rate levy imposed on all consumption using the sophisticated version of the method—an approach that is based on invoices and is virtually indistinguishable from the credit method. The accounts required would be substantially different both from those now kept for income tax purposes and from those envisaged under the naive subtraction method.

7. Conceptually, the retail sales tax is a perfect example of a destination-based tax. In fact, however, state retail sales taxes are often levied on some capital assets, intermediate goods, and other business inputs. Thus some retail sales tax is commonly included in the price of exports. Moreover, retail sales tax levied on imports is not fully equivalent to taxes levied on domestic production, so that the destination principle is not fully applicable. For more on these and other defects of retail sales taxes as actually levied, see chapter 7.

8. Given the virtual certainty that the origin principle would not be considered seriously in the United States, there is no purpose in going further into details of its implementation. I might note, however, that it is probably best implemented through the addition or the subtraction method for an income-based VAT. Using the credit method to implement an origin-principle tax is practically impossible. For a further discussion, see Carl S. Shoup, *Public Finance* (Chicago: Aldine Publishing Co., 1969), pp. 262–64; or "Criteria for Choice among Types of Value Added Tax" (Paper presented at World Bank Conference on Value Added Taxation in Developing Countries, Washington, D.C., April 21–23, 1986).

9. Zero rating is not to be confused with exemption; both terms are explained in chapter 6.

10. Sijbren Cnossen, "Harmonization of Indirect Taxes in the EEC," in Charles E. McLure, Jr., ed., *Tax Assignment in Federal Countries* (Canberra, Australia: Centre for Research on Federal Financial Relations, 1983), pp. 150–68, notes that the European Economic Community is adopting this approach, which has long been used in the Netherlands.

11. We would expect the price of imports to reflect whether tax is paid at the import stage or at the first stage after importation.

12. As mentioned in note 7 and explained more fully in chapter 7, retail sales taxes do not handle foreign trade as precisely as the VAT. While this may lead one to favor the VAT over the retail sales tax, it should not be allowed to obscure the basic truth that there is no special magic about the

BTAs allowed under a VAT; they only render the VAT a destination-based levy similar to the more familiar retail sales tax.

13. U.S. Department of the Treasury, *Tax Reform for Fairness, Simplicity, and Economic Growth* (Washington, D.C., 1984), vol. 3, chap. 7.

14. The generic term "exclusion" is used at this point to encompass both exemptions and zero rating. The two are not, of course, the same, as explained further in chapter 6, and their differences have important implications for the size of the tax base. Chapter 8, as summarized in the rest of this chapter, indicates which treatment is more appropriate or likely for various items of consumption expenditures.

15. These estimates are based on consumption figures for 1984, the latest available. The important result from the calculation reported here is not the tax base at 1984 levels of income but the percentage of 1984 consumption included in the tax base under various assumed exclusions. This percentage can be applied to projected consumption in future years to calculate the potential tax base in those years.

16. Cedric Sandford and Michael Godwin, in "Administrative and Compliance Problems Unique to VAT: The Rebate System, Invoicing Issues, and Related Problems" (Paper presented at World Bank Conference on Value Added Taxation in Developing Countries, Washington, D.C., April 21–23, 1986), note with regard to the VAT levied in the United Kingdom: "Because of the zero rating and exemptions, a positive VAT rate extended to not much more than half the value of total consumption."

17. To tax food provided for employees in full, it would be necessary either to value the food served employees or to disallow a deduction for purchase of food by the employer; see also the discussion of the taxation of employee benefits in chapter 8.

18. Under zero rating such an organization would receive refunds of all taxes paid on purchases; under exemption it would not. See also the discussion of zero rating and exemption in chapter 6 and that of the tax treatment of nonprofit institutions in chapter 8.

19. This assumption is quite extreme. It seems unlikely that even under an extremely liberal policy of exclusions all inputs into housing would be allowed to escape tax fully through zero rating of sales of new houses.

20. U.S. Department of the Treasury, *Tax Reform*, vol. 3, pp. 85–87.

21. Sandford and Godwin, in "Administrative and Compliance Problems," state, "Clearly, VAT is not a tax to impose at low rates." Of course, this does not mean that the federal government would need to collect VAT of at least 5 percent entirely for its own use. It might, in principle, collect a tax of 7 or 8 percent, turning 5 or 6 percent over to state governments. For more on this see chapter 9.

22. U.S. Department of the Treasury, *Tax Reform*, vol. 2, chap. 9.

23. Of course, both taxes also entail important compliance costs; these may well be higher in relative terms for the income tax, unless the VAT is levied at a very low rate.

4
Economic Effects

The economic effects of introducing a value-added tax are, for the most part, not very interesting. True, imposition of a VAT would probably cause a one-time increase in prices, and the tax would be regressive unless explicit steps were taken to reduce its regressivity. But the tax would have relatively little effect on the allocation of economic resources or on the competitiveness of U.S. industry in world markets, except to the extent that it reduced the deficit and caused the dollar to weaken. That the economic effects of the VAT are rather bland—we might call it a vanilla tax—is one of its chief advantages. After all, the primary purpose of taxation is (or at least should be) to raise revenue, not to change economic behavior; certainly unintended changes in behavior induced by taxation are not likely to be desirable.

That the VAT does not have very interesting economic effects does not mean that the effects of substituting it for part of the present tax system would not be significant. If a relatively neutral VAT were substituted for part of the highly distortionary income tax system, the allocation of resources might be greatly improved. Moreover, the VAT can be expected to be more conducive to saving than the income tax. But, strictly speaking, most of any such effects should be attributed to reduction of the income tax, not to imposition of the VAT. Analogous statements can be made about using the relatively neutral VAT, rather than the income tax, to raise additional revenue.

In this chapter I examine the economic effects of introducing a VAT. For the most part I focus on the likely effects of the VAT, since it is novel and relatively unknown in the United States. But in several instances—most notably in the discussion of international aspects—I explicitly discuss the consequences of substituting the VAT for part of the existing corporate income tax.

Purists might argue that the entire discussion should be cast in terms of substituting the VAT for other taxes, even if the VAT is being considered as a new source of additional revenue. According to this argument, the VAT should not be considered in a vacuum since an alternative tax could almost always be used instead of the VAT as a source of additional revenue; thus the VAT should be compared explicitly with alternative taxes that could be imposed or raised. I do not follow that approach, because to do so would make the presentation unduly tedious.[1] Moreover, the economic effects of the major alternative sources of revenue have been thoroughly documented elsewhere and are sufficiently well known that they need not be described in detail here.[2]

The final two sections of this chapter examine European experience with the VAT and its relevance for the United States. One key fact should be kept in mind in examining European experience. Most of the six original members of the European Economic Community (EEC) levied gross receipts taxes that virtually all tax experts agreed were highly defective (for reasons explained in chapter 7) and needed to be replaced. The situation is quite different in the United States, where there is no federal sales tax to replace. Moreover, federal introduction of the VAT would constitute entry into a new fiscal realm—one traditionally reserved for the states (see also chapter 9).

Economic Neutrality

Most advocates of free-market capitalism believe—as a general principle, if not in specific instances—that free markets do a reasonably good job of guiding economic decision making.[3] That is, they believe that if government interference can be minimized, the millions of independent decisions made daily by households and businesses will result in generally satisfactory choices—choices of what goods and services should be produced and consumed, of the production technology best suited to producing a given good or service, of how best to organize and finance production, and so on. If the government interferes with economic decision making, whether through taxation, regulation, or other means, economic decisions and the resulting allocation of the nation's scarce resources are likely to be less satisfactory.

Government interference in the economy cannot be completely eliminated. In particular, the need to finance government operations inevitably entails taxation, and even the most nearly ideal tax system would induce some distortion of economic decision making.[4] Nonetheless, one objective of sensible economic policy should be to interfere in free-market decision making as little as is consistent with other objectives and constraints, such as taxpayers' perceptions and administrative feasibility.[5] In the income tax sphere, this can be achieved by taxing all real economic income uniformly and consistently, without regard to its source or use.[6] In the field of indirect taxation, neutrality would be achieved by subjecting all goods and services consumed by households to the same rate of ad valorem taxation.[7] Deviations from either of these principles will, in general, result in suboptimal allocation of resources and loss of economic well-being.

Unless shot through with exemptions and differential rates, a VAT would go far to meeting the requirements of neutrality. In comparison, income taxes are notoriously distortionary; they distort choices of methods of finance (especially debt-equity ratios and dividend payout rates of corporations), choices of business organization (corporate versus noncorporate forms of organization), choices of production technology (capital- versus labor-intensive methods of production), and consumption decisions (corporate versus noncorporate products and tax-deductible expenditures versus others). Moreover, the income tax discriminates in favor of current consumption, because it taxes the return to saving; this fault is not shared by the consumption-based VAT, which treats present and future consumption equally. One estimate of the benefits of using revenues from a flat-rate VAT to replace the existing corporate income tax with an integrated system of personal and corporate taxation suggests that gains in economic welfare of as much as 1 percent of the present value of future output could be achieved.[8]

Distributional Issues

It is generally assumed that an American VAT would be regressive if levied in the conventional way as a destination-based tax on sales of goods and services to consumers. This section summarizes evidence on this score and considers four options for dealing with the potential regressivity of the VAT. First, however, it may be useful to digress briefly to consider the likely incidence of the VAT. In the discussion that follows the likely incidence is discussed in isolation. That is, the VAT is considered as a source of new revenue rather than as a replacement or substitute for another revenue source. The appendix to this chapter discusses the incidence of the corporate income tax.

The Incidence of a VAT. In examining the likely incidence of any kind of VAT or sales tax, including the business transfer tax (BTT) and the Hall-Rabushka personal-exemption VAT, it is useful to distinguish between two idealized potential bases of indirect, or sales, taxation—

production and consumption. The difference between these two bases hinges on how transfer payments and international transactions in goods and services are treated. For now I ignore the existence of transfer payments, returning to consider their implications in the second part of this section.

Under a destination-based tax, imported goods are subject to the same tax as domestically produced goods, and exports are free of tax. In other words, the base of a destination-principle tax is consumption rather than production. The base of an origin-principle tax is production. Imports from abroad are not taxed (since they are not produced domestically), but exports of domestically produced goods are taxed like other production.

Retail sales taxes are inherently destination-based levies; that is, they are levied on consumption rather than on production. Because of the use of border tax adjustments, the VATs employed in Europe and in most other countries are also destination-based taxes; that is, they are taxes on consumption.

International competitive pressures ensure that the likely incidence of consumption-based taxes is on consumers; by comparison, producers are likely to bear the burden of production taxes.[9] Although these statements may appear to be tautological, they are not. Rather, they state results that are indicated by economic analysis. The simplest case is that of a tax on production. Suppose that the output of a given country constitutes only a small portion of the worldwide supply of a product. If that country decides to introduce or increase a production- or origin-based VAT, it cannot expect to be able to increase the price of its exports by the amount of that tax. Rather, since its producers face essentially fixed world prices, they must absorb the tax. In other words, the production-based VAT is borne by producers.[10]

The analogous result holds for a consumption-based VAT. Suppose that a relatively small country decides to increase its taxes on consumption. (In carrying through this mental experiment, it may be useful to think in terms of the retail sales taxes that are common in the United States. A destination-based VAT and a retail sales tax are merely two ways of implementing a destination-based consumption tax.) Producers in countries that export to a country levying a destination-based tax will probably not be forced to absorb such a tax. Since producers faced with a destination-based tax in one country have the alternative of selling elsewhere if they cannot pass the tax forward to consumers in the taxing country, prices in the taxing nation will probably rise by the amount of the tax, and the tax will be borne by consumers in that nation. This result is, of course, totally consistent with the usual assumption that consumption taxes such as state retail sales taxes are borne by consumers.

Some may think that the BTT would not have the same incidence as a more conventional credit-method VAT, just because it is based on the subtraction method. There is, however, little reason for this belief, unless the difference in methods of calculating tax liabilities results in significant differences in the tax base.[11] Proponents of the BTT emphasize that the tax would be imposed on the destination principle. Receipts from foreign sales would be excluded from the tax base, and imports would be subject to tax. The BTT is clearly a tax on consumption rather than production. As such, it can be expected to be borne by consumers.[12]

The Hall-Rabushka personal-exemption VAT, however, is clearly designed to be a production-based levy. Export sales are included in receipts, and imports are deductible, though not taxed at the point of importation. Thus it can be expected that the Hall-Rabushka tax would be reflected in lower factor incomes rather than in higher product prices. Low-income recipients of wage income would be protected from the implied drop in net wages by the personal-exemption feature unique to this tax.

Four Ways to Reduce Regressivity. The VAT has generally been opposed by those who are concerned about its potentially adverse effects on the distribution of tax burdens among income classes. Simply stated, as a tax on consumption, the VAT would be regressive; since consumption falls as a percentage of income as income rises, the VAT would take relatively more of the income of low-income than of higher-income households. The first line of table 4 shows Treasury Department estimates of the distribution by income class of the burden of a broad-based VAT (one applying to about 80 percent of consumption) levied at a rate of 10 percent in a world without adjustment of transfer payments for price increases induced by the VAT.[13] VAT burdens decline steadily as a percentage of income from more than 14 percent for families with annual incomes below $10,000 to less than 2 percent for families with annual incomes greater than $200,000.[14]

A more troublesome aspect of this pattern of incidence is the heavy burden on low-income households per se.[15] After all, regressivity among families subject to the income tax can be offset by adjusting the personal exemptions, rate structure, and other features of the income tax. No such remedy is available for those not subject to income tax, short of expanding refundable credits or introducing a

TABLE 4
Net Burden of 10 Percent Value-added Tax as a Fraction of Economic Income, by Income Class

	Family Economic Income Class (thousands of dollars)								Cost of Alternatives[a]
	0–10	10–15	15–20	20–30	30–50	50–100	100–200	200 and over	
1. Value-added tax on broad base without adjustment of indexed transfers	14.2	9.2	7.5	6.1	5.0	3.9	3.0	1.8	—
Alternatives									
2. VAT on broad base with adjustment of indexed transfers	9.6	6.9	6.0	5.2	4.5	3.6	2.9	1.8	11.0
3. VAT on broad base without adjustment of indexed transfers and with food prepared at home zero rated	11.0	7.3	6.0	5.0	4.1	3.3	2.7	1.8	14.5
4. VAT on narrow base without adjustment of indexed transfers[b]	8.9	5.9	4.8	4.1	3.3	2.7	2.3	1.7	28.8
5. VAT on broad base without adjustment of indexed transfers and with refundable phased-out credit based on 100 percent of poverty-level income (low credit)	10.5	7.8	6.7	5.8	4.9	3.9	3.0	1.0	4.8

(Table continues)

33

TABLE 4 (continued)

	Family Economic Income Class (thousands of dollars)								Cost of Alternatives[a]
	0–10	10–15	15–20	20–30	30–50	50–100	100–200	200 and over	
6. VAT on broad base without adjustment of indexed transfers and with refundable phased-out credit based on 150 percent of poverty-level income (high credit)	8.7	7.1	6.3	5.6	4.8	3.9	3.0	1.8	7.2

NOTE: Restricted to families with non-negative income.

a. The cost of each alternative is expressed as a percentage of the revenue from a value-added tax on the comprehensive base (as described in U.S. Department of the Treasury, *Tax Reform*, vol. 3, chap. 7) at 1988 levels.

b. The narrow base provides for zero-rating expenditures on home-prepared food, new housing, prescription drugs and medicines, household energy, and water and sanitation services.

SOURCE: U.S. Department of the Treasury, *Tax Reform*, vol. 3, p. 111.

negative income tax. In what follows I focus on the problem of reducing the burden of taxation on low-income families.

The regressivity of the VAT and its burden on low-income families could be partially offset in at least four ways. First, transfer payments received by low-income households could be increased by enough to offset the burden of the VAT. Under current law this would occur automatically for social security payments and several other kinds of transfers, which are indexed for increases in the consumer price index (CPI). Although an explicit decision to adjust the definition of the CPI to eliminate the effect of the VAT is conceivable, such a step seems highly unlikely. Line 2 of table 4, which allows for the indexing of transfer payments under current law, is thus probably more indicative of the actual effect of the VAT on the distribution of tax burdens than line 1.

Table 5 shows that while the VAT is regressive, even with indexing of transfers, indexing dramatically reduces the aggregate effect of the VAT on low-income families. The Treasury Department has estimated, however, that 4 million of the 14 million families with incomes below $10,000 do not receive indexed transfers.[16] Thus indexing of transfers is a highly uneven means of dealing with the regressivity of the VAT.

Second, a few necessities that figure prominently in the budgets of low-income households could be exempted or zero rated. Lines 3 and 4 of table 4 show the effects of eliminating tax on food prepared at home by zero-rating foodstuffs and the effects of defining the tax base even more narrowly (but without adjusting transfers in either case).[17] These alternatives distort economic choices, complicate compliance and administration, and are extremely blunt and expensive instruments to use in the effort to avoid regressivity.[18] They are complicated because of the compliance and administrative problems caused by differentiation between taxed and zero-rated sales.[19] They are blunt because so much revenue must be lost on consumption by the non-poor to relieve the tax burden on the poor, especially if zero rating extends beyond food.[20] As line 3 of table 5 shows, to reduce taxes on households with incomes below $15,000 by just over 20 percent, it is necessary to reduce taxes on those with incomes of $20,000-50,000 by 18 percent and taxes on those with incomes of $50,000-100,000 by 15 percent.[21]

In appraising the desirability of using zero rating and multiple rates to reduce the regressivity of the VAT, it is important to keep in mind the following conclusions drawn from a conference devoted to examination of lessons from European experience with the VAT:

TABLE 5
REDUCTIONS OF VALUE-ADDED TAX BURDENS UNDER ALTERNATIVE SCHEMES, BY INCOME CLASS
(percent)

	Family Economic Income Class (thousands of dollars)								Cost of Alternatives[a]
	0–10	10–15	15–20	20–30	30–50	50–100	100–200	200 and over	
1. Value-added tax (VAT) on broad base without adjustment of indexed transfers	14.2	9.2	7.5	6.1	5.0	3.9	3.0	1.8	—
	Reductions in Tax as Percentage of Economic Income								
Alternatives									
2. VAT on broad base with adjustment of indexed transfers	32	25	20	15	10	8	3	0	11.0
3. VAT on broad base without adjustment of indexed transfers and with food prepared at home zero rated	23	21	20	18	18	15	10	0	14.5

4. VAT on narrow base without adjustment of indexed transfers[b]	37	36	36	33	34	31	23	6	28.8
5. VAT on broad base without adjustment of indexed transfers and with refundable phased-out credit based on 100 percent of poverty-level income (low credit)	26	15	11	5	2	0	0	0	4.8
6. VAT on broad base without adjustment of indexed transfers and with refundable phased-out credit based on 150 percent of poverty-level income (high credit)	39	23	16	8	4	0	0	0	7.2

NOTE: Restricted to families with non-negative income.

a. The cost of each alternative is expressed as a percentage of the revenue from a value-added tax on the comprehensive base (as described in U.S. Department of the Treasury, *Tax Reform*, vol. 3, chap. 7) at 1988 levels.

b. The narrow base provides for zero-rating expenditures on home-prepared food, new housing, prescription drugs and medicines, household energy, and water and sanitation services.

SOURCE: Table 4.

The central technical lesson of European experience is that multiple rates can be used to eliminate the regressivity of the value-added tax, but that the penalties in administrative complexity, increased compliance costs, and distortions in consumption decisions have been high and probably unjustified. Most conference participants agreed . . . that it would be preferable to use other taxes and transfer payments to alleviate the undesirable distributional consequences generated by value-added tax imposed at uniform rates.[22]

Third, the existing system of earned-income tax credits could be extended to allow, in effect, for refund of average VAT paid by low-income households. Lines 5 and 6 of table 4 illustrate the effects of two such schemes that differ in the level of credit provided.[23] This is easily the most cost-effective means of avoiding regressivity; relief is targeted to low-income families, and there is far less loss of revenue or reduction in taxes paid by high-income families. The high-credit alternative in line 6 produces the greatest reduction in taxes on low-income families; the low-credit option in line 5 shows somewhat less dramatic results.

Although theoretically this approach may be the most appropriate means of dealing with the problem of regressivity, it raises troublesome issues. Such a system of potentially universal refundable tax credits would constitute in embryonic form a negative income tax.[24] Whether a negative income tax is appropriate for the United States should be debated explicitly on its merits; such a policy should not merely be adopted without sufficient thought as an adjunct of a VAT. If a negative income tax were introduced, no other means of dealing with the regressivity of the VAT would be necessary, aside from some adjustment of income tax paid on incomes above the poverty level. Of course, significant issues in the design of a negative income tax would need to be addressed.

Fourth, the personal-exemption form of VAT could be implemented. Unfortunately the Treasury Department does not present estimates of the distributional effects of this form. I can, however, make the following observations. Given the method of implementing this form of VAT, it is more likely to be reflected in lower factor payments (for example, wages) than in higher prices.[25] Thus it would not be necessary or appropriate to zero-rate necessities, and indexation of transfers would appear to be largely irrelevant. To the extent that value added reflected labor income paid to families with income below the tax threshold, tax would not be collected. The primary low-income group not protected by this method would be low-income recipients of nonlabor income, such as dividends and interest.

Effects on Prices

In appraising the effects of a VAT on prices and on the rate of inflation, it is important to distinguish between imposing or raising a VAT as a new source of revenue, substituting a VAT for an existing direct tax such as the income tax, and substituting the VAT for another indirect tax such as a sales or excise tax. Significant effects on prices would not be expected from replacing one form of indirect tax with another or from substituting a VAT for a direct tax that is reflected in product prices. Thus the rest of this section is relevant only for the introduction of a VAT as a new source of revenue or a replacement of a direct tax that is not shifted to consumers.

The VAT increases the cost of taxable goods and services sold to households for consumption. (It is not a cost in other circumstances, since businesses are allowed a credit for the VAT.) Monetary policy would be expected to accommodate this increase in costs; if so, prices would probably rise by the amount of the VAT.[26] Thus, for example, if the VAT applied to 80 percent of consumption, a 10 percent VAT would probably raise the cost of consumption by about 8 percent.[27] The alternative of a monetary policy sufficiently restrictive to prevent a price increase would probably cause enough unemployment to be politically unlikely as well as economically unwise.

The price rise induced by the VAT would be a one-time phenomenon; although it might be measured as a spurt of inflation, it would not be a rise in the rate of inflation. Under some conditions, however, imposing a VAT might create further rounds of price increases and aggravate inflation. Most obviously, an increase in the CPI induced by the VAT might trigger wage increases because of provisions for cost-of-living allowances in labor contracts. These would create pressures for further price increases and further rounds of wage increases. These ripple effects are difficult to predict with confidence, but they would probably not be important for the nation as a whole, especially if they were not accommodated by monetary policy.

International Aspects

The VAT first drew significant attention in the United States during the 1960s, when it was recognized that under the General Agreement on Tariffs and Trade (GATT) border tax adjustments are allowed for VAT on products entering international trade. Some observers believed that U.S. reliance on the corporate income tax, for which no border tax adjustments are allowed, together with European reliance on national VATs, placed American producers at a competitive disadvantage in international markets and was therefore deleterious to the

39

U.S. balance of payments.[28] Moreover, the argument went, the United States could improve its balance of payments by substituting a VAT for part of the corporate income tax. Arguments similar to these still figure prominently in the debate over VAT. But since exchange rates are no longer fixed, attention now focuses primarily on improving the competitive position of the United States rather than its balance of payments.

The claim that U.S. imposition of a VAT would improve the nation's competitive position (or its balance of payments) can be appraised at several levels.[29] The crudest version of this argument is that imposing the VAT would in itself improve our competitive position because the tax is rebated on exports and imposed on imports.[30] This argument is quite unpersuasive, for reasons given in chapter 3. The border tax adjustments on both imports and exports are necessary to prevent the producers of a nation levying a VAT from being at a competitive disadvantage; they do not give that nation a competitive advantage.[31]

Exponents of the contrary view presumably see the rebate of VAT as no more than an export subsidy and the imposition of the VAT on imports as merely a protective tariff; of course, export subsidies and import duties would improve our competitive position (and our balance of payments, for a given exchange rate). But the border tax adjustments required to place the VAT on a destination basis are not merely export subsidies and import duties. The VAT is imposed on imports precisely to prevent them from competing unfairly with domestic products, which are subject to the VAT; similarly, the VAT is rebated so that exports will not enter world markets burdened by the tax paid at prior stages.

Another way to appreciate this crucial point is to recall the basic similarity between a VAT and a conceptually pure retail sales tax. Like the VAT the retail sales tax applies to imports as well as to domestically produced goods. Similarly, like the VAT the retail sales tax is not levied on exports. Yet hardly anyone would seriously argue that imposing a national retail sales tax would in itself improve the competitive position of U.S. industry.

A more sophisticated argument accepts the reasoning of the preceding paragraph but suggests that substituting the VAT for part of the corporate income tax would improve the ability of U.S. industry to compete in international markets, at least for a while.[32] Whether such a tax substitution would have the postulated effect depends on how it would affect domestic prices. According to the standard incidence analysis summarized above and the discussion of likely price effects, the VAT, with its compensating import levy, would be reflected in higher prices for all goods sold in U.S. markets, including imports. By comparison, since the tax would be rebated on exports, it would leave the price of exports unchanged. The VAT by itself should have no significant structural effect on international trade. If the tax substitution is to have any important structural effects on trade, they must be traced to the reduction of the corporate income tax.

The GATT rules, which were formulated during World War II, are based on the traditional assumptions that indirect taxes are reflected in product prices but that the corporate income tax is borne by shareholders and thus has no effect on product prices. Removing a corporate tax with the effects postulated by the authors of the GATT would not affect the competitive position of U.S. industry, and substituting the VAT for part of such a tax would also be neutral in its effects on international competitiveness. Thus the argument that the tax substitution would improve the competitive position of the United States challenges the results of traditional incidence theory.

If the corporate income tax is reflected in higher prices of corporate output, removing part of the tax should lower the prices of goods produced by U.S. corporations. Combining this effect with the lack of effect of imposing the destination-based VAT would produce a fall in the prices of domestically produced goods in relation to those of goods produced abroad, both in other countries and in U.S. import markets. Under these conditions the tax substitution would improve the short-run competitiveness of the United States. Long-run improvements, however, are less likely.

Another way of making this argument is to think of the corporate income tax as having effects on prices similar to those of a very complicated form of sales tax. In such a case the corporate tax and the VAT might have generally similar effects on domestic prices, but only the VAT would provide border tax adjustments. This being the case, the postulated tax substitution would improve the competitive position of domestic producers in both U.S. and foreign markets. This way of phrasing the question highlights the crucial issue: Does the corporate income tax raise prices, as a sales tax does? The jury is still out on this issue, as explained further in the appendix to this chapter, but it seems reasonable to believe that substituting a VAT for part of the corporate income tax might improve U.S. competitiveness in the short run.

The argument just presented must be modified in one important respect. Under current law many American industries that are active in international trade pay little or no corporate income tax at the margin on income from investment.[33] In these circumstances reducing the corporate tax rate would cause little improvement of the competitive position of such industries; indeed a reduction in corporate tax rates might actually raise the cost of capital and be detrimental to the competitive position of such industries.[34] This qualification should be somewhat less important under the recently enacted tax reform.

Growth of Government

The fear has often been expressed that introduction of a VAT would lead to a rise in government spending.[35] For example, in appraising European experience, Henry Aaron of the Brookings Institution has written:

> The value added tax in Europe was intended as a substitute for other taxes, but it has been associated with an increase in taxation. . . . Statistics strongly suggest that the value-added tax was a handy instrument at a time when government expenditures were rising. . . . While the value-added tax might be used to reduce other taxes and as part of a program of fiscal retrenchment in the United States, it is important to recognize that the United States would be blazing a trail of fiscal forbearance not traversed by any of the countries covered in this book.[36]

Among the evidence commonly cited for the "money machine" hypothesis—that government will grow more rapidly if the Congress has this relatively painless source of revenue—is the difference in ratios of tax to gross domestic product (GDP) found in countries that do and do not have national sales taxes.[37] None of the four countries listed in table 6 that have the lowest ratios of tax to GDP have national sales taxes, whereas all the rest do. Although it appears that adoption of a VAT has not caused the ratio of tax to GDP to grow any faster than in countries without a VAT, this evidence is not dispositive.[38]

The money machine argument is difficult to appraise. To some extent it must rely on the perception that the VAT is less apparent than other taxes or is even hidden. But this view is not really convincing; the VAT is not (or need not be) hidden.

A somewhat different view is that raising additional tax revenues from existing revenue sources would be difficult because of taxpayers' resistance, erosion of the tax base, and fear of adverse economic consequences but that the VAT could be used for this purpose. This argument seems somewhat more compelling but raises another issue: Would an expansion of government spending, if it were facilitated by adoption of the VAT, be good or bad? Answers to this question are likely to reflect political views about the proper size of governments. Liberals are likely to argue that various defects in the political process

42

TABLE 6

FEDERAL, STATE, AND LOCAL TAX REVENUES AS PERCENTAGE OF
GROSS DOMESTIC PRODUCT, SELECTED COUNTRIES, 1982

	Total Tax Revenue	Total Indirect Taxes
Sweden	50.3	12.2
Belgium	46.6	12.1
Netherlands	45.5	10.8
Denmark	44.0	16.2
France	43.7	13.0
United Kingdom	39.6	11.5
Italy	38.3	6.6
Luxembourg	37.7	8.4
Germany	37.3	9.9
Canada	34.9	12.1
Switzerland	30.9	6.1
United States	30.5	5.3
Japan	27.2	4.2

SOURCE: Organization for Economic Cooperation and Development, *Revenue Statistics of OECD Member Countries, 1965–1983* (Paris, 1984), reported in U.S. Department of the Treasury, *Tax Reform*, vol. 3, p. 24.

cause the government to be starved for revenue and result in inadequate government spending. Conservatives counter that the political process results in too much government spending and taxes that are too high. Examination of whether federal tax revenues and government spending should be higher lies well beyond the scope of this monograph.[39] Needless to say, however, views on this basic issue condition responses to the prospect that adoption of a VAT might lead to greater growth of government.

Economic Effects of the Value-added Tax in Europe

Some thirty countries now impose comprehensive VATs, that is, VATs extending through the retail stage. About half of them are in Europe, and a dozen are in Latin America. New Zealand is the most recent convert to VAT; its tax was imposed beginning October 1, 1986.[40]

Among the questions that naturally arise in considering the adoption of a federal tax on value added in the United States are, How is it done in Europe? and What have been its effects in Europe? This section provides brief and necessarily incomplete answers to these questions.

The first VAT in Europe was adopted by France in 1954. But it was applied only through the wholesale stage and was extended to the retail stage and to services only on January 1, 1968, the date when Germany substituted a VAT for its notoriously defective "cascade" turnover tax. (The defects of such taxes are described in chapter 7.) Thus the Danish VAT, adopted in 1967 as a replacement for a tax levied at the wholesale stage, was the first truly general VAT in Europe. The VAT was adopted by the Netherlands and Sweden in 1969, by Norway and Luxembourg in 1970, by Belgium in 1971, by Ireland in 1972, and by Italy, the United Kingdom, and Austria in 1973.

Only Denmark and Norway have adopted single-rate taxes on value added, although the disadvantages of multiple-rate systems are well known. Sweden nominally has one rate, but it applies the tax to a reduced tax base in the case of construction. The United Kingdom has only one positive rate but provides extensive zero rating; most food-stuffs, fuel and power, drugs and medicine, and children's footwear and clothing are zero rated. See table 7 for VAT rates in Europe.

Not surprisingly, the reduced rates and exemptions commonly apply primarily to items that might reasonably be considered necessities: food, housing, transportation, electric utilities and telecommunications, newspapers, and social and medical services. Conversely, differentially high rates apply primarily to luxuries.[41] In this regard it has been noted, "Possibly by coincidence, the single-rate countries are also those with the most developed social welfare systems, and the most progressive direct tax scales; as a result they least need to attempt income redistribution via high VAT rates on luxuries and low ones on necessities."[42] Finally, the financial sector is usually exempt for the services it provides, though not for its purchases. Those in certain activities can generally choose whether or not to be in the VAT system and thus be able to take credit for taxes paid on purchases.

It is difficult to generalize about the economic effects of adopting the tax on value added in Europe. Effects on the efficiency of resource allocation are not directly observable and can only be surmised from theoretical arguments and the nature of the preexisting tax systems. Where the VAT replaced a cascade turnover tax, as in Germany, Luxembourg, and the Netherlands, the gains in economic efficiency are almost certain to be great. Where it replaced a retail sales tax, as in Norway and Sweden, or even a wholesale tax, as in Denmark, the gains are not likely to be as important. Where it replaced a variety of indirect taxes, as in Belgium and France, or a system of differential

TABLE 7
RATES OF EUROPEAN VALUE-ADDED TAXES, 1983 AND 1985
(percent)

	Standard Rate	Reduced Rate[a]	Higher Rate
European Economic Community (March 1985)			
Belgium	19	6, 17	25, 33
Denmark	22	None	None
France	18.6	5.5, 7	33.3
Ireland	23	10[b]	None
Italy	18	2, 9	38
Luxembourg	12	3, 6	None
Netherlands	19	5	None
United Kingdom	15	None[c]	None
West Germany	14	7	None
Other countries (1983)			
Austria	18	8, 13	30
Norway	20	None	None
Sweden	23.46	None[d]	None

a. Books, newspapers, and periodicals, as well as exports, are commonly zero rated.
b. Also zero rating of medicine and most foodstuffs and clothing and a 2.3 percent rate for live animals.
c. But zero rating of most foodstuffs, fuel and power, drugs and medicines, and children's footwear and clothing.
d. Also zero rating of medicines, most fuels, and electricity.

SOURCES: For EEC countries, Commission of the European Communities, *Completing the Internal Market* (white paper to the European Council, June 1985), p. 49; for other countries, Claudia Scott and Howard Davis, *The Gist of GST: A Briefing on the Goods and Services Tax* (Wellington, New Zealand: Victoria University Press, Institute of Policy Studies, 1985).

rates on selected items, as in the United Kingdom, an intermediate result is likely. Since the United States has no federal sales tax to replace with a VAT, the European evidence on this score is of little relevance to the United States. The VAT has not replaced an important direct tax except in France, where the social security payroll tax was eliminated.

Similar statements can be made about the effect of adopting a VAT on the rates of saving and investment. First, the effects would probably not be large, since the VAT would primarily replace other indirect taxes. Second, the effects would be difficult to isolate, even with sophisticated econometric techniques.

Probably the question most often asked about the European taxes on value added is how they affected prices when they were introduced. The answer to this question is crucial for the likely effects on international competitiveness, as well as in itself. Here the evidence is mixed and difficult to evaluate.[43] Germany was perhaps the most successful in its efforts to prevent a large increase in prices from accompanying its introduction of the VAT.[44] It is generally agreed that substituting the VAT for the German cascade tax had little effect on prices.[45] Tait identifies Belgium and Luxembourg as other members of the EEC in which introducing the VAT had little or no effect on prices.

France, Italy, and the United Kingdom seem to have been only slightly less successful in their attempts to prevent the VAT from setting off inflation. In all three countries the introduction of the VAT appears to have coincided with the acceleration of inflation. But Tait suggests that in each case the increase in the rate of inflation can arguably be attributed to other causes. Considering all circumstances, he assigns these three important countries to the "little or no change" category.[46]

Most of this European experience is not directly relevant to appraising the likely effects on prices of introducing a federal tax on value added in the United States, since in these cases the VAT replaced existing indirect taxes. The most relevant experience appears to be that in Denmark and Norway. In Denmark, where the shift to the VAT was used to increase revenues substantially, prices rose by 8 percent. But authorities appear to have expected and condoned this, since the adverse distributional effects of the price increase were mitigated by a general increase in wages and special relief for low-income persons. Perhaps for this reason, the price increases accompanying introduction of the VAT were a one-time event and did not lead to a rise in the rate of inflation. In Norway a switch in the composition of revenues from direct to indirect taxation occurred simultaneously with introduction of the VAT. There prices increased by almost 6 percent, and inflation accelerated. A wage-price spiral based on increased inflationary expectations and accommodated by monetary policy appears to explain this difference.[47]

This experience contains some lessons for the United States: introducing an American VAT would probably result in an increase in prices, especially if the VAT were a source of additional revenue, but this could be a one-time event that would not lead to further inflation if the transition were handled properly.

Because European experience is not directly relevant to the United States, we must rely on theoretical analysis. It is probably safe to say that introducing a VAT would raise prices of taxable goods and services by about the percentage amount of the tax. The effect on overall prices would also depend on the fraction of consumption subject to the VAT.

Only if the VAT were substituted for part of the corporate income tax or another direct tax and that tax had been shifted forward in the form of higher prices could we expect prices not to rise markedly with introduction of a VAT. If the corporate tax had not been shifted, prices would probably rise by about the amount of the tax.

The view that introducing a VAT would lead to greater government spending has recently been challenged, on the basis of experience in countries that belong to the Organization for Economic Cooperation and Development (OECD). Stockfisch argues that the change in ratios of tax to GNP over the period during which the VAT was adopted in many advanced countries appears to be no different for VAT countries than for OECD members without VATs.[48] This evidence is, however, far from conclusive, since the statistical test used by Stockfisch sheds little light on the money machine hypothesis.

All the countries included in Stockfisch's sample of countries adopting a VAT already had a national sales tax (that is, they already had a money machine, though perhaps a less efficient one). Stockfisch is thus merely demonstrating that a change in the *form* of national sales tax did not have a dramatic effect on the rate of growth of tax collections, compared with experience in countries with no VAT. That finding is hardly surprising and sheds virtually no light on whether introducing a VAT in a country with no national sales tax would cause the growth of government spending to accelerate.

Relevance of the European Experience

When the six original countries of the EEC decided in the early 1960s to switch to the VAT, they clearly made the right choice. But their decision was based on considerations that have little relevance for the United States. The American discussion of whether to introduce a VAT occurs in a context that raises issues that did not arise or were quite secondary in the European debate.

At the time the EEC was formed, most of the member states levied gross receipts taxes (turnover taxes) of the kind described in chapter 7. Given the manifest defects of such taxes, a revenue-neutral shift to a relatively neutral VAT was a clear improvement.

The VAT would distort economic choices less than the turnover tax, and accurate border tax adjustments would be possible, as they were not under the turnover taxes. Moreover, effects on prices, the rate of inflation, and the distribution of tax burdens among income classes would probably be minimal. Nor did such a shift create substantial problems of taxpayers' compliance and administration; the primary change was to require issuance of invoices to business customers and allow taxpayers to take credit for taxes paid on purchases as shown on invoices.

Consider now the situation in the United States. There is no defective federal sales tax to replace with a VAT. An American VAT would be a source of additional revenue or a replacement for part of the existing income tax or both. Therefore, the need for additional revenue must be assessed, and the VAT must be compared explicitly with existing or potential alternative sources of revenue. The decision is thus much more complicated than it was in Europe. An American VAT would probably raise prices, and it would be regressive unless explicit steps were taken to avoid burdens on low-income taxpayers. Moreover, a substantially greater educational effort would be required than in Europe to introduce this new form of tax.

The American decision is further complicated by a factor that played little role in Europe, our federal system of government. State and local governments have long seen the general sales tax as their private fiscal preserve. Introduction of a federal VAT would be seen as an intrusion into that preserve and as such would not be welcomed by state and local governments.

Because almost all states levy retail sales taxes, introducing a federal VAT would also raise tricky issues of fiscal coordination. These include harmonization of federal and state bases, state piggybacking on a federal sales tax, and sharing of revenues from a federal VAT with the states—issues that are discussed further in chapter 9. They were largely absent from the European debate on VAT.[49]

Appendix: The Incidence Debate

Much of the discussion of the desirability of an American VAT has been in the context of substituting it for part of the corporate income tax. Almost any careful consideration of the effects of such a substitution quickly moves to a discussion of the incidence of the two taxes, since several of the most important effects of the substitution depend crucially on the answer to that question. Most obviously, the distributional implications depend directly on the incidence of the taxes, that is, on who bears their burdens. A consumption-based VAT would almost certainly be borne by households in rough proportion to consumption expenditures, for reasons noted in the text. Thus this appendix focuses on the incidence of the corporate income tax, which is far less certain. Although I cannot hope to settle the issue, I can lay out the arguments.[50]

Traditional theory holds that any tax on economic profits can only be borne by recipients of profit income, at least in the short run. According to that theory, prices in competitive industries equal the marginal costs of marginal firms that, having no profits, pay no tax. A firm that has a monopoly position in an industry maximizes profits by setting marginal costs equal to marginal revenue. In either case the existence of the profits tax, which affects neither marginal costs nor marginal revenue, has no effect on output, price, or payments to productive inputs. Thus, the reasoning goes, the tax is reflected in lower profits net of tax. That is, the tax is borne by owners of the firm.

A multitude of reasons exist, however, for believing that the corporate income tax can be at least partly shifted either to consumers or to labor, even in the short run. First, corporate income for tax purposes is not made up solely of economic profits; it includes the normal return to equity capital. Thus part of the tax does constitute an element of costs.[51] Second, important portions of the corporate sector of the U.S. economy fit neither the perfect competition nor the pure monopoly mold, and oligopoly behavior is quite consistent with substantial shifting of the corporate tax. The tax may act, for example, as a signal for firms setting prices in a consciously parallel fashion, whether with or without an established price leader, to raise prices. Moreover, wage settlements with strong unions may result in labor's sharing the burden of such a tax. Third, corporate goals other than short-run profit maximization (such as avoidance of antitrust action, constrained sales maximization, or limit pricing based on long-range profit maximization) may lead to shifting of the tax. Finally, if capital is mobile internationally, the corporate tax is more likely to be borne by consumers and by land and labor.[52] Thus one can find strong theoretical support on both sides of the incidence argument.

Unfortunately, empirical work on this subject leaves us very much in the dark. The pioneering work by Kryzaniak and Musgrave during the 1960s found the tax to be completely shifted in manufacturing, a result not theoretically inconsistent with the oligopoly structure of much manufacturing, but this analysis has been subjected to considerable criticism.[53] Moreover, the relevance of this earlier analysis to the current debate is substantially reduced by the much greater interdependence that now characterizes the world economy. Faced with competition from abroad, U.S. corporations are not likely to be able to shift the tax easily. It seems best to report only that the jury is still out on the question of the short-run incidence of the corporate income tax.

Finally, it is not even clear whether the short- or the long-run incidence of the tax is of more importance for policy purposes. For questions of immediate effects on income distribution and on prices and the balance of payments, short-run effects are crucial. But where equity is concerned, it is also useful to consider the incidence in the long run.

In the long run the corporate income tax can be expected to induce two effects that dramatically change the traditional short-run result that the tax is borne by shareholders. First, the tax is likely to produce a shift in the relative prices of corporate and noncorporate output and a reallocation of capital from the corporate to the noncorporate sector. This drives down the return to noncorporate investors and partially restores the return to corporate investment. As a result the tax is borne by all owners of capital, not just by shareholders. Moreover, it induces a shift in the relative prices of corporate and noncorporate output, making the former relatively more expensive. Second, by depressing capital formation, the tax reduces the productivity of labor and thus is borne in part by workers.

Given the uncertainty about the answers to important questions about the incidence of the corporate income tax, it seems best simply to present the arguments of the text under two alternative assumptions—that the tax is borne entirely by shareholders and that it is shifted to consumers. Neither intermediate positions, such as 50 percent shifting, nor alternative assumptions, such as a partial shifting to labor or a sharing of the burden by all recipients of capital income, are considered. Intermediate shifting assumptions lead to intermediate results and need not be considered explicitly. The assumption of short-run shifting to labor, though theoretically possible, does not have widespread professional support, and the added complication of including it in the analysis does not seem justified. Sharing of the burden by all owners of capital would not produce distributional results dramatically different from those of the burden solely on shareholders. It is, however, consistent with a shift in the relative prices of corporate and noncorporate output that suggests that a reduction in the corporate income tax might help American competitiveness.

Notes

1. I do take such an approach, however, in earlier analyses of the VAT; see, for example, Charles E. McLure, Jr., "The Tax on Value Added: Pros and Cons," in Charles E. McLure, Jr., and Norman B. Ture, *Value Added Tax: Two Views* (Washington, D.C.: American Enterprise Institute, 1972), pp. 1–68; "The Tax Restructuring Act of 1979: Time for an American Value Added Tax?" *Public Policy*, vol. 28 (Summer 1980), pp. 301–22; "VAT versus the Payroll Tax," in Felicity Skidmore, ed., *Financing Social Security* (Cambridge, Mass.: MIT Press, 1981), pp. 129–64; and "Value Added Tax: Has the Time Come?" in

Charls E. Walker and Mark A. Bloomfield, eds., *New Directions in Federal Tax Policy for the 1980s* (Cambridge, Mass.: Ballinger, 1983), pp. 185–213.

2. For defects of the current income tax, see U.S. Department of the Treasury, *Tax Reform for Fairness, Simplicity, and Economic Growth* (Washington, D.C., 1984), vols. 1, 2; or Henry J. Aaron and Harvey Galper, *Assessing Tax Reform* (Washington, D.C.: Brookings Institution, 1985).

3. The sentence in the text is intended to be a qualified statement of the theoretical argument that under certain conditions resource allocation determined by decisions made in competitive markets maximizes consumer welfare. That theoretical conclusion must be qualified in recognition that the conditions necessary for the proof of welfare maximization do not prevail in the real world.

4. If taxes are not levied explicitly, inflation acts as a tax by reducing the real value of assets fixed in nominal (monetary) terms.

5. Economic purists will note that the theory of optimal taxation does not lead to minimization of interference in free-market decision making as the objective of public policy. Since the dictates of optimal taxation theory are probably neither administratively feasible nor politically viable, it seems sensible in the absence of a compelling argument to the contrary to interfere as little as possible with free-market decision making, especially in indirect taxation.

Henry J. Aaron, ed., *The Value Added Tax: Lessons from Europe* (Washington, D.C.: Brookings Institution, 1981), suggests the same conclusion (p. 6): "A case can be made for the differentiation of tax rates on various commodities. In practice, the required differentiation would be hard to carry out, and the view persists that the potential neutrality (in other words, uniformity) of the value-added tax is one of its chief advantages." Similarly, J. A. Kay and E. H. Davis argue in "The VAT and Services" (Paper presented at World Bank Conference on Value Added Taxation in Developing Countries, Washington, D.C., April 21–23, 1986) that there is "a presumption of uniformity in commodity taxation which implies a VAT at a common rate across all goods and services."

6. U.S. Department of the Treasury, *Tax Reform*, takes this as its objective. It can, of course, be objected that the taxation of income, rather than consumption, constitutes an important form of interference with market forces: preference for present versus future consumption. For more on the decision to pursue reform of the income tax rather than introduction of a tax on consumed income, see ibid.; Charles E. McLure, Jr., "Reflections on Recent Proposals to Rationalize the U.S. Income Tax," in *Proceedings of the 41st Congress of the International Institute of Public Finance, Madrid*, August 26–30, 1985; and idem, "Where Tax Reform Went Astray," *Villanova Law Review*, vol. 31 (forthcoming 1986).

7. Again, neutrality (as described by the theory of optimal taxation) may not be optimal when compared with a system that takes account of administrative reality or perceptions of fairness. See also note 5.

8. See Charles L. Ballard, John Karl Scholz, and John B. Shoven, *The Value-added Tax: A General Equilibrium Look at Its Efficiency and Incidence* (Paper

presented at NBER Conference on the Effects of Taxation on Capital Formation, West Palm Beach, Florida, February 14–16, 1986). Interestingly enough, gains in economic welfare in this case are relatively insensitive to whether a flat-rate VAT or a system with differentiated rates is considered. This study also reports results of simulations of using revenues from a VAT to reduce personal income tax rates by a constant fraction and by a constant number of percentage points, as well as to finance integration of the income taxes. Moreover, it compares the welfare costs of financing a 10 percent increase in government spending with a VAT and with the income tax. A multiplicative increase in the income tax reduces welfare by one-third more than using a VAT to raise the same amount of additional revenue.

The complete integration option examined by Ballard et al. is only one way of reducing the corporate income tax; though perhaps conceptually the best way of doing so in the context of an income tax, it may not be administratively feasible. See Charles E. McLure, Jr., *Must Corporate Income Be Taxed Twice?* (Washington, D.C.: Brookings Institution, 1979), chap. 5.

Allowing relief from double taxation of dividends, through either a corporate deduction for dividends paid or a shareholder credit for dividends received, may provide most of the allocative benefits of complete integration, and it is clearly feasible, as European experience shows. Simply reducing corporate tax rates would probably also improve economic efficiency, by making the distortions created by the corporate tax less important. Reducing corporate taxes by accentuating existing distortionary tax preferences (such as the special tax treatment of oil and gas, timber, and investment in certain industries) or introducing new preferences could very well worsen allocative efficiency rather than improve it.

9. Strictly speaking, the arguments that follow may be valid only if exchange rates are fixed; a fundamental theorem of international trade asserts that under certain conditions a general tax on consumption and a general tax on production are equivalent, the only difference being the exchange rate. (A shift from a production tax to a consumption tax is equivalent to devaluation.) Even with fixed exchange rates the choice of origin or destination principles may simply be reflected in movements in domestic price levels. The conditions required for this equivalence theorem to hold are sufficiently unrealistic that the statements in the text do not seem unreasonable. See Sijbren Cnossen and Carl S. Shoup, "Value-added Tax Coordination," in Sijbren Cnossen, ed., *Tax Coordination in the EC* (Daventer, The Netherlands: Kluwer, 1986).

10. In general, producers in one nation can raise prices in response to a production tax by a fraction of the price increase that would result from a worldwide production levy equal to the nation's share of worldwide output. See Charles E. McLure, Jr., "Market Dominance and the Exporting of State Taxes," *National Tax Journal*, vol. 34 (December 1981), pp. 483–85. Similar statements apply to the effects of consumption taxes levied by one nation.

11. See, however, the discussion of the effects of an extremely high exemption for small business in chapter 8. To the extent that exempt businesses dominate certain sectors, it might be difficult for nonexempt firms to pass the tax on to consumers.

12. The statements in the text ignore the effects of the proposed FICA offset, which is unlikely to be enacted, for reasons given in chapter 6.

13. These estimates are taken from U.S. Department of the Treasury, *Tax Reform*, vol. 3, p. 111. For earlier attempts to estimate the distributional effects of an American VAT, see Charles L. Schultze, Edward R. Fried, Alice Rivlin, and Nancy H. Teeters, *Setting National Priorities: The 1973 Budget* (Washington, D.C.: Brookings Institution, 1972); and Charles E. McLure, Jr., "Economic Effects of Taxing Value Added," in Richard A. Musgrave, ed., *Broad-based Taxes: New Options and Sources* (Baltimore: Johns Hopkins University Press for the Committee for Economic Development, 1973), pp. 155–204. The various papers in Aaron, *Value Added Tax*, report on the incidence of the VAT in several European countries. The analysis of incidence in Ballard et al., *Value-added Tax*, is difficult to compare with that reported in studies such as these, since it considers changes in total economic welfare induced by taxation rather than merely who pays the tax.

14. Estimates such as these are generally acknowledged to overstate the regressivity of the VAT. According to the "permanent income hypothesis," a household with a temporarily low income will continue to consume more or less at its accustomed level, which is likely to be higher than that of a household permanently at the same lower income. Life-cycle considerations are especially important in this context. Young families may base current consumption decisions, especially on the purchase of consumer durables, on expectations of lifetime income. Similarly, retired couples with little current income continue to consume by running down amounts previously saved for retirement. This helps explain how in table 4 a 10 percent VAT assumed to be levied on only about 80 percent of consumption can constitute more than 14 percent of economic income in the lowest income bracket (under $10,000) and more than 9 percent of income in the second bracket ($10,000–15,000).

Edgar K. Browning, "The Burden of Taxation," *Journal of Political Economy*, vol. 86 (April 1978), pp. 649–71, and Edgar K. Browning and William R. Johnson, *The Distribution of the Tax Burden* (Washington, D.C.: American Enterprise Institute, 1979), have questioned the traditional view that sales taxes are regressive, noting that if transfer payments are indexed for inflation or otherwise adjusted to reflect consumption taxes, only those who receive factor incomes actually pay the tax. Since these are likely to have incomes higher than those of recipients of transfers, they argue, the tax would be progressive.

More recently Edgar K. Browning, "Tax Incidence, Indirect Taxes, and Transfers," *National Tax Journal*, vol. 38 (December 1985), pp. 525–34, has argued that the validity of this argument does not depend on the indexing of transfers. Rather, he argues, the basic assumption of differential incidence analysis—the constancy of real government expenditures—calls for this result. The empirical significance of this qualification (but not the underlying methodological issues) is considered immediately below.

15. In evaluating this argument it is important to note that in the Treasury Department method underlying table 4 contributions to (and earnings on funds invested in) pension plans and retirement accounts were treated as

current income in the year in which contributions were made (and accrual of earnings occurred) rather than in the year in which withdrawals were made. See U.S. Department of the Treasury, *Tax Reform*, vol. 1, pp. 57–59. Thus, in principle, a retired taxpayer consuming his or her pension wealth might show virtually no current income, and the VAT paid by the retiree would be interpreted as contributing to regressivity. This state of affairs obviously has different implications from those of a low-income family stuck permanently in poverty.

16. See ibid., vol. 3, p. 91. Of course, transfers may be indexed de facto if legislated increases match increases in the cost of living.

17. Unfortunately the Treasury Department source of table 4 does not present estimates of the effects of both indexing transfers and adopting any of the three other policies simultaneously.

18. In appraising the distortions and administrative headaches created by differential rates, it is worthwhile to consider the following quotations from Richard Hemming and John A. Kay, "The United Kingdom," in Aaron, *Value Added Tax*.

> It is important, therefore, to note that as soon as any complication in rate structure is introduced, the pattern of uniformity flies apart completely. For example, most food is zero rated in Britain, but restaurant meals are taxed at 15 percent. Because the 15 percent rate is applied to the whole value of the output while there is no input tax to be refunded on the food content of inputs, the value added in catering is taxed at a much higher rate than 15 percent. . . . The range of effective rates [on selected input-output industries], from − 24.3 percent to 37 percent, is far broader than the range of nominal rates. It is important to note that these differences in effective rates affect decisions by individual consumers about whether to buy a particular commodity or produce it themselves, and in some cases there is no real option. Effective rates do not, in general, represent the rates that businesses would face in deciding whether to produce a good themselves or to obtain it from another supplier (pp. 80–81).

> The dispersion of effective rates creates distortions beyond those explicitly intended. A customer of a British branch of McDonald's is offered two prices depending on whether he wishes to take his hamburger away (buy food, a zero-rated transaction) or eat it on the premises (consume a restaurant meal and pay value-added tax at the standard rate). It is probably not entirely coincidental that the Westminster branch of McDonald's has chosen a location immediately adjacent to the piazza of Westminster Cathedral (p. 81).

19. If nontaxation took the form of exemption rather than zero rating, the complexity would be even greater, because of the necessity of prorating purchases of many vendors between exempt and taxable sales. Moreover, exemption is a less efficient way to achieve distributional objectives than zero rating, since tax would be collected on some early stages of production of

goods that are ultimately to be exempt. See also chapters 6 and 8.

20. Claudia Scott, "VAT and Tax Reform" (Paper presented at World Bank Conference on Value Added Taxation in Developing Countries, Washington, D.C., April 21–23, 1986), notes: "Selective exemptions have only a minor impact on the overall incidence of sales taxes since the distribution of consumption expenditure on any particular item is not sufficiently different from the distribution of consumption expenditure overall to have a marked impact on the incidence of taxes."

21. Line 4 of table 4 tells an even more dramatic story about the inefficiency of this approach: if an attempt is made to reduce regressivity by extending zero rating beyond food, taxes on those with incomes of $50,000-100,000 must be reduced by 31 percent to reduce taxes on families with incomes below $15,000 by 36 percent.

22. Aaron, *Value Added Tax*, p. 16. U.S. Department of the Treasury, *Tax Reform*, reaches very much the same conclusion (vol. 3, p. 45):

If a single rate of value-added tax is politically unacceptable, the only other rate should be zero. It should be applied to necessities such as food and medicine, assuming other alternatives for removing the burden of the tax from the poor are not feasible. If zero rates are used, there is little need for, and much complexity created by, the use of reduced "semi-necessity" and increased "luxury" rates of tax.

23. In the high-credit option, the credit would be based on VAT paid at an income of 150 percent of the poverty level, in the low-credit option on VAT paid on a poverty-level income. In both cases the credit would be phased out between the poverty level and 150 percent of that level. Over the phase-out range the VAT system would increase marginal tax rates by some twenty-four or thirty-two percentage points. A 10 percent VAT levied on 80 percent of consumption would equal 8 percent of additional consumption—which is likely to be approximately equal to additional income. In addition, for the low option the credit would be 8 percent of poverty income. As income rose to 150 percent of the poverty level, the credit would be phased out, producing a marginal tax rate of 16 percent over the phase-out range, in addition to the VAT itself. Under the high-credit option the phase-out would produce a 24 percent marginal tax rate by itself.

24. To some extent it can be said that the earned-income tax credit (EITC) already constitutes an embryonic negative income tax. But the EITC is available only to those who are employed (being based on earnings) and support children. A credit intended explicitly to offset the VAT for low-income households would presumably contain neither of these limitations and would therefore be much more widely available and more expensive.

25. This assertion seems especially valid for the origin-based levy proposed by Robert E. Hall and Alvin Rabushka in *Low Tax, Simple Tax, Flat Tax* (New York: McGraw-Hill, 1983), and in *The Flat Tax* (Stanford, Calif.: Hoover Institution Press, 1985). Even for a destination-based variant it seems reasonable, if less certain.

26. Alan A. Tait, "The Value-added Tax: Revenue, Inflation, and the Foreign

Trade Balance" (Paper presented at World Bank Conference on Value Added Taxation in Developing Countries, Washington, D.C., April 21–23, 1986), makes the following observation on European experience:

> However, in VAT legislation it is often implied that traders are expected to pass the tax forward. Examples in government distributed literature have explained the VAT introduction and show margins fixed with the VAT passed forward in the chain of production to end up in the price to the final consumer. This is not to say that traders will do this in practice, but if the authorities expect it and if the government acquiesces in an increase in the money supply to finance trade at the higher prices, an increase in the CPI seems more probable than a decrease in factor rewards.

See also the further discussion of European experience in the next-to-last section of this chapter.

27. This does not necessarily mean that the consumer price index (CPI) would rise by exactly 8 percent. That would depend on the degree of correspondence between the base of the VAT and the market basket employed in calculating the CPI.

28. Chapter 3 discusses border tax adjustments and how they convert an origin-principle VAT into a destination-principle tax. The important point in the present context is that under the GATT BTAs are allowed for indirect taxes but not for direct taxes. Thus the corporate income tax, considered a direct tax, cannot be rebated on exports or levied on imports, as can the VAT, an indirect tax.

29. This section considers only the possibility that imposing an American VAT or partially substituting it for other taxes would alter the competitive position of the United States by changing the structure of relative prices. It does not consider whether deficit reduction made possible by imposition of a VAT would improve international competitiveness by causing a decline in the value of the dollar. In principle, any such effects would be common to other forms of deficit reduction, including alternative sources of revenues and expenditure reduction. Thus the interesting question in the present context is whether the VAT would be any more likely than increases in other taxes to increase American competitiveness by altering the structure of relative prices.

30. Although this patently absurd argument is heard less frequently now than in earlier episodes of the continuing debate of the pros and cons of the VAT, it is encountered often enough that it deserves brief discussion.

31. Thus U.S. Department of the Treasury, *Tax Reform*, states (vol. 3, p. 22):

> Imposing a value-added tax without any reduction in the income tax, or some other direct tax, would not directly improve the U.S. balance of trade. Export subsidies and import taxes could, in a system of fixed exchange rates, increase a country's exports and reduce its imports. But the export rebate and import tax allowed for the value-added tax are merely border tax adjustments required to put the value-added tax on a destination basis. The export rebate merely allows exports to

enter world markets free of value-added tax, not at a subsidized price below the pre-tax price. Similarly, imposing a value-added tax on imports merely places imports on an equal footing with domestically produced goods; it does not penalize imports. A comparison with state retail sales tax is illustrative; in any particular state, charging retail sales tax on a Toyota does not make a Chevrolet more competitive in that state, because the same sales tax applies to both automobiles. Nor would the Chevrolet be more competitive abroad just because it could be exported free of sales tax. As with a retail sales tax, the imposition of a value-added tax, with no offsetting change in any other taxes, would not directly improve the U.S. trade balance.

32. As mentioned in note 9, a standard proposition in the theory of international trade is that there is no fundamental difference between a tax levied on all consumption (for example, a retail sales tax or a destination-based VAT) and a tax levied on all production (for example, an origin-based VAT); any differences in effects on absolute price levels will simply be reflected in changes in exchange rates. Even though no real world VAT is likely to be truly universal in its coverage, there is enough truth in this proposition to suggest that in the long run a shift in tax policy that involves greater use of border tax adjustments will be reflected primarily in domestic price levels or in exchange rates and will have little long-run effect on patterns of international competition. Of course, this does not imply that such shifts in tax policy cannot have important short-run effects, since exchange rates do not adjust instantaneously to their long-run equilibrium levels.

33. See U.S. Department of the Treasury, *Tax Reform*, vol. 2, chap. 8.

34. There is an important question of which margin is at issue. If more sales can be made with existing capital, the marginal effective tax rate may approximate the statutory rate. If, however, additional investment is required to make additional sales, the relevant marginal effective tax rate will be substantially lower, because of generous capital consumption allowances. Indeed, marginal effective tax rates may actually be negative and respond inversely to changes in the statutory rate. For this discussion the second of these is probably the more relevant margin.

It is also important to note that when one tax replaces another (or part of the revenue from another), as the Michigan VAT did, there is strong political pressure to preserve in the successor tax the preferences in the predecessor. Thus it may be easier to adopt a "clean" VAT as a source of added revenue than as a replacement for revenue from an existing tax.

35. See, for example, McLure, "Tax on Value Added"; "Tax Restructuring Act"; "VAT versus the Payroll Tax"; and "Value Added Tax."

36. Aaron, *Value Added Tax*, pp. 15–16.

37. See U.S. Department of the Treasury, *Tax Reform*, vol. 3, pp. 23–26.

38. See also the brief discussion in the text at note 48.

39. Note, however, that I have (for example, in McLure, "Tax Restructuring Act" and "VAT versus the Payroll Tax") appraised the possibility that adopting a VAT would cause an increase in the size of government as a disadvan-

tage (and have been criticized by Peter A. Diamond, "Comments" on Charles E. McLure, Jr., "VAT versus the Payroll Tax," in Skidmore, *Financing Social Security*, pp. 165–66, for doing so without adequate justification).

40. See Carl S. Shoup, "Criteria for Choice among Types of Value Added Tax" (Paper presented at World Bank Conference on Value Added Taxation in Developing Countries, Washington, D.C., April 21–23, 1986); and Scott, "VAT and Tax Reform." Tait, "The Value-added Tax," indicates that thirty-nine countries now use the VAT.

41. For a somewhat more extended overview of the structure of VAT rates in Europe, see Cnossen and Shoup, "Value-added Tax Coordination."

42. "VAT in Europe," *The Economist*, March 25, 1972.

43. The following discussion is based on Tait, "The Value-added Tax"; he notes:

> The major reason why there have been few studies of the effect of VAT introduction on retail prices is not through disinterest but because it appears too difficult (or even impossible) to disentangle the changes in prices attributable to VAT from other influences on prices. "How can we know the dancer from the dance?"

44. Tait notes (ibid.): "The Federal Republic of Germany is the country most frequently referred to when commentators wish to show that the introduction of a VAT need not affect the CPI."

45. Tait notes (ibid.) that "the CPI rose by only 1.5 percent over the whole of 1968 and of this no more than 0.4 to 0.6 percentage points were ascribed to the VAT."

46. Tait also classifies Sweden, Ireland, and Austria in the "little or no change" category, "considering all circumstances," although on the basis of data alone they would fall in the "acceleration" category; he does not discuss in detail experience in these countries or in the Netherlands, in which he says introduction of the VAT had a one-time effect on prices (ibid.).

47. Ibid.

48. J. A. Stockfisch, "Value-added Taxes and the Size of Government: Some Evidence," *National Tax Journal*, vol. 38 (December 1985), pp. 547–52. For a mixed verdict on similar evidence, see U.S. Department of the Treasury, *Tax Reform*, vol. 3, pp. 23–26.

49. West Germany, the only federation among the original six members of the EEC, shares revenues from its VAT with the German states. See Ewald Nowotny, "Tax Assignment and Revenue Sharing in the Federal Republic of Germany and Switzerland," in Charles E. McLure, Jr., ed., *Tax Assignment in Federal Countries* (Canberra, Australia: Centre for Research on Federal Financial Relations, 1983), pp. 260–86.

50. For a more complete discussion, see Richard A. Musgrave and Peggy B. Musgrave, *Public Finance in Theory and Practice*, 3d ed. (New York: McGraw-Hill, 1980), chap. 19; or Joseph E. Stiglitz, *Economics of the Public Sector* (New York: W. W. Norton, 1986), chap. 21.

51. Further complicating matters is the fact that the corporate income tax contains a hodgepodge of provisions that accord special treatment to various

industries and types of investment.

52. For further elaboration on this theme, see Arnold C. Harberger, "The State of the Corporation Income Tax," in Walker and Bloomfield, *New Directions in Federal Tax Policy*, pp. 161–71.

53. Marian Krzyzaniak and Richard A. Musgrave, *The Shifting of the Corporation Income Tax* (Baltimore: Johns Hopkins University Press, 1963). For references to this literature, see Musgrave and Musgrave, *Public Finance*, p. 436. It is interesting to note that there has been relatively little econometric analysis of this issue for almost two decades.

5
Alternative Revenue Sources

Several sources of revenue from indirect taxation, in addition to the value-added tax, have been mentioned prominently in recent months, primarily in the context of income tax reform, as a means of avoiding the large increases in corporate tax liabilities that would otherwise be necessary to finance substantial reductions in income taxes paid by individuals. Concern with deficit reduction could once again bring several of these taxes to congressional attention as alternatives to a federal VAT. This chapter discusses several of these alternative revenue sources: an oil import fee, a tax on all imported and domestic oil, a tax on all sources of energy, a tax on gasoline—or, more accurately, on all motor fuels—and an increase in excise taxes and tariffs.[1] The discussion of the VAT is deliberately quite brief; it merely summarizes the major points of the discussion of chapters 4 and 6.

The criteria used to assess these taxes are economic neutrality, international competitiveness, distributional equity or fairness, and administrative feasibility. The discussion of international competitiveness, fairness, and administrative simplicity probably requires little introduction; those concepts should be clear from context. The merits of economic neutrality are briefly discussed in chapter 4.

Oil Import Fee

An oil import fee has little to recommend it beyond administrative feasibility.[2] Since virtually all imported oil comes into the country either in large tankers or through a limited number of major pipelines, implementing an oil import fee should be fairly simple and straightforward. Moreover, such a fee could be employed to yield a moderate amount of revenue fairly quickly. It is unlikely that a major contribution to deficit reduction could be financed in this way, however.

The distortionary effects of an oil import fee could be quite severe. Since the United States buys oil in highly and increasingly competitive world markets, a high proportion of an oil import fee would presumably be reflected in higher prices of imported crude oil. Those higher prices would create upward pressure on costs of petroleum products and petrochemical feed stocks. Moreover, to some extent an oil import fee would form a price umbrella over alternative sources of domestic energy, such as coal and nuclear power, as well as domestic oil and gas. Thus all energy-intensive activities would be more expensive than in the absence of the oil import fee.

Since the free-market price of oil reflects its opportunity cost, why should the United States make oil artificially expensive in relation to other goods and services by imposing a tax on imported oil? Such a tax would distort consumption decisions away from the use of oil and petroleum-intensive products. Similarly, it would distort choices of production technology by inducing substitution of other sources of energy for oil and discouraging the use of energy-intensive means of production.

Because a tax on imported oil would raise prices of petrochemical feed stocks, refined petroleum products, and other energy-intensive products, it would place such products at a competitive disadvantage in relation to similar products purchased abroad. A natural tendency would be to rebate the import fee on exports of refined petroleum products and petrochemical feed stocks and to extend the fee to imports of such products to avoid an adverse effect on U.S. competitiveness. This would greatly complicate tax administration, because it would necessitate estimating the fraction of the cost of thousands of products represented by imported oil. But that is only the beginning of the problem. If competitive effects are truly to be avoided, it would also be necessary to allow export rebates and apply compensating import duties to industries using fuel oil, refined petroleum products, and petrochemicals. This would be an overwhelming administrative task.

The distributional effects of an oil import fee are also of questionable merit. The prices of heating oil and other petroleum products would be higher than in a free market. Most obviously, such a tax would be regressive; after all, heating fuel and gasoline are hardly luxury items in the United States. Perhaps less obvious is the fact that the price umbrella created by an import fee would allow recipients of oil income from domestic sources, who are generally among the wealthiest segments of American society, to receive artificially inflated prices for their products. It is difficult to be sympathetic to the distributional implications of an oil import fee.[3]

The regional effects of such a fee would also be significant. It would create a substantial redistribution of income from the industrial Northeast to the oil-producing states. The most adverse effects of such shifts could be avoided by exempting fuel oil from the tax, but only at the expense of further administrative costs and economic distortions. Moreover, the price umbrella would protect the revenue position of the energy-producing states—states that only a few years ago were being decried for exploiting consuming states by exporting resource taxes to them.[4]

Two possible counterarguments in favor of an oil import fee deserve brief discussion. First, spokesmen for the domestic oil industry may argue that such a fee is necessary on national defense grounds, to encourage exploration, development, and production of domestic resources in the face of depressed world prices for oil. Simply put, this is an argument for tariff protection of the domestic oil industry. General economic arguments against tariff protection are persuasive and well known and need not be repeated here. What should be noted, however, is that the national defense argument cuts both ways in the case of a nonrenewable natural resource.

The national defense argument is, essentially, an argument that private markets will underprovide resources required for national defense in the absence of protection or some other form of subsidy. When tariff protection is accorded to a manufacturing industry, the welfare of the nation is likely to suffer from the consequent distortion of the allocation of economic resources; but at least the encouragement of current production does not reduce possibilities for future production. Indeed, future production may be enhanced through learning by doing, exploitation of economies of scale, and other attributes of infant industries.

The situation is, of course, quite different in the case of a nonrenewable natural resource such as oil. Increased production today *does* imply reduced production tomorrow. Although higher prices might lead to improved recovery methods, the total amount of domestic oil available for eventual production is more or less fixed. Thus increasing current production in the name of national security may constitute a myopic policy that simply postpones and aggravates the problem of depletion that must eventually arise.[5]

Tax on All Oil

A tax on all oil would be markedly preferable to a tax on imported oil only. The adverse effects on resource allocation and international competitiveness would probably be roughly similar to those of an oil import fee. As with the oil import fee, pressure would be brought to bear to convert the tax into a destination-based levy, to avoid adverse effects on international competitiveness. The distributional effects would probably also be quite similar, except in one important respect. The higher prices paid by consumers because of the tax would flow into the federal Treasury, rather than into the pockets of owners of oil or the treasuries of energy-producing states.

Energy Tax

In principle a tax on all energy would be preferable to a tax either on imported oil or on oil from both foreign and domestic sources. It would, of course, discriminate against energy-intensive activities, and pressure would probably be felt for border tax adjustments to prevent competitive damage. Because it would apply to all competing sources of energy, it would create less distortion of economic choices than a tax on oil alone.

A tax on all energy would, however, give rise to numerous policy issues and administrative controversies. Should the tax be levied at the same ad valorem rate on all energy sources, or should an equal amount of tax be collected from energy of a given Btu content? Would petrochemical feed stocks be subject to the tax, or would they be exempt? How would self-supply of energy be treated? Would a firm that generated its own electricity pay tax only on the fuel used to generate it? What if gases that would otherwise be lost were used for generation? Would electrical energy bought from a public utility be taxed in full, so that labor and capital costs as well as the cost of oil or gas used in the boilers would be subject to tax? How would coke used in producing steel be treated? If coke were subject to the energy tax, what method would be used to value coke produced in ovens owned by a steel company from coal extracted from its own mine? Depending on how these and many other questions were answered, substantial distortions in the markets for energy, petrochemicals, steel, and other commodities might occur. All things considered, energy does not seem to be a sensible base for taxation.

Gasoline (Motor Fuels) Tax

Probably the least objectionable form of taxation of energy would be what is commonly called a gasoline tax. More accurately, such a tax almost certainly would—and certainly should—apply to all motor fuels, including diesel fuel, liquefied petroleum gas, and alcohol, rather than only to gasoline. To limit the tax to gasoline would distort economic decisions in favor of other forms of motor fuel; indeed, it would perversely favor diesel fuel, one of the greatest sources of air pollution.

For many reasons a tax on motor fuel would be superior to the various energy taxes described. First, the necessary administrative apparatus to collect such a tax is already in place, thanks to the existing federal motor fuel taxes. The tax could therefore be implemented much more quickly than any of the other energy taxes. Moreover, its administration would be vastly simpler than that of a tax on all energy and somewhat simpler than that of a tax on all oil. It would not necessarily be simpler than a tax on all imported oil; but if border tax adjustments were made for the latter, its administration would be substantially more difficult than that of a tax on motor fuels.

It can be argued that motor vehicles and their drivers impose social costs not adequately reflected in the prices of the vehicles and of motor fuels, including existing taxes on motor fuels. Such external costs include pollution and congestion, as well as the cost of constructing and maintaining highways, roads, and streets. Thus, at least within limits, an increase in motor fuel taxes might improve resource allocation rather than worsen it.

A large percentage of the motor fuel tax would be borne by consumers rather than by business. Since the tax would be a deductible expense in calculating income tax liability, even the portion ultimately paid by business would be diminished. Of course, that is also true of other taxes considered above. The relatively minor effect on business has several advantages. First, business decision making would suffer relatively little distortion. To the extent that present motor fuel taxes fail to reflect adequately the social costs of users of motor fuels, the case against increased business costs of this type would be weak. The primary discrimination would be against industries for which motor fuel is an important input.[6] If necessary to prevent such discrimination, a credit against income tax could be allowed for the motor fuel tax. Since the tax would be a relatively unimportant cost in most industries, adverse effects on international competitiveness per dollar of revenue would probably be smaller than for other energy-related taxes. Thus border tax adjustments would probably not be needed.

The primary arguments against a tax on motor fuels are the distortion of economic decision making (if total taxes on motor fuels exceeded social costs created by users of the fuels) and the adverse distributional consequences. Being applied to consumption rather than to importation, however, a motor fuel tax would not artificially protect domestic producers by propping up prices, as an import fee would. Thus its effects on income distribution would be far less perverse than those of an oil import fee.

A tax on motor fuels has a substantial political advantage in the present environment. At least within limits, it would be reflected in smaller reductions from recent pump prices for motor fuels rather than in price increases.

Increased Excise Taxes and Tariffs

A final possibility for indirect taxation would be to increase excise taxes. This could be done explicitly or implicitly, as in Senator Robert Packwood's recent proposal to make excise taxes and tariffs nondeductible in calculating taxable income.[7] Since motor fuel excises have been discussed in the previous section, only potential increases in other excises are discussed here.

In general, increased federal excises have little to recommend them. At best they can be defended as offsetting inflation that has occurred since they were last raised, reflecting the social costs of such harmful activities as smoking and consuming alcoholic beverages, and raising revenues in a relatively painless way.

These defenses can usefully be considered in reverse order. First, painless taxes are not necessarily good taxes. The problem goes well beyond the issue of whether citizens fully appreciate the cost of government. Excises tend to be regressive, and they create horizontal inequities between those who do and those who do not consume the excisable commodities. If these objections based on vertical and horizontal inequities are not to prevail, it is necessary to believe strongly, indeed, that excises reflect the social costs of the excisable activity or that they will inhibit socially harmful activity.[8]

Clearly excises do have these benefits, but the generally accepted view is that their inequities outweigh any such benefits. Resort to excises as an important source of revenues is usually associated with developing countries that lack the administrative capacity to impose better taxes, such as income and general sales taxes; the federal government of the United States clearly does not fit that description. If excises are to be raised purely for revenue reasons, it would be better to let the state governments do so, since their options for raising revenue are more limited than those of the federal government. Of course, if federal excises make no sense, raising them to keep up with inflation has little appeal.

As a general matter, it makes no sense to disallow income tax

deductions for excise taxes and tariffs.[9] At best, this is only a complicated and disingenuous indirect means of raising excise tax rates that
suffers from the defects just described. Moreover, in the case of tariffs
it would almost certainly create loud protests from our trading
partners, and perhaps retaliation.[10]

Conventional Value-added Tax

A broad and comprehensive consumption-based VAT using the standard credit method has substantial advantages over any of the four
energy-related taxes or increases in excises discussed. First, the VAT
could easily yield substantial revenue with a low rate; indeed, the
possibility that a VAT might become a money machine has often been
cited as a potentially important disadvantage.

Second, being extremely broad in its impact, the VAT tends to
interfere less with economic neutrality than more narrowly defined
taxes on imported oil, all oil, energy, motor fuels, or goods subject to
excises. Being levied on relatively narrow bases, those taxes would
require high rates to raise a given amount of revenue. Of course, this
advantage can easily be overstated, because for both administrative
and political reasons it is unlikely that an American VAT would be
truly comprehensive.

Third, a VAT would be relatively easy to implement; but implementation would not be costless or immediate. It has been estimated
that 20,000 additional employees and an annual expenditure of $700
million would be required to administer a VAT and that it could not be
implemented until eighteen months after it was enacted.[11]

Fourth, the VAT would probably not have the adverse effects on
international competitiveness that the energy-related taxes would
have. Nor would it have positive effects on international competitiveness, as is commonly asserted. Under commonly employed methods
the VAT would automatically apply to imports and would exempt
exports. Thus it would be neutral in its effect on international competitiveness.

The VAT (or other form of sales tax) also has the attraction that it
might be the most popular means of raising substantial additional
revenue. Evidence on the relative popularity of a general sales tax and
other forms of indirect taxes is scanty. But substantial evidence suggests that a national sales tax would be preferred to an increase in
income tax rates. In a 1984 survey of public opinion on government
and taxes, the Advisory Commission on Intergovernmental Relations
found a national sales tax (with an exemption for food and similar
necessities) preferred over an increase in income tax rates by a margin

of 32 percent to 7 percent. Similarly, when asked which is the "worst tax, that is, the least fair," 46 percent of respondents chose either the federal income tax (36 percent) or the state income tax (10 percent); only 15 percent chose the state sales tax. This pattern of responses was fairly uniform across income classes, sex, age, race, and level of education.[12]

Of course, the VAT also has important disadvantages. The possibility that it might lead to increased government spending and the cost and delay of implementing it have already been mentioned. Perhaps its primary added disadvantage is its inherent regressivity; as a tax on consumption it naturally takes a higher percentage of income from low-income than from higher-income families. Although various means are available to deal with this problem, none is truly satisfactory.

Finally, the VAT raises issues of fiscal federalism that are absent (or at least much less prominent) in the case of the energy-related taxes. These are described in detail in chapter 9. In particular, state and local governments have strongly opposed federal intrusion into the sales tax area, a domain traditionally reserved for subnational governments. Federal imposition of a sales tax, however, might help to bring greater uniformity to the retail sales taxes levied by state governments. Moreover, it might help eliminate the inequities, distortions, and revenue loss resulting from the ability of mail-order houses to make interstate sales without paying sales tax to the states of residence of their customers. Federal imposition of one of the energy-related taxes would probably create less opposition from subnational governments.

All things considered, a well-designed VAT or some other form of general sales tax would be far superior to any of the four forms of energy-related taxation or an increase in excises. It would interfere with economic decision making less than any of the energy-related taxes, and its distributional effects are likely to be better and unlikely to be worse. Because it could not be implemented quickly, the VAT should not be seen as a quick fix. It should be considered only if an additional long-run source of revenue is thought desirable. It would clearly be much more satisfactory for this purpose than any of the energy-related taxes.

The Business Transfer Tax

The business transfer tax (BTT) proposed by Senator William Roth has substantial disadvantages not shared by a conventional VAT. First, use of the subtraction method constitutes a serious gamble. A subtraction-method tax works reasonably well provided it has only one rate and no preretail exclusions from the tax base. In such a case it is basically equivalent to a credit-method VAT. With multiple rates or exclusions, a subtraction-method tax makes little economic or administrative sense, and accurate border tax adjustments cannot be made. Given the likelihood that pressures for exclusions and multiple rates would not be successfully withstood, it seems inadvisable to adopt a naive subtraction-method tax such as the BTT.[13]

Some of Senator Roth's BTT provisions would constitute especially unwise tax policy. First, an exclusion for organizations with gross receipts of less than $10 million would create an enormous distortion in favor of sectors, such as services, with high ratios of value added to sales, especially those in which it would be relatively easy to qualify for the small-business allowance. Moreover, it would create strong incentives for manipulation of organizational form (such as the tax-induced use of franchises and subsidiaries) and of transfer prices on sales between related entities to take advantage of this exception. With an exception of this kind, accurate border tax adjustments would be impossible, and our trading partners would surely object to border tax adjustments based on an implicit assumption that the full rate of BTT was being paid on domestic production.

Senator Roth has asserted that the BTT would be preferable to an ordinary European-style VAT. Because tax liability under the BTT would be based on figures already available in a firm's books of accounts, it would entail little additional compliance or administrative burden for taxpayers or the Internal Revenue Service.[14] In comparison, the credit method requires application of tax to every transaction in the economy.

This judgment seems naive at best. A fully comprehensive subtraction-method VAT might be preferable on administrative grounds to a credit-method VAT. But that is not what Senator Roth is proposing. Rather, he is proposing a tax that discriminates in favor of selected firms and sectors through the small-business exemption. It is unrealistic to believe that substantial efforts would not be undertaken to use this liberal exemption to escape the tax or that enormous efforts would not be required to prevent manipulation. Once the ramifications of these considerations are taken into account, it is unlikely that the BTT will be preferable on administrative grounds to a conventional VAT; it may simply be unworkable.

Senator Roth's proposal makes no reference to the tax treatment of financial institutions and insurance, among the most troublesome areas of application of a VAT. Nor does it discuss the tax treatment of purchases and commercial activities of tax-exempt organizations and governments. By handling the troublesome issues of farming, small business, and used goods through the meat-ax approach of an extremely high exemption, it creates the problems mentioned. More satisfactory treatment of these and other issues would substantially reduce the apparent attraction of the Roth BTT.

The proposed credit of the BTT against liability for the social security (FICA) tax would not be legal under standard international practice, as described by the General Agreement on Tariffs and Trade. Our trading partners would thus object strongly to the form of BTT proposed.[15] If their objections went unheeded, they might retaliate, either by providing compensating export subsidies and countervailing import duties or by allowing similar credits for their own VATs against their payroll taxes. Given the likelihood that no net gain in international competitiveness could be achieved, it seems extremely unwise to embark deliberately on a beggar-thy-neighbor tax policy that would increase international tensions by running directly counter to accepted international practice. The FICA credit for the BTT might also distort the choice of production technology in favor of labor-intensive activities (particularly those paying relatively low wages) and against capital-intensive means of production.

Notes

1. The Treasury Department has estimated the following five-year revenue yields from three of these alternatives: $8 oil import fee, $81.4 billion; twenty-one-cent per gallon increase in gasoline tax, $92 billion; and 6 percent tax on the value of all energy, $102.2 billion.

2. This discussion concentrates on microeconomic effects of an oil import fee. Robert E. Hall, "The Adverse Economic Consequences of an Oil Import Fee" (Testimony before the Subcomittee on Energy and Agricultural Taxation of the Senate Finance Committee, February 27, 1986), focuses on macroeconomic effects, noting that an oil import fee of $10 per barrel might cause a needless sacrifice of almost 2 percent of GNP.

3. Hall provides the following appraisal of these effects: "An oil import fee is bad for the economy in general. It is bad for consumers. It is bad for workers. It is bad for farmers. Its only favorable impact is on domestic oil, coal, and gas producers. That benefit is far outweighed by the general adverse effect of an oil import fee" (ibid.).

4. On this issue see, for example, the papers in Charles E. McLure, Jr., and Peter Mieszkowski, eds., *Fiscal Federalism and the Taxation of Natural Resources* (Lexington, Mass.: Lexington Books, 1983), pp. 1–10.

5. For a similar assessment, see Hall, "Adverse Consequences."

6. Industries producing goods and services that are complements in consumption to motor fuel, such as tourism, would also be adversely affected.

7. U.S. Congress, Joint Committee on Taxation, *Tax Reform Proposals in Connection with Committee on Finance Markup* (Washington, D.C., 1986), p. 62. The Packwood proposal would also presume that a firm's taxable income at least equaled its excise tax collections.

8. If the goal is to inhibit socially harmful activity, it seems more appropriate to disallow deductions for expenses of advertising the products or even to place an excise on such advertising.

9. Consider a firm that buys the taxed product for $100 and sells it at the same price plus the excise. Under the Packwood proposal taxable profits would be presumed to equal the amount of the excise, even though economic profits are zero, by assumption. J. Roger Mentz (Testimony before the Senate Finance Committee, April 21, 1986) notes that this provision might violate many foreign tax treaties.

10. Mentz confirms this view (ibid.).

11. See U.S. Department of the Treasury, *Tax Reform for Fairness, Simplicity, and Economic Growth* (Washington, D.C., 1984), vol. 3, chap. 9.

12. See Advisory Commission on Intergovernmental Relations, *1984 Changing Public Attitudes on Governments and Taxes* (Washington, D.C., 1984), pp. 19, 16. One must be somewhat suspicious of results such as these, since 47 percent of respondents would raise revenues by "reducing special tax treatment for capital gains and cutting tax deduction allowances for charitable contributions, state and local taxes, medical expenses, etc." (14 percent offered no opinion). Recent congressional action on federal tax reform has shown the deductions for state and local income and property taxes and for charitable contributions to be among the most sacrosanct and the deduction for sales taxes to be relatively vulnerable.

13. In chapter 6 I show that it is possible to construct a more sophisticated subtraction-method tax that avoids some of the problems of the BTT. Since such a levy must be based on invoices, like the credit method, rather than on existing books of account, it lacks one of the apparent advantages of the subtraction method.

14. See William V. T. Roth, "The Roth Reforms" (Speech to the National Press Club, Washington, D.C., February 20, 1986, and supporting documents).

15. Allowing this credit would be tantamount to providing border tax adjustments for payroll taxes, a practice that is clearly contrary to the GATT. See chapter 6. The assertion by Senator Roth that his proposal "harmonizes our tax system with that of our major trading partners" is patently false. None of our major trading partners allows its VAT to be credited against its payroll taxes. Moreover, none uses the subtraction method or allows a small-business exemption that approaches the size of that proposed by Roth.

6

Issues in the Design of
a Value-added Tax

In appraising the economic effects of the value-added tax and thus the desirability of an American VAT, it is generally satisfactory to consider whether the United States should adopt a tax with the economic effects of a federal retail sales tax. Although the two taxes and their economic effects would not be exactly equivalent, they would be sufficiently similar to make the comparison valid for most purposes. Having said that, however, I must emphasize that the administrative techniques employed to collect a VAT do matter. First, the VAT treats capital investment, services, and international trade more satisfactorily than a retail sales tax, at least as levied by the states; this is explained further in chapter 7.

Second, the textbook descriptions of the subtraction and credit methods presented in chapter 3 obscure important differences between the two methods. This chapter explains that in its simplest form—what I call the naive subtraction method—the subtraction method is truly satisfactory only if the VAT is levied at a single rate on a comprehensive tax base.[1] Once multiple rates and exclusions from the tax base enter the picture, this system breaks down.

Some of the defects of the naive subtraction method can be remedied by adopting a more sophisticated version that allows deductions only for purchases on which tax has been paid. But even this sophisticated subtraction-method VAT, which is essentially equivalent to a credit-method VAT, functions satisfactorily only if levied at a uniform rate (with at most a zero rate in addition to the uniform positive rate). Given the likelihood that political pressure for multiple rates would be irresistible, this conclusion throws considerable doubt on the wisdom of enacting a subtraction-method VAT, such as the business transfer tax (BTT) proposed by Senator William Roth. As the Treasury Department concluded in its 1984 assessment of VAT: "While there are different forms of value-added tax and alternative methods for calculating tax liability, the only form suitable for the United States would be a consumption-type value-added tax with tax liability determined under the credit method."[2]

A third set of technical issues in the design of a VAT concern the tax treatment of small businesses, used goods, and such activities as financial institutions, services, housing, and farming. These are considered in chapter 8.

Exemption and Zero Rating under the Credit Method

An important administrative feature of the credit-method VAT is the difference between exemption and zero rating. Although the two terms may sound synonymous, they have quite different effects. A firm selling zero-rated items is a registered taxpayer (is "in the system") and can therefore receive credits for taxes paid on purchases. Thus its sales really occur free of tax on inputs, as well as tax on value added at the zero-rated stage.

In comparison, a firm selling only exempt items is not registered and can obtain no credit for taxes paid on purchased inputs. Therefore, although exemption entails less administrative effort and compliance costs than zero rating, it is also less favorable to the taxpayer. This is shown by two examples (see table 8). Exempt sales made at retail (stage C in the example) are not tax-free sales; because no credit

TABLE 8

ILLUSTRATION OF EXEMPTION AND ZERO RATING OF RETAILER UNDER
CREDIT-METHOD VALUE-ADDED TAX
(dollars)

| | Stage of Production | | | |
	A	B	C	Total
Exemption of retailer				
Gross tax liability	30	70	0	100
Credit	0	30	0	30
Net tax liability	30	40	0	70
Zero rating of retailer				
Gross tax liability	30	70	0	100
Credit	0	30	70	100
Net tax liability	30	40	−70	0

SOURCE: Based on table 1.

TABLE 9

ILLUSTRATION OF EXEMPTION AND ZERO RATING OF
INTERMEDIATE STAGE UNDER CREDIT-METHOD VALUE-ADDED TAX

(dollars)

	Stage of Production			
	A	B	C	Total
Exemption of wholesaler				
Gross tax liability	30	0	100	130
Credit	—	0	0	0
Net tax liability	30	0	100	130
Zero rating of wholesaler				
Gross tax liability	30	0	100	130
Credit	0	30	0	30
Net tax liability	30	− 30	100	100

SOURCE: Based on table 1.

can be taken for taxes paid on inputs, such sales contain a tax component from previous stages that were taxed.

This result can be contrasted with that for zero rating of the retail stage. The taxpayer at stage C is allowed a credit (and refund, if appropriate) for taxes paid on purchases even though no tax is collected on sales; in effect, all taxes paid at previous stages are rebated or refunded. Zero-rated sales to consumers are thus totally free of tax. Zero rating is far more effective than exemption in freeing such items as food from tax for distributional reasons. Export sales are virtually always zero rated, so that they can enter world markets free of tax.

Even worse (from the point of view of the taxpayer and perhaps of economic neutrality) is the situation where exemption occurs before the last stage (see table 9). An exempt firm (stage B in the example) pays no tax on sales but can take no credit for taxes paid on inputs ($30 in the example). Yet its customers must pay tax on the full amount of their sales ($100 in the example) and have no tax on inputs for which to take credit. Because of this break in the chain of credits, the total tax load ($130 in the example) is actually increased by exemption.[3] This places exempt activities at a disadvantage in both domestic and international markets, distorting resource allocation and reducing international competitiveness.

By comparison, zero rating of intermediate stages in the production-distribution process (stage B) has no effect on ultimate liability. The zero-rated stage pays no tax on sales but is allowed credit for tax paid on purchases, unlike the situation under exemption. Not surprisingly, many observers believe that zero rating is far preferable to exemption from an economic point of view, despite the need to include in the system firms that receive net refunds rather than pay tax, since it avoids the distortions of exemption.[4]

Exemption creates an additional administrative problem under a credit-method VAT. Suppose that a given firm sells both exempt and zero-rated items or both exempt and taxable items. It might appear that the distinction between zero-rated and exempt sales would be irrelevant for a firm making both kinds of sales, since tax would be collected on neither. In fact, this is not the case, since the distinction between exempt and taxable sales has implications that go beyond the need to distinguish whether tax must be collected on sales.

Presumably such a firm should be allowed credit for taxes paid on inputs used to produce the zero-rated or taxable goods and services. But it cannot be allowed credit for all purchases, including those used in the production of exempt sales. Otherwise, the exemption would, in effect, be converted to zero rating for firms selling both zero-rated and exempt goods, giving such firms a competitive advantage over those selling only exempt goods. Similarly, allowing no credit for inputs to zero-rated sales would be equivalent to the less favorable exemption of such sales.[5]

In some instances, particularly goods bought for resale without further processing, distinguishing between inputs for exempt sales and those for taxable or zero-rated sales would pose no problem. But for many other productive inputs, including commercial rent (if subject to tax), utilities, fuels, and transportation expenditures, it would be impossible to allocate costs precisely between exempt and taxable or zero-rated sales. That being the case, it would be necessary to resort to approximate methods to apportion costs between the two kinds of sales. Costs that cannot be attributed directly might be apportioned on the basis of the fraction of the firm's total sales that were exempt, rather than taxable or zero rated.[6] It would then be necessary to record separately sales that are exempt, taxable, and zero rated. Thus exemption creates a layer of complexity that is missing if only zero rating is allowed.

Zero rating is most appropriately employed where there is a conscious desire to eliminate tax on certain commodities (say, for distributional reasons) or transactions (most notably, exports). Exemption may be chosen when administrative considerations make it undesirable to require registration of certain firms (for example,

74

farmers and small businesses) but eliminating tax on final consumption does not have high priority.[7] The disadvantage created by exemption of sales occurring before the retail stage can be substantially relieved by allowing optional registration and in some cases by zero-rating inputs used primarily by exempt sectors (such as farming).

Exclusion under the Subtraction Method

Under the naive subtraction method described, the distinction between exemption and zero rating is meaningless. Liability for VAT is determined by applying the tax rate to value added, which is calculated by deducting all purchases from sales. It clearly makes no difference whether a zero rate is applied to value added calculated in this way or whether the value added is simply exempted. Nor is there any need to distinguish between inputs used for the production of zero-rated and tax-exempt sales; deduction is allowed for all purchases under this version of the subtraction method.

This feature of the naive subtraction method is, however, a mixed blessing. Under the credit method, as long as there is no break in the chain of credits, the only tax rate that ultimately matters is the rate applied to sales to final consumers.[8] Any advantage that might otherwise result from failure to collect tax at an earlier stage, whether because of zero rating or evasion, is eliminated at the next stage because credit for taxes paid on purchases is lower by a corresponding amount. (Of course, if exemption causes a break in the chain of credits, aggregate taxation is greater than indicated by the statutory rate applied at the final stage.)

Such is not the case under the naive subtraction method. Because of the method of calculation, value added that is not taxed at a given stage is also not subsequently taxed. This result is illustrated in table 10. In this example the value added at stages A and C is taxed, but that at stage B, assumed to be exempt, escapes tax.[9]

This characteristic of the naive subtraction method means that a real advantage is to be gained from evasion and from lobbying and other political activities intended to produce preferential treatment of various stages of production.[10] Moreover, in the absence of strong requirements for mandatory consolidation, transactions would be likely to be channeled through affiliates operating at the exempt stage at prices that would artificially inflate the fraction of value added at that stage. To the extent that these efforts were successful and tax was not paid on value added, whether because of evasion, manipulation of transfer prices, or the natural effect of exemption, resource allocation would be distorted, inequities would result, and revenues would be lost. Imports pose a particular problem, because the effects of undervaluing imports do not simply wash out at later stages, as under the credit method. Besides resulting in lost revenue, such undervaluation would allow importers to undersell domestic producers.

It is possible to construct a more sophisticated subtraction-based VAT in which the effects of both exemption and zero rating under a credit-method tax can be replicated. This possibility deserves examination for several reasons. First, understanding the sophisticated subtraction method further highlights the defects of the naive version. Second, once the problems of the naive method are more fully appreciated, there may be a tendency to try to avoid those problems while

TABLE 10
ALTERNATIVE TREATMENTS OF EXCLUDED INTERMEDIATE STAGE
UNDER SUBTRACTION-METHOD VALUE-ADDED TAX
(dollars)

| | Stage of Production | | | |
	A	B	C	Total
Basic information				
Sales	300	700	1,000	2,000
Purchases	0	300	700	1,000
Value added	300	400	300	1,000
Naive subtraction method				
Taxable sales	300	[a]	1,000	1,300
Purchases	0	[a]	700	700
Taxable value added	300	0	300	600
VAT	30	0	30	60
Exemption equivalent				
Taxable sales	300	[a]	1,000	1,300
Deductible purchases	0	[a]	[b]	0
Taxable value added	300	0	1,000	1,300
VAT	30	0	100	130
Zero-rate equivalent				
Taxable sales	300	0	1,000	1,300
Deductible purchases	0	300	0	300
Taxable value added	300	−300	1,000	1,000
VAT	30	−30	100	100

a. Not in system: sales not taxable and purchases not deductible.
b. Purchases from nonregistered vendor: not deductible.

retaining the subtraction method, rather than simply moving to the more common credit method. This exposition indicates the form such remedies might take and notes that this improved subtraction method differs little from the credit method. Finally, it is important to realize that even the sophisticated subtraction method cannot accommodate multiple rates.

Suppose that deductions can be taken in calculating taxable value added only for purchases on which tax has previously been paid. This might be implemented by distinguishing between registered (tax-paid) purchases and unregistered purchases (on which tax has not been paid). Table 10 (under "exemption equivalent") illustrates the use of this sophisticated subtraction method to replicate the result of a break in the chain of credits when an intermediate stage is exempted under the credit method.[11] Firms at stage C are allowed no deduction for purchased inputs; since their suppliers (firms at stage B) are exempt from tax, their sales purchases are not registered. Tax is paid at stage C on the entire value of retail sales to households, with no deduction for purchases. As a result, the aggregate taxable value added at stages A and C exceeds the value of retail sales. The result is equivalent to a break in the chain of credits under the credit method. (The result is identical with the results for exemption under the credit method reported in table 9. Problems for firms selling both exempt and taxable or zero-rated goods would be the same as under the credit method.)

Exemption under the credit method has little to recommend it. Zero rating, generally superior, can, however, also be replicated in this more sophisticated version of the subtraction method. In this case, illustrated in the bottom part of table 10, firms at stage B are zero rated rather than exempt. Thus they are allowed to take a deduction for purchases even though their sales are not taxable. This produces negative taxable value added and a refund of the full amount of tax paid on purchases from stage A. Being zero rated, the purchases of stage C from stage B would not be considered tax paid; thus no deduction would be allowed for them, and firms at stage C would pay tax on the full $1,000 of their sales to consumers. Comparison of the last lines of tables 10 and 9 indicates that the tax paid at each stage and the total tax are the same under the conventional credit-method tax with zero rating of stage B and this sophisticated version of the subtraction method designed to replicate zero rating.[12]

The results in these two situations are identical in another important respect. If the undesirable effects of breaking the chain of deductions by exempting intermediate stages are to be avoided without excluding value added at that stage from the tax base, taxpayers at the zero-rated stage must be registered, and the fiscal authorities must pay refunds to taxpayers at that stage. Thus the administrative convenience of exemption must be sacrificed if the benefits of zero rating are to be realized.

Compliance with the sophisticated subtraction method might be slightly less onerous than compliance with the credit method. Under the credit method invoices or receipts for sales to registered taxpayers must identify VAT paid so that the purchaser can claim credit for it. The purchaser must record credits as well as purchases. Under the

TABLE 11
ILLUSTRATION OF BORDER TAX ADJUSTMENTS
WITH EXCLUDED INTERMEDIATE STAGE
UNDER SUBTRACTION-METHOD VALUE-ADDED TAX
(dollars)

| | Stage of Production | | | |
	A	B	C	Total
Benchmark case: no exclusion				
Domestic sales	300	700	0	1,000
Purchases	0	300	700	1,000
Value added	300	400	−700	0
VAT	30	40	−70	0
Exempt sales by B, naive subtraction method				
Taxable sales	300	a	0	300
Purchases	0	a	700	700
Taxable value added	300	0	−700	−400
VAT	30	0	−70	−40
Exempt-equivalent sales by B				
Taxable sales	300	a	0	300
Deductible purchases	0	a	b	0
Taxable value added	300	0	0	300
VAT	30	0	0	30
Zero-rate equivalent of sales by B				
Taxable sales	300	0	0	300
Deductible purchases	0	300	0	300
Taxable value added	300	−300	0	0
VAT	30	−30	0	0

a. Not in system: sales not taxable and purchases not deductible.
b. Purchases from nonregistered vendor: not deductible.

sophisticated subtraction method the seller need only record whether tax has been paid on a given sale, since only tax-paid purchases are allowed as a deduction. The purchaser must, of course, record deductible and nondeductible purchases separately. The primary substantive difference in compliance obligations is the need for the seller to record the amount of tax paid under the credit method, rather than simply whether the transaction is subject to tax under the sophisticated subtraction method. The purchaser's need to distinguish taxable and nontaxable purchases under the subtraction method seems to be roughly as onerous as the need to keep track of taxes paid under the credit method.

The distinction is more apparent than real, however, because if the VAT is levied at a single rate, the credit method can be administered in exactly the same way as the sophisticated subtraction method, with credit being calculated from creditable purchases.[13] Compliance with the credit method is more onerous than with the sophisticated subtraction method only if multiple rates are employed under the former but not the latter; under the latter multiple rates are infeasible.

Border Tax Adjustments under the Subtraction Method

As long as only one tax rate applies to all value added, border tax adjustments (BTAs) pose no more of a conceptual problem under the subtraction method than under the credit method. Under these circumstances the two methods of calculating tax liabilities are basically identical in effect. Thus in the benchmark case of table 11, exports occur tax free, as under the credit method, since taxes paid on domestic production before the export stage are rebated at export, and imports are subjected to the same tax as domestically produced goods.

If, however, coverage is not universal or if differential rates are applied to various goods and services, it is extremely difficult to provide precise BTAs under the naive subtraction method.[14] Moreover, problems of valuing and classifying imports are much more serious under the subtraction method than under the credit method. This section describes the difficulty of making precise BTAs if coverage is not universal and how the subtraction method can be modified to handle this problem as long as only one tax rate is employed. The following sections discuss the even greater problems that occur if differential rates are employed, problems that even the sophisticated subtraction method cannot handle; the subtraction method; the business transfer tax (BTT); and the illegality of the FICA offset for the BTT proposed by Senator Roth, which is not an inherent feature of a subtraction-method VAT.

Consider first the case in which sales by stage B to firms at stage C, assumed for purpose of this example to be exporters, are tax exempt. Straightforward application of the naive subtraction method would produce a negative tax base for stage C equivalent to its $700 of purchases from stage B (the result of allowing a deduction of $700, even though export sales are excluded from taxable receipts) and a refund of $70 (see table 11). This more than offsets the $30 VAT collected at stage A. Thus the aggregate tax collected on exports of $1,000 would be −$40 rather than zero, as is appropriate under the destination principle of taxation. Our trading partners would not quietly tolerate this result, which amounts to an export rebate for taxes not paid. It is worth repeating that under the credit method used in other countries BTAs are much more accurate.

Nor would it be satisfactory simply to disallow purchases as a deduction for firms engaged in exporting. If that were done, exports would be burdened with the tax collected at stage A, rather than occurring tax free. Table 11 also illustrates this exemption-equivalent approach.

If coverage is not complete, the only satisfactory way of implementing BTAs under the subtraction method is to adopt the sophisticated method described in the previous section. This is illustrated in the last part of table 11. Stage B would be accorded the equivalent of zero rating rather than exemption and would receive credit for tax paid at stage A. Export sales would not be included in taxable receipts of firms at stage C, and untaxed purchases from stage B would not be deductible to the exporter. Thus exports would occur free of tax.

Compensating taxes on imports also function satisfactorily only if this more sophisticated version of the subtraction method is employed, for both conceptual and administrative reasons. Accurate valuation and classification of imports are necessary if BTAs are to compensate for taxes on domestic products, but the difficulty goes well beyond that.[15] The conceptual problem is not with the taxation of imports per se. If the statutory rate of tax is applied to them, goods imported directly by consumers will be taxed "properly." Moreover, if intermediate goods employed in further production are imported and taxed, it is fully appropriate to allow a deduction for imports in calculating taxable value added.

The problem arises because under the naive subtraction method domestically produced goods are not taxed at the statutory rate (except by accident) if the VAT is not applied universally at a single rate. The exclusion of preretail sales from taxable receipts results in omission of value added at that stage from the tax base. Thus any domestically produced product that involved such an exempt stage would have a competitive advantage over imports, which would be fully taxed.

This state of affairs would not escape the notice of our trading partners, who can be expected to demand that BTAs for imports, as well as for exports, reflect exclusion of slices of value added of domestic goods from the VAT base, to prevent overcompensating for the American VAT. Of course, attempting to calculate the appropriate compensating import tax accurately would be a hopeless undertaking. It would inevitably involve compensation for average amounts of taxes on particular import-competing products, and distortions in both directions around the average would exist.[16]

Under the exemption-equivalent version of the subtraction method, the problem would be just the opposite; taxation of imports at the statutory rate would fail to reflect adequately the full amount of tax paid on domestically produced goods. American producers would clamor—with justification—for BTAs greater than the statutory rate. Just what the appropriate BTA should be would be controversial and subject to uncertainty. This problem would, of course, also exist under the credit method.

If, finally, the sophisticated subtraction method were adopted and no break in the chain of deductions occurred, the tax content of goods sold after the tax-free or zero-rated stage would be the statutory rate. Then applying the statutory rate to imports would produce the proper result.

Differential Rates under the Subtraction Method

Differential rates make compliance and administration under the credit method cumbersome but are not a fatal defect; however, they render the naive subtraction method unworkable.[17] This explains why it would be unwise to adopt the BTT proposed by Senator Roth. Although Roth originally proposed that the BTT be a uniform single-rate levy, both administrative feasibility and political pressures would probably soon dictate differential rates. Moreover, even as proposed, the BTT would have a large exemption for small business.

The problem posed by differential rates can be understood by recalling how the credit and subtraction systems operate. Under the credit method any tax paid before sales to ultimate consumers has no lasting significance; the tax paid on purchases of intermediate goods and other productive inputs is allowed as a credit. If such inputs are taxed at a rate lower or higher than the standard rate, the credit is correspondingly smaller or greater. Only the tax rate applied to exports or to retail sales to households, which are not allowed a credit, ultimately matters.

Under the subtraction method the result is quite different. Under the naive subtraction method the tax rate is applied to slices of value added. Suppose that each of the stages in the production process of table 1, which is reproduced in table 12, is subject to a different tax rate, and let these three rates be 5 percent, 10 percent, and 15 percent. (How these stages would be differentiated in practice is not obvious; I return to that issue below.)

In the factual situation assumed, aggregate tax liability would be $100, exactly the same as under the uniform-rate 10 percent VAT used as our benchmark. But suppose that the composition of value added at various stages differed from what we have assumed thus far. In the extreme case, illustrated in the two other parts of table 12, virtually all

TABLE 12
ILLUSTRATION OF MULTIPLE-RATE VALUE-ADDED TAX
LEVIED UNDER THE SUBTRACTION METHOD
(dollars)

| | Stage of Production | | | |
	A	B	C	Total
Benchmark case				
Sales	300	700	1,000	2,000
Purchases	0	300	700	1,000
Value added	300	400	300	1,000
VAT rate (%)	5	10	15	10[a]
VAT	15	40	45	100
Early-value-added case				
Sales	960	980	1,000	2,940
Purchases	0	960	980	1,940
Value added	960	20	20	1,000
VAT rate (%)	5	10	15	5.3[a]
VAT	48	2	3	53
Late-value-added case				
Sales	20	40	1,000	1,060
Purchases	0	20	40	60
Value added	20	20	960	1,000
VAT rate (%)	5	10	15	14.7[a]
VAT	1	2	144	147

a. VAT rates in the total column are calculated from total VAT and total value added.

value added might occur at either stage A or stage C. The aggregate tax burden would be approximately $50 or $150 (5 percent or 15 percent of retail value) rather than $100 (10 percent of retail value).

Needless to say, strong incentives would exist to minimize taxation both by reorganizing production and by engaging in artificial transactions that would give that appearance. In the example of the table, this would entail adopting production and distribution techniques that would subject as much of value added as possible to the 5 percent rate or manipulating transactions to produce that effect. Attempting to prevent such manipulation would create severe administrative problems and interfere with legitimate business decisions on the organization of production and distribution.

Differential rates also render accurate BTAs impossible under the subtraction method. Consider first the naive subtraction method. If all domestic production followed the pattern described in the benchmark case of table 12, it would be satisfactory to apply BTAs on imports at the average rate of 10 percent. Of course, this is not the case; at the very least, a different average rate would be needed to calculate BTAs for imports competing with each domestic industry. In addition, even if the BTAs applied to various products were accurate on the average for each industry, particular firms would be placed at a competitive advantage or disadvantage in relation to imports, as well as to domestic competitors. Again, this is in marked contrast to the precise BTAs under the credit method.

The situation is at least as troublesome on the export side under the naive subtraction method. Suppose that stage C in the benchmark case of table 12 is an exporter. Subtraction of purchases from exempt exports would produce a negative figure for taxable value added of −$700. Ideally exporters would receive a rebate of $55, the amount that has been paid at previous stages as output moved through the production process. The particular configuration of value added by stages assumed in this example implies a rebate rate of just under 8 percent. If, however, the assumed tax rates applied to stages A and C had been reversed, a rebate of $85, or more than 12 percent of the $700 "negative value added" at the exempt stage, would be required. Simple variations in the composition of value added and tax rates applied at various stages produce results that appear even more peculiar. As for imports, it would be necessary to choose an average rebate rate, with all the distortions, inequities, and room for controversy that entails.

We saw earlier that it was possible to avoid most of the problems inherent in failure to tax certain stages under the subtraction-method tax by adopting a sophisticated version of that method. That solution is not adequate to overcome the difficulties in making accurate BTAs

83

for a multiple-rate VAT levied under the subtraction method just described.

The sophisticated subtraction method treats purchases differently, depending on whether tax has been paid at the immediately prior stage; deduction is allowed for tax-paid purchases but denied for purchases on which tax has not been paid. Once the system has more than one non-zero rate, the simple binary decision of whether purchases are deductible is inadequate, because the decision to allow deduction has very different implications in a system with multiple rates.

In the example of the benchmark case, it makes no sense to allow firms at stage B a deduction for purchases taxed at a rate of 5 percent in calculating value added to be taxed at a rate of 10 percent. At stage C the situation is even worse: $300 of purchases carry a VAT rate of 5 percent (from stage A) and $400 a rate of 10 percent (from stage B), even though the value added at stage C will be taxed at a rate of 15 percent. Taxing the retail stage at the highest rate would probably create cries of outrage: a deduction for purchases taxed at an average rate between 5 and 10 percent may seem inadequate if value added at the retail stage is taxed at a rate of 15 percent.

In short, even the sophisticated subtraction method makes sense only in the context of a system with one non-zero rate. Under the credit-method tax, credit is subtracted from tax liability; so there is no difficulty in allowing credit for taxes on purchases taxed at one rate against tax on sales calculated at another rate. Under the subtraction method this simply cannot sensibly be done if there are multiple positive rates.

Line drawing could be extremely important under a multiple-rate naive subtraction-method VAT. Since different rates would be applied to various slices of value added and the differences would not be neutralized by subsequent credits, both taxpayers and tax administrators could be plagued by the need to make hairline decisions on classifications, with millions of dollars riding on the resolution of definitional issues. By comparison, such decisions would be much less important under the credit method (or the sophisticated subtraction-method equivalent of the credit method), even with multiple rates. Differential rates are important under the credit method only if applied at the final stage on sales to households.

Appraisal of the Subtraction Method

The naive subtraction method is clearly unworkable, except in the unlikely event that the tax is levied on all goods and services at a uniform rate. This defect is doubly troublesome since the very existence of this method would create political pressures for exclusions and preferential rates and would encourage cheating. Many of the problems of exclusions from the base for the VAT could be overcome by employing a sophisticated version of the subtraction method based on invoices. Ironically, the sophisticated subtraction-method tax would be virtually identical with a single-rate credit-method VAT and would therefore involve little saving in taxpayer compliance or administrative effort.

The inability of the subtraction method (even the sophisticated version) to accommodate differential rates can be seen as either a strength or a weakness of that method. If differential rates are thought appropriate or inevitable for political reasons, the subtraction method cannot be used. In that context the problems just described pose insuperable difficulties. If it is thought that differential rates can be avoided, the problems caused by multiple rates would not be a drawback; indeed, they might be an advantage of the subtraction method: since the subtraction method cannot function with differential rates, adopting that method would foreclose the option of multiple rates.[18] This is a risky approach, however, since experience with VAT in other countries, as well as with the U.S. income tax, suggests that multiple rates might be adopted for a subtraction-method tax despite the overwhelming difficulties inherent in doing so.[19]

The VAT is often attacked as a hidden levy and therefore easier to raise than other, more visible taxes. This concern is not particularly valid—or need not be—under the credit method. VAT on sales to registered businesses is always stated separately, so that it can be claimed as a credit; it could be stated separately on all transactions with unregistered buyers, as under the retail sales tax in the United States. Failing that, the VAT rates applied to various transactions could be displayed prominently, since there would presumably be only a few rates (ideally no more than three, including zero).[20] In short, the VAT is probably not inherently as hidden as is sometimes thought.

The subtraction-method tax is likely to be somewhat more hidden, even if imposed at a uniform rate, unless extraordinary means are taken to force its revelation. It is impossible for the tax content of many items to be known if differential rates are levied under the naive subtraction method.

Given the way the subtraction method works, the amount of VAT on a given transaction need not be separately stated. It would be quite artificial to require separate quotation of the tax. Under a single-rate VAT merchants could state the product of the tax rate and the selling price, but this calculation would be required for no other purpose.[21] Alternatively, the single rate could be posted.

Of course, if a single rate did not apply to all transactions, even this calculation would be misleading. The tax content of a particular item depends on the tax rate applied to each slice of value added—something that a merchant could not ordinarily know for each of hundreds or thousands of items. Thus a multiple-rate, subtraction-method VAT (if it were feasible) would inevitably be hidden.[22]

The Business Transfer Tax

The business transfer tax proposed by Senator Roth is what I have characterized as a naive subtraction-method VAT. That is, it is calculated from books of account rather than from invoices and makes no distinction between purchases on which tax has been paid and for which deductions are allowed and those for which tax has not been paid and no deductions are allowed. It thus suffers from the potential administrative and economic drawbacks inherent in the naive subtraction method, unless levied at a single rate on a comprehensive base. It may be objected, of course, that Senator Roth has proposed that the BTT be levied at a single rate with no exclusions. But experience in the United States and elsewhere does not inspire hope that rate differentiation and exclusions from the base could be avoided. The large exemption for small business allowed in the Roth plan is a particular source of difficulty.

The BTT could, of course, be transformed into the more sophisticated subtraction method. That would be tantamount to converting it to a single-rate credit-method tax; like the credit-method VAT, the sophisticated subtraction-method tax would be based on invoices. Exemptions, including that for small business, would be less troublesome, but multiple rates would still cause problems. On balance the subtraction method underlying the BTT has little to recommend it.

FICA Offset for the Business Transfer Tax

Senator Roth's latest proposal for a BTT includes a provision that the tax should be offset against the employer's portion of the payroll taxes levied to finance social security (the FICA taxes). Even though that provision may eventually be dropped, it deserves explicit examination, so that its defects can be fully understood.

Senator Roth has asserted that BTAs could be made for the BTT despite the FICA credit; that is, that the full BTT would be rebated on exports and levied on imports.[23] It seems highly unlikely that the BTT would pass muster under the General Agreement on Tariffs and Trade if it contained the FICA offset. Consider the rationale underlying the GATT rules on BTAs and the likely effects of the BTT with FICA offset.

The GATT allows that BTAs can be provided for indirect taxes but not for direct taxes. These rules seem to reflect the view current when the GATT was formulated, that indirect taxes are reflected in higher product prices but direct taxes are not.[24] Although the propriety of these rules might reasonably be challenged, they continue to guide international practice.

To see why the BTT with FICA offset would not survive a challenge under the GATT, consider the example in table 13. This table is based on the example of table 1, under the assumption that a product is either exported at production stage C or imported into the United

TABLE 13
ILLUSTRATION OF PROTECTIVE NATURE OF
BUSINESS TRANSFER TAX WITH FICA CREDIT
(dollars)

| | Stage of Production | | | |
	A	B	C	Total
Basic information				
Sales	300	700	1,000	2,000
Purchases	0	300	700	1,000
Value added	300	400	300	1,000
FICA base	200	300	200	700
FICA tax (at 7%)	14	21	14	49
Exports by sector C				
Taxable value added[a]	300	400	−700	0
VAT before FICA credit[a]	30	40	−70	0
Net VAT after FICA credit[b]	16	19	−70	−35
Sector C competes with imports				
Taxable value added	300	400	300	1,000
VAT before FICA credit	30	40	30	100
Net VAT after FICA credit	16	19	16	51
VAT on $1,000 of imports	—	—	100	100

a. See table 11, benchmark case.
b. Assumed for this purpose that no FICA offset is allowed the exporter, who has a negative liability for VAT. If FICA offset is allowed the exporter, perhaps because of VAT liability on domestic sales, the entire $49 of FICA tax would provide a subsidy to exports.

States at that point in the production process.[25] Two additional lines have been added to the examples used earlier, showing how much of the value added at each stage is assumed to consist of wages and salaries subject to the FICA tax (the FICA base) and the amount of the FICA tax due in the absence of the FICA offset.

The section on exports indicates that in the absence of the FICA credit (and assuming universal coverage of prior stages by a uniform rate) exports would occur tax free, as they do under a conventional credit-method tax. It also shows that allowing a credit for FICA tax, as well as ordinary BTAs, creates a negative total net VAT burden on exports, that is, a net subsidy.[26] Of course, this result would violate the GATT.

Analogous results occur in the case of domestic goods competing with imports, illustrated in the last part of table 13. The last line emphasizes that imports are subject to the full BTT. In the absence of the FICA credit, domestic production would be taxed at the same rate, in the aggregate, as imports. The FICA credit would reduce the net cost of the BTT to domestic producers to well below that borne by imports.[27] Again, the FICA credit produces a result that would not be legal under the GATT.

The BTT with FICA offset has been justified as combining imposition of a VAT with repeal of the FICA tax. Of course, our trading partners could not object to combining explicit repeal of the FICA tax with imposition of a VAT. But that is not what is being proposed here. Rather, the net effect is, in effect, to provide BTAs for the FICA tax, which is quite inconsistent with the GATT rules.

Taken by itself, the FICA credit for the BTT appears to constitute a strange and economically inefficient distortion in favor of labor-intensive means of production. But Senator Roth has also proposed an extremely generous system of capital consumption allowances that would provide a substantial incentive for capital-intensive production.[28] This combination of incentives targeted at both labor and capital (and therefore at neither) seems to have the primary effect of reducing tax on American production. Indeed, that objective goes hand in hand with the protectionist thrust of the proposed legislation: to increase taxes on imports through the BTT while reducing taxes on domestic production, including exports. This transparent fact will not be lost on our trading partners.

The Superfund Value-added Tax

One potential source of finance of the Superfund would be a subtraction-method VAT levied at a rate of 0.08 percent on value added in manufacturing. For reasons stated earlier in this chapter, the proposed Superfund VAT is severely flawed and should not be adopted. Moreover, because it would apply only to value added in manufacturing, it would have even greater defects, which are described in the next chapter.[29]

Some observers may think that the concern expressed here is misplaced, since no tax on value added levied at such a low rate could do much harm, no matter how badly it is structured. This view may be correct but is extremely shortsighted.[30] Once the Superfund VAT was in place, there would be a natural tendency to turn to it whenever additional revenue was needed. The tax rate might easily drift upward to 1, 2, or even 5 or 10 percent, especially if a consensus developed that the federal budget deficit should be substantially reduced. At these rates the limitation of coverage to manufacturing value added would cause serious distortions. Extension to the retail stage would alleviate this problem but would be strongly resisted.

Moreover, given the nature of the subtraction method, substantial political pressures would arise to exempt various activities or at least to apply preferential rates to them. This, of course, would create all the difficulties documented in earlier sections of this chapter. In short, we would have created a monster. To forestall the unfolding of such a series of events, an alternative means of financing the Superfund should be found.

The Hall-Rabushka Personal-Exemption Value-added Tax

Robert Hall and Alvin Rabushka of the Hoover Institution have proposed replacing both the corporate and the individual income taxes with a low flat-rate tax on a much broader base.[31] Although the Hall-Rabushka tax would be implemented in much the same way as the income tax, it is, in effect, a particularly ingenious version of the naive subtraction-method VAT.

As under the BTT, the base of the Hall-Rabushka tax on business would be calculated by subtracting purchases from receipts. Unlike the Roth BTT, the Hall-Rabushka tax does not contain a small-business exemption. If not applied universally at a single rate, as proposed, it would suffer from the allocative defects of a naive subtraction-method VAT.

The Hall-Rabushka tax differs from the prototypal subtraction-method tax and from the BTT in several respects. First, wages and salaries (but not fringe benefits) are treated as deductible expenses of business and an item of taxable receipt for wage earners, who pay tax on labor income at the same rate applied to business "income." In a

TABLE 14
THREE-STAGE EXAMPLE OF 10 PERCENT HALL-RABUSHKA
(PERSONAL-EXEMPTION) VALUE-ADDED TAX
(dollars)

| | Stage of Production | | | |
	A	B	C	Total
1. Sales	300	700	1,000	2,000
2. Purchased inputs	—	300	700	1,000
3. Labor payments	200	300	200	700
4. Business tax base $(1-2-3)$	100	100	100	300
5. Business tax (10% of 4)	10	10	10	30
6. Personal tax (10% of 3)	20	30	20	70
7. Total tax	30	40	30	100

NOTE: This example is constructed to be consistent with tables 1 and 13. Lines 1, 2, and 7 are identical with lines 1, 2, and 4 in table 1. Line 3 and the resulting figures in lines 4, 5, and 6 are added to demonstrate the mechanics of the Hall-Rabushka tax. Line 3 of table 1 is the sum of lines 3 and 4 above. The distinguishing personal-exemption feature of the Hall-Rabushka tax is ignored for the purpose of this example to focus on the tax treatment of labor payments; either exemption is set at zero or labor income exceeds exemption.

sense, workers are treated as being "in the system," as far as the provision of labor services is concerned. They are not, however, allowed deductions for their own purchases of goods and services. The mechanics of the Hall-Rabushka tax are illustrated in table 14. The exemption is available, however, only for wage and salary income. Since income of the self-employed is taxed as business income, it is not eligible for personal exemptions. But the self-employed can take advantage of personal exemptions by paying themselves wages and salaries. Once full advantage has been taken of personal exemptions, it makes no difference for liability under the Hall-Rabushka tax whether self-employment income is characterized as business income or as wages and salaries.

Because of the personal-exemption feature, which is novel in the context of a VAT, though not in the context of an income tax, Hall and Rabushka are able to reduce the regressivity of the VAT through personal exemptions for the taxpayer and dependents, as under an ordinary income tax. Without the personal exemption, the Hall-Rabushka tax would be borne in rough proportion to factor incomes, for reasons given in chapter 4. The personal exemption would, in effect, free labor income below the exemption level from the tax.

Second, the Hall-Rabushka plan does not provide for zero rating of exports. Nor would it apply to imports. It thus follows the origin principle, rather than the more common destination principle. For this reason it would not pose problems of calculating accurate BTAs, even if it were not imposed uniformly on all activities. It would, however, involve serious problems of valuation of both imports and exports that do not exist under the credit-method destination-based VAT.

If the tax is viewed as a direct tax, this treatment of foreign transactions may be politically acceptable. But in the context of a VAT, it is extremely questionable from a political point of view. All other countries employ the destination principle, and pressures to do so in the United States would be enormous.[32] The questions, then, are whether the Hall-Rabushka tax could be converted to the destination principle (presumably it could) and, if so, whether it would be deemed eligible for BTAs under the GATT. Since the personal exemption is a feature usually associated with direct taxes, it could reasonably be argued that no BTA should be allowed for the portion of VAT offset by the personal exemption. There is relatively little difference, however, between employing the personal-exemption VAT and levying an ordinary VAT and using demogrants or family allowances to avoid regressivity; the latter approach would, of course, unquestionably be legal under the GATT.[33]

If the tax were converted to the destination principle, the problems of accurate BTAs would arise. These problems could be avoided by using the credit method. There thus seems to be little reason that the personal exemption that distinguishes this approach could not be included in a credit-method tax as a personal credit. Thus restructured, the Hall-Rabushka approach may offer promise as a means of overcoming the regressivity of the VAT.

Appendix: Other Inferior Forms of Value-added Tax

The discussion of techniques of computing the VAT in the text concentrated on a consumption-based VAT using either the subtraction or the credit method. Thus it set aside the question of how capital goods should be treated in the computation of liability by assuming that a consumption-based VAT was at issue. Moreover, it did not consider an alternative means of calculating value added, the addition method. I now consider explicitly the tax treatment of capital goods under an income-based VAT and the use of the addition method.

Income-based VAT. Under the consumption variety of subtraction-method VAT, purchases of capital goods and additions to inventories, as well as intermediate goods consumed currently and other business inputs, are offset immediately against gross sales in computing taxable value added. (Although the income-based VAT would be most naturally implemented through the addition method, for ease of exposition the initial explanation in this appendix is based on the subtraction method. Exactly the same problems would be encountered under the credit method.) There is thus no need to distinguish between various kinds of business purchases in calculating value added, and the example in table 1 is directly applicable. (This appendix focuses on the tax treatment of capital goods, neglecting for the most part the treatment of international transactions. Note, however, that the tax base equals consumption only if the destination principle

TABLE 15
COMPARISON OF INCOME AND CONSUMPTION BASES
FOR TAXES ON VALUE ADDED
(dollars)

| | Stage of Production | | | |
	A	B	C	Total
1. Sales	300	700	1,000	2,000
a. Intermediate goods	300	500	—	800
b. Capital goods	—	200	—	200
c. Consumer goods	—	—	1,000	1,000
2. Purchased inputs				
a. Intermediate goods	—	300	500	800
b. Capital goods	—	—	200	200
3. Capital stock				
a. Initial (assumed)	800	1,000	1,200	3,000
b. Purchases of capital goods (2b)	—	—	200	200
c. Depreciation [.05 × (3a + 3b)]	40	50	70	160
d. End of period (3a + 3b − 3c)	760	950	1,330	3,040
e. Net investment (3d − 3a)	−40	−50	130	40
4. Value added				
a. Income base (1 − 2a − 3c)	260	350	430	1,040
b. Consumption base (1 − 2a − 2b)	300	400	300	1,000
5. Factor payments plus net profits				
a. Wages	160	220	300	680
b. Rent	40	30	20	90
c. Interest	30	50	60	140
d. Net profit	30	50	50	130
e. Total	260	350	430	1,040

is adopted; under the origin principle the tax base is production.)

Under the income-based VAT, only depreciation on capital goods and amortization of other multiperiod assets (as well as purchases of currently consumed intermediate goods and other single-period inputs), rather than the entire purchase price, can be offset against sales in the period of acquisition or expenditure.[34] Capital goods and other multiperiod assets must be distinguished from intermediate goods, and depreciation or amortization schedules for tax purposes must be established for the former. Moreover, no deduction should be allowed for additions to inventories, but costs of goods sold from inventory should be deductible. Table 15 gives an example of the calculation of value added under the income-based VAT and compares it with the calculation under the consumption variety.[35] (The tax base is income originating in the taxing jurisdiction only if the origin principle is employed.)

Because purchases of both intermediate goods and capital goods are offset immediately against sales under the consumption-based VAT, the net tax base equals sales of final products to ultimate consumers, or consumption. Thus it is equal to the base of an ideal retail sales tax, that is, of a single-stage sales tax applied only to sales to final consumers.

The tax base under the income-based VAT equals income rather than consumption, since for capital goods only depreciation is allowed as an offset against sales. This distinction can be seen in table 15, where value added under the income VAT equals the sum of factor payments and net profits. For this reason a comprehensive VAT of the income variety is equivalent to a flat-rate integrated tax on corporate and personal income, with no exemptions or deductions other than those needed to measure income. Of course, the base of the income VAT exceeds that of the consumption VAT by the amount of net investment. Because the base for a VAT would be income or consumption and not some new or different tax base, it is proper to think of the VAT as an administrative device for collecting a tax on one of these bases rather than as a tax on a wholly new base.

In the text attention focuses on the consumption-based VAT because it is the most likely to be adopted in the United States, for several reasons. First, the consumption-based VAT is used in Europe, and pressure to use it here would be strong.[36] Compounding this influence is the fact that only the origin principle is fully consistent with the income base; the BTAs necessary to implement the destination principle are consistent only with a consumption-based levy. Moreover, BTAs could not be made accurately under an income-based VAT, even if enactment of such a conceptually impure approach were thought desirable. That is, zero rating of exports would not eliminate tax on capital goods used to produce exports under an income-based VAT, and imports would be taxed less heavily than domestic production subject to an income-based VAT. Of course, it is highly unlikely that the origin principle, or even these smaller biases in favor of foreign products over domestic products, would be politically acceptable.

Second, much of the impetus for a VAT can be attributed to the desire to switch to relatively greater reliance on consumption-based taxes. A consumption-based VAT would meet this objective; an income-based VAT would not. Moreover, an additional tax on income could far more easily be implemented directly, by reforming the present income tax or by adding several percentage points to existing income tax rates, than by imposing an income-based tax on value added.

Finally, the treatment of capital goods and other multiperiod assets is far simpler under the consumption variant than under the income variant. At the most basic level, the income-based VAT would require depreciation and amortization schedules and accounting. Thus all the legislative and regulatory battles that have been fought over the years in the income tax context would be fought again in the VAT arena. They would include the need to index depreciation allowances for inflation, as well as the question of asset lives and patterns of depreciation.[37] Moreover, those constructing their own capital goods would have to apply depreciation accounting to them rather than simply expense the costs of inputs used in constructing such assets.[38]

The issues of the timing of deductions for capital consumption allowances go well beyond depreciation to include all issues in which expenditures in one year create economic income in subsequent years. These include intangible drilling expenses of the oil and gas industry, the costs of growing timber, cattle, and grapes, the tax treatment of defense contractors, and other expenses of multiperiod production. Issues of inventory accounting go beyond the relatively simple issues of choosing between first-in, first-out (FIFO) and last-in, first-out (LIFO) and whether to allow indexed FIFO. Particularly important are choices of which taxpayers must use inventory accounting and the valuation of inventories.[39] Given the political difficulty of gaining the conceptually correct decisions in these areas, as demonstrated by the debate over income tax reform, and the complexity of such approaches, it seems best not to attempt them.

The Addition Method. Under the addition method the statutory tax rate is applied directly to value added, as under the subtraction

94

method. The addition method recognizes that under the income concept value added equals the sum of factor payments and profits. It is the natural choice for implementing an income-based VAT; indeed, by its very nature the addition method is directly suitable only for the implementation of the income-based VAT, and only the calculation of that type of tax is illustrated in tables 15 and 16.[40] Liabilities are, of

TABLE 16

COMPARISON OF THREE METHODS OF CALCULATING LIABILITIES
UNDER VALUE-ADDED TAXATION

(dollars)

	Stage of Production			
	A	B	C	Total
1. Subtraction method				
a. Value added (from table 15)				
1. Consumption base	300	400	300	1,000
2. Income base	260	350	430	1,040
b. Tax liability at 10% rate				
1. Consumption base	30	40	30	100
2. Income base	26	35	43	104
2. Credit method				
a. Sales (from table 15)	300	700	1,000	2,000
b. Purchases (from table 15)				
1. Intermediate goods	—	300	500	800
2. Capital goods	—	—	200	200
c. Depreciation (from table 15)	40	50	70	160
d. Gross tax liability on sales at 10% rate	30	70	100	200
e. Tax on purchases and depreciation at 10% rate				
1. Consumption base (10% of b1 + b2)	—	30	70	100
2. Income base (10% of b1 + c)	4	35	57	96
f. Net tax liability				
1. Consumption base (d − e1)	30	40	30	100
2. Income base (d − e2)	26	35	43	104
3. Addition method				
a. Sum of factor payments and profits (from table 15)	260	350	430	1,040
b. Tax liability at 10% rate (income base only)	26	35	43	104

course, the same as under the subtraction and credit methods of computing an income-based VAT, as long as the base is defined comprehensively and tax is imposed at a single rate.

If, as seems likely, American interest were to focus primarily on the consumption-based VAT, the addition method would have little attraction. The credit method is the natural way to implement a consumption-based VAT. The addition method is markedly inferior for several reasons. First, exclusions and preferential rates would pose the same problems under the addition method as under the naive subtraction method. Distortions and inequities would occur, and accurate BTAs would be impossible.

Second, all the components of income to be added together to calculate the base for the VAT must be defined. A natural place to start would be with the calculation of income for income tax purposes; using different measures of income for the income tax and the VAT would entail annoying and inexcusable complexity. Given existing problems under the income tax, this is hardly appealing. It appears quite unlikely that factor incomes would be defined substantially more appropriately under the addition-method VAT than they are under the income tax.

Notes

1. I use the terms "naive" and "sophisticated" merely to describe two variants of the subtraction method, not to be pejorative. An alternative terminology would distinguish between a method based on books of accounts, which would allow deduction for all purchases, and a method based on invoices, which would permit differentiation between tax-paid (deductible) purchases and tax-free (nondeductible) purchases. I rejected this alternative terminology to avoid confusion with the existing use of "invoice method" to describe the credit method.

Like almost everyone else writing on the VAT, including such a renowned authority as Carl S. Shoup in "Criteria for Choice among Types of Value Added Tax" (Paper presented at World Bank Conference on Value Added Taxation in Developing Countries, Washington, D.C., April 21–23, 1986), I have previously simply assumed implicitly that the subtraction-method VAT would follow the lines of the naive version described here. Some experts may have appreciated the potential equivalence between the credit method and the sophisticated subtraction method, but there is little published evidence of this. It appears more likely that most experts on the VAT never considered the issue.

2. U.S. Department of the Treasury, *Tax Reform for Fairness, Simplicity, and*

Economic Growth (Washington, D.C., 1984), vol. 3, p. 2. See also Shoup, "Criteria for Choice." He notes (p. 6): "The countries that have introduced the comprehensive VAT have shown a remarkable degree of unity in selecting among the possible combinations. Virtually all of them have opted for the consumption type . . . employing the destination principle . . . [and] computing by the tax credit method." John F. Due, "The Tax Treatment of Farmers and Small Firms under Value Added Taxes" (Paper presented at World Bank Conference on Value Added Taxation in Developing Countries, Washington, D.C., April 21–23, 1986), has noted that the Philippines used the subtraction method before switching to the credit method.

In conversations with numerous experts attending the recent World Bank conference, I confirmed that there is relatively little literature on the subtraction-method VAT for one simple reason: since the subtraction method was early widely realized to be inferior to the credit method, it received little attention. U.S. Department of the Treasury, *Tax Reform*, vol. 3, is an exception; it devotes attention to explaining problems with the subtraction method because of the realization that those who do not appreciate its defects might propose its adoption in the United States. The government of Canada is said to favor the subtraction method of implementing the VAT as a means of minimizing conflicts with provincial retail sales taxes; see chapter 9 for further discussion of intergovernmental issues.

3. Using the notation of note 5 to chapter 3, this proposition can be stated as follows:

$$\sum_{i=1}^{3} T_i = \sum_{i=1}^{3} (t_3 S_i - C_i)$$
$$= t\, S_3 - C_3 + t\, S_1 - C_1$$

Since neither stage 3 nor stage 1 has evidence of tax paid on invoices, both C_3 and C_1 are zero, and total tax collections are $t(S_3 + S_1)$. That is, value added before the exempt stage is, in effect, taxed twice because the chain of credits is broken.

Strictly speaking, exemption of only the initial stage in a linear production-distribution process would not cause a break in the chain of credits, since there is no stage before the exempt stage. Of course, in most modern economies there is really no important "initial" stage that has no purchased inputs.

4. For example, Sijbren Cnossen, "The Netherlands," in Henry J. Aaron, ed., *The Value Added Tax: Lessons from Europe* (Washington, D.C.: Brookings Institution, 1981), pp. 43–59, writes (p. 58): "The neutrality of the tax would be improved . . . if exemptions were replaced by zero rating."

5. Consider the following example. Three retail firms sell $100 of merchandise, consisting of (1) only zero-rated items, (2) only exempt items, and (3) half exempt and half zero-rated items. Each firm makes taxable purchases of $60; for the third firm these are assumed to be proportionately related to exempt and zero-rated sales. The following table summarizes tax consequences for the first two firms and three ways of treating purchases of the third.

	Firm 1 (zero-rated)	Firm 2 (exempt)	Firm 3 (½ exempt; ½ zero-rated)		
			Prorated purchases	Credit for all purchases	No credit for purchases
Tax on purchases	6	6	6	6	6
Tax on sales	0	0	0	0	0
Credit on purchases	6	0	3	6	0
Net tax	0	6	3	0	6

Allowing credit for all purchases is equivalent to zero rating; allowing no credit is equivalent to exemption. Prorating purchases gives the correct result for the firm selling both exempt and zero-rated items.

6. This is especially troublesome for capital goods, which produce output primarily in periods after their purchase. It would often be difficult to know at the time credit should be taken the extent to which capital assets will be used for taxable (or zero-rated) and exempt production.

7. For further discussion along these lines, see U.S. Department of the Treasury, *Tax Reform*, vol. 3, pp. 39–42.

8. The equation in note 5 of chapter 3 can be rewritten as follows for the case of multiple rates:

$$\sum_{i=1}^{3} T_i = \sum_{i=1}^{3} (t_i S_i - C_i)$$

Since $C_i = t_{i-1} S_{i-1}$,

$$\sum_{i=1}^{3} T_i = t_3 S_3$$

9. In the notation of note 3 of chapter 3,

$$\sum_{i=1}^{3} T_i = \sum_{i=1}^{3} t_i V_i$$

If one stage is exempt, value added at that stage is not taxed subsequently, as under the credit method.

10. Thus U.S. Department of the Treasury, *Tax Reform*, warns (vol. 3, p. 10): "Under the subtraction approach, virtually every sector of the economy would exert political pressure for special treatment. . . . They would try to minimize their value-added tax liability by seeking preferential, or perhaps even zero, rates of value-added tax on their own sector or industry."

11. There is no need to illustrate exemption of only the final stage, since the result is the same under both the naive and the sophisticated versions of the subtraction method (and the credit method)—exclusion of value added at the exempt stage from VAT.

12. The similarity to the credit method could be carried even further. As noted in chapter 8, in the situation of this example some European countries would allow firms at stage C to take credit for taxes deemed to have been paid

by the exempt firm at stage B on purchases from stage A, despite the absence of an invoice documenting actual payment of tax. Under the sophisticated subtraction method, firms at stage C could be allowed analogous deductions for purchases deemed taxable by exempt firms at stage B.

13. This is the approach proposed for the Superfund VAT.

14. The same point is made in U.S. Department of the Treasury, *Tax Reform*, vol. 3, p. 10; and Shoup, "Criteria for Choice."

15. An extremely naive approach would not even include matching of values on customs declarations used in calculating VAT on imports against deductions claimed for imports in calculating liability for VAT. But problems could easily arise under less outrageously weak administrative procedures. Suppose that foodstuffs are exempt and that a particular kind of vegetable oil can be used either to produce food preparations or for industrial purposes. Misclassification at the import stage (in either direction) would result in the wrong amount of tax. The error would not be corrected at a subsequent sale, as under the credit method.

16. These problems would be similar to those encountered in providing BTAs for turnover taxes; see chapter 7.

17. U.S. Department of the Treasury, *Tax Reform*, states (vol. 3, p. 13): "To determine the correct amount of border tax adjustment it would be necessary to know the number of previous stages, the value added at each of those stages, and the tax applied at each of those stages."

18. This attitude, plus the difficulties posed by preexisting provincial retail sales taxes, may explain the preference of the Canadian government for the subtraction method.

19. In this regard it is instructive to consider the following assessment by Aaron, *Value Added Tax*, based on European experience (p. 16):

> European experience . . . suggests, however, that this advice may be a counsel of perfection. In varying degrees all European countries except Denmark employ differentiated rates, to pursue distributional objectives and make the distributional pattern of the value-added tax resemble that of taxes it replaced. In either case, no country treated in this book has followed the advice of the majority of the conference participants to do away with varied rates and to reduce the number of exemptions; all conferees thought that the United States would follow the European pattern of differentiated rates and exemptions if it adopted the value-added tax. None, for example, believed that Congress would be able to resist the pressure to impose lower than average rates of taxation on such necessities as food, housing, and medicines, although most participants agreed that it would be unfortunate if Congress deviated from uniform rates.

20. For instance, in countries that impose the VAT restaurant menus commonly indicate that prices include VAT.

21. The tax paid by the merchant is, moreover, the product of the tax rate and the merchant's value added. Of course, this is not calculated on a transaction-by-transaction basis.

22. Note that Senator Roth's proposal for a BTT contains no provisions to prevent the tax from being hidden. Because it is calculated from books of account, it could not easily be stated separately even if applied universally. The large exemption for small business and the FICA offset aggravate the difficulties of knowing the tax content of a given transaction.

23. William V. T. Roth, "The Roth Reforms" (Speech to the National Press Club, Washington, D.C., February 20, 1986, and supporting documents).

24. For a description and analysis of the GATT rules and the rationale behind them, see Robert H. Floyd, "GATT Provisions on Border Tax Adjustments," *World Trade Journal*, vol. 7 (1973).

25. To facilitate comparison with other tables, this example is based on the 10 percent VAT rate used in other examples in this monograph, rather than the 8 percent rate in the latest Roth proposal for a BTT. The FICA rate is rounded to 7 percent to facilitate calculation in the examples.

26. Table 13 refers to the "net VAT after FICA credit," even though, strictly speaking, it appears to be the FICA tax, rather than the BTT, that is reduced by the offsetting of BTT against FICA. The key point is that the table reports the net effect on tax liability of imposing the BTT, after allowance is made for ordinary BTAs and the FICA credit.

The results reported here may actually understate the net subsidy entailed by the BTT with FICA credit, because it is assumed that none of the FICA tax paid at the export stage can be offset by the BTT, since VAT before credit is negative. If the exporter has enough VAT liability on domestic sales, the full FICA tax could be offset. Business would presumably be organized and transactions structured in such a way that the full benefits of both BTAs and the FICA credit could be realized.

27. In this case, unlike the situation for exporters described in note 26, the entire FICA offset is assumed to be usable by firms competing with imports.

28. See Roth, "Roth Reforms."

29. Whether a VAT limited to manufacturing is an appropriate vehicle for financing the Superfund should be considered explicitly. Although this important question is beyond the scope of this analysis, the case for using such a tax does not seem compelling, compared either with using general revenues to clean up preexisting wastes or with using effluent charges to finance disposal of future wastes.

30. This discussion ignores the crucial question of whether this "mini-VAT" could be administered effectively with little or no additional expense. There is, however, a prima facie case against the proposition.

31. See Robert E. Hall and Alvin Rabushka, *Low Tax, Simple Tax, Flat Tax* (New York: McGraw-Hill, 1983); and Hall and Rabushka, *The Flat Tax* (Stanford, Calif.: Hoover Institution Press, 1985). The X-plan described in David F. Bradford, *Untangling the Income Tax* (Cambridge, Mass.: Harvard University Press, 1986), closely resembles the personal-exemption VAT of Hall and Rabushka. It is not discussed here because progressive rates are applied to compensation, rather than the flat rate applied to business income.

32. Moreover, as noted in the appendix to this chapter, the origin principle is really not consistent with the consumption-based VAT; the destination

principle is conceptually more compatible with the consumption base.

33. For a more detailed discussion of these issues, see George N. Carlson and Charles E. McLure, Jr., "Pros and Cons of Alternative Approaches to the Taxation of Consumption," in *Proceedings of the 1984 Conference of the National Tax Association–Tax Institute of America* (Nashville, Tenn., 1984), pp. 147–54.

34. Carl S. Shoup, *Public Finance* (Chicago: Aldine Publishing Co., 1969), also describes the gross-product and wage VATs (pp. 251–53). U.S. Department of the Treasury, *Tax Reform*, provides a negative evaluation of the gross-product VAT (vol. 3, p. 6). Under the gross-product tax no deduction for capital investment or credit for tax on such investment would be allowed. The aggregate tax base would thus be gross national product. This variant of the VAT has, unfortunately, received altogether too much attention in discussions of VATs.

First, the gross-product tax would not even be a true tax on value added; it would be a turnover tax, to the extent that capital is used in production. (See chapter 7 for an explanation of the nature and defects of turnover taxes.) By comparison, an income tax can be faulted for the timing of capital consumption allowances but not their total absence.

Second, the gross-product tax would create a substantial disincentive for saving, investment, and capital-intensive production. It would not be a serious candidate for adoption—and should not be—unless other policies result in artificial stimulus to capital-intensive production, as in some developing countries that suffer from shortages of capital.

Third, there would be a sharp discontinuity between the treatment of repairs and maintenance (expensed) and investment (totally nondeductible). Under a consumption-based tax these expenditures are treated identically, and under an income-based VAT the issue is the less important one of the timing of deduction. Other issues of what to expense and what to capitalize (and therefore never deduct) would also be magnified. See the discussion in the text of this appendix at note 37 for more on the issue of which expenditures should be capitalized under an income-based VAT. Presumably the same expenditures would be nondeductible under the gross-product VAT.

In short, the assessment by the Treasury Department in *Tax Reform* (vol. 3, p. 6) that the gross-product VAT "is best relegated to the realm of conceptual curiosities and should not receive serious consideration" is too generous; it should be relegated to the junkpile of conceptual monstrosities and never need to be mentioned again in works such as this.

35. Table 15 also illustrates the calculation of value added under the addition method, to be explained in the second part of this appendix.

36. Shoup ("Criteria for Choice") notes that Finland employs a gross-product VAT. Turkey allows credit for taxes on capital goods to be taken only over a period of five years, except by industries that benefit from investment incentives under the income tax.

37. See U.S. Department of the Treasury, *Tax Reform*, vol. 2, chap. 8.

38. For further elaboration of the points made in this paragraph and the next in the context of the income tax, see ibid., chaps. 9–12.

39. See ibid., chap. 10.

40. Shoup ("Criteria for Choice") notes, "For the income type of VAT, which is based on the sum of the factor incomes of the firm, the addition method is the obvious one to use. The subtraction and credit methods are not suitable. Conversely the addition method is not suitable for the consumption type." Theoretically a consumption-based VAT could be implemented under the addition method, but only if profits were reduced by the amount of net investment. Alternatively, profits for tax purposes could be adjusted by adding back all capital consumption allowances and deducting all investment expenses. Advisory Commission on Intergovernmental Relations, *Strengthening the Federal Revenue System: Implications for State and Local Taxing and Borrowing*, A-97 (Washington, D.C., 1984), indicates that this is the approach followed in the Michigan VAT.

This suggests that the addition method is merely a variant of the subtraction method, a fact that can be appreciated from the manipulation of the following definitional identities:

$$V_A = I + F$$
$$V_S = S - E - P$$

where V_A and V_S are value added calculated under the addition and subtraction methods, respectively, I is business profits, F is factor payments, S is sales, E is purchases that would be allowed as an immediate deduction under either an income- or a consumption-based VAT, and P is either purchases of capital goods and other multiperiod assets or the depreciable amount of such purchases, depending on whether the income or subtraction method is being examined. But $I = S - F - E - P$; thus $V_A = S - E - P$. With V_A, as with V_S, the crucial issue is the definition of P, that is, the tax treatment of capital goods and other multiperiod assets.

7
Alternative Forms of General Sales Tax

In recent years the value-added tax has been the form of general sales tax most commonly proposed for introduction by the federal government. But any serious discussion of a federal VAT should include consideration of the retail sales tax, a much more familiar and quite productive source of state and local revenue in the United States. The first section of this chapter compares the retail sales tax and the VAT. A VAT that would exclude the retail stage and a gross receipts tax have also occasionally been mentioned in the recent debate. The second and third sections indicate why these alternatives should not receive serious consideration.

Value-added Tax versus Retail Sales Tax

In theory the VAT and a pure form of the retail sales tax are economically equivalent. But in actuality the two taxes are likely to be different for administrative reasons, quite aside from any differences in their tax bases arising from policy decisions. These differences and the resulting administrative advantages and disadvantages of the two ways of implementing sales taxes are reviewed in this section. It may be worth noting at the outset that most of the differences are not inherent in the two approaches and are easily overstated. For the sake of holding the discussion to manageable proportions, the retail sales tax is compared only with a consumption-based VAT imposed under the credit method, the most likely candidate for adoption in the United States.[1]

The retail sales tax has the substantial advantage of familiarity. The five states that do not levy sales taxes—Alaska, Delaware, Montana, New Hampshire, and Oregon—are among the least populous in the nation. The retail sales tax is also somewhat easier to understand and implement than the VAT. Thus far less education would be required by introduction of a federal retail sales tax than of a VAT.

The existence of exemptions would create less difficulty under a retail sales tax than under a VAT. First, a firm selling both exempt and taxable or zero-rated items would not need to allocate costs between the categories, as under a VAT. Second, the problem of overtaxation that arises when the chain of exemptions is broken under the VAT would not exist under the retail sales tax.

A credit-method VAT (or its equivalent under the sophisticated subtraction method) requires the payment of substantial refunds as a matter of course. This is especially true of exports, but it can also arise when a firm's sales are taxed at a lower rate than its purchases or when tax paid on capital expenditures in a given period is large in relation to tax due on sales or exceeds it.[2] Under the retail sales tax no refunds are necessary in any of these cases. There may, however, be cascading of taxes on previous stages.

A further advantage of the retail sales tax over the VAT is the smaller number of firms that must be registered. This difference is not as great as might be thought, however, since many firms in the manufacturing and wholesale sectors also make sales to retail customers.[3] Moreover, the firms that would be liable for the VAT but not for the retail sales tax are likely to be large and easy for the tax administration to deal with.

One reason for the popularity of the credit method of implementing the VAT in Europe is the automatic production of documents that can—at least in theory—be used in enforcement of the tax both up and down the line in the production-distribution process. A firm's need to have proof of taxes paid on purchases creates demands for invoices that provide information to the revenue agents about sales of the firm's suppliers. Viewed from the other end, invoices and receipts issued by a supplier contain information that is useful in validating the purchasing firm's claims of credits for taxes paid on purchases. Information gained in this way is also potentially useful in enforcement of income and other taxes. These self-enforcing features can, however, be easily exaggerated; invoices can be faked, and claims for credits can be overstated unless taxes paid and credits claimed are actually cross-checked. Moreover, this feature may be relatively less important in the United States, where taxpayer compliance is—or at least was—generally agreed to be higher than in Europe.[4]

Probably the primary economic advantage of the VAT over the retail sales tax is in the treatment of capital goods and other business inputs, international transactions, and services. Under a consumption-based VAT, registered business purchasers are allowed credit for taxes on all inputs, whether of capital, services, intermediate goods, or other business purchases. Thus only consumer goods and services are ultimately taxed under the VAT.[5]

Under the retail sales tax the solution is not so simple. Since some goods and services can be employed either as productive inputs or as consumer goods, a way must be found to exempt them from tax when purchased for business use. Otherwise the retail sales tax will contain elements of a gross receipts tax and share its defects: investment will be penalized; discrimination will occur between various domestically produced goods and services; vertical integration will be encouraged; and accurate border tax adjustments (BTAs) will be impossible because of taxes paid on inputs at earlier stages and incorporated in prices.

One approach to this problem is to exempt from tax the sales of specific items used largely for business purposes. This clearly cannot produce totally satisfactory results, since this kind of distinction is untenable for many products; steam turbines can be exempted from the tax with little danger of an error in classification, but hammers and shovels cannot. Moreover, businessmen object to dividing sales into taxable and exempt categories and accounting for them separately, especially since any categorization is likely to involve hairsplitting that defies reason.

A second and more common approach is to exempt purchases by registered firms on the assumption that purchases by nonregistered customers will be made almost entirely by consumers. An obvious problem is, of course, guaranteeing both that production inputs are largely free of tax and that not too much otherwise taxable output intended for the private use of the firm's owner passes through tax-exempt transactions.[6] Dealing with exemption certificates, especially for small purchases, causes delays, compliance problems for vendors, and administrative difficulties.

A further problem, not inherent in retail sales taxation, is that in actual practice no effort is usually made to exempt all purchases of business firms from the tax. States commonly adopt rules providing exemption only for goods that are to become "component parts" of final products or that are for "direct use" in the production process. If the retail sales tax is truly to be a consumption tax that avoids multiple taxation of value added, exemption should be allowed for *all* purchases by business firms.[7]

Services pose a somewhat different problem. They are often exempt from retail sales tax, either to prevent cascading in the case of business services or because legislators fail to understand that taxation of services provided to households is required for economic neutrality and equity or because of successful political activity by those who provide services. (See chapter 8 for elaboration of the argument that services to consumers should be taxed.) Pressures to exempt services offered primarily to households would also be strong under a VAT. But efforts to exempt business services from a VAT would be substantially weaker if the credit method were adopted. Complete exemption of any stage of the productive process (besides the last) from paying a credit-method VAT on its sales poses problems.

The problem is not that the final output would be undertaxed, since tax on the exempt sector would be made up at later stages; it is rather that the firms in the exempt sector would not be allowed credit for taxes paid on their purchases. When the chain of credits is broken, the product is overtaxed, rather than undertaxed. By comparison, under the retail sales tax, exemption means freedom from tax. The problem of overtaxation may be important, for example, for professional services, which are often outside the VAT system. The importance of this source of double taxation of services depends on the tax rates and the importance of business purchases of various services. Since most providers of professional services to business would want to be in the system under a VAT, it would be relatively simple to approximate the correct solution of taxing all services.[8] Authorities differ about the relative effectiveness of the retail sales tax and the VAT in handling purchases of business firms, including services and capital goods, but on balance it appears that the verdict must favor the VAT.[9]

The credit-method VAT automatically produces precise BTAs, except when a sector before the export stage is exempt. By comparison, to the extent that the retail sales tax is applied to purchases of capital goods, intermediate goods, and other business purchases, it will produce an effective rate of tax on domestic production that exceeds the statutory rate. Thus application of the statutory rate to imports will not fully compensate for the retail sales tax on domestic products; they will be placed at a competitive disadvantage in relation to imports. Similarly, exports will contain some element of tax, even if they are exempt from the retail sales tax, and will thus be at a disadvantage in foreign markets.[10]

A final issue in the choice between a federal retail sales tax and a VAT involves important questions of intergovernmental relations.[11] Federal use of either a VAT or a retail sales tax would constitute an intrusion into a field of taxation heretofore reserved for the exclusive use of state and, more recently, local governments.[12] If a state's autonomy in determining its sales tax base is deemed important, the federal government should probably adopt a retail sales tax, rather than a credit-based VAT, if it adopts either.[13] This contention rests on the ease of piggybacking state and local levies on a federal retail sales tax and the difficulty of doing so on a federal VAT. If, however, it were decided that states should have the freedom to set sales tax rates but that fiscal autonomy need not extend to the tax base, a federal VAT with federal collection of state supplements might be preferred.

In the final analysis, the choice between a VAT and a retail sales tax may depend crucially on the rate of tax envisaged. At a low rate a retail sales tax might be preferable, but at rates higher than about 10 percent the enforcement and efficiency advantages of the VAT probably outweigh the advantages of the retail sales tax.[14] Since half the states (three-fourths if local sales taxes are included) have sales taxes of at least 5 percent, it appears that the choice should probably be a VAT.[15]

Preretail Taxes

Single-stage sales taxes are sometimes levied at the manufacturing or wholesale stage, rather than on retail sales. Moreover, some VATs do not extend through the retail stage; they are applied only through the manufacturing or wholesale stage, usually for administrative reasons. Several recent proposals for subtraction-method VATs would extend only through the manufacturing stage.[16]

Exclusion of the retail stage from a national sales tax, though sometimes necessary in a developing country for administrative reasons, would be unnecessary and a serious mistake in a developed country such as the United States.[17] First, it would create substantial economic distortions. Industries in which a high proportion of value is added at the retail stage would be favored over those in which relatively more value is added at earlier stages. Thus, for example, services would be placed at a competitive advantage in relation to the sale of goods. Goods characterized by high retail margins would also be given a tax advantage. Since distortions of consumer choices reduce the total satisfaction realized from economic activity, they should be avoided.

Normal business decisions would also be distorted by such a tax. The natural tendency would be to shift as much value added as possible to stages not covered by a preretail tax. For example, advertising, distribution, or other activities normally conducted by a manufacturer might be shifted to the retail stage to remove them from the scope of a manufacturing-stage tax. The retail business might be a wholly owned subsidiary or an unrelated firm.[18]

Excluding the retail stage from a VAT or imposing a single-stage tax on either manufacturing or wholesaling would also create substantial administrative difficulties. Most obviously, distinguishing between taxable and nontaxable transactions would be intractably difficult. Manufacturers and wholesalers that make both exempt retail sales and taxable preretail sales would experience particular difficulty in complying and would cause administrative problems.

Moreover, to establish parity with competitors, notional prices would need to be established for any good produced by a company both selling at retail and engaged in taxable transactions, whether manufacturing or wholesaling. Such notional prices could sometimes be established by reference to arm's-length transactions with unrelated parties. More commonly, however, such transactions might not exist, and the notional prices would be determined arbitrarily. Experience in the international sphere demonstrates how difficult it is to determine whether transfer prices for transactions between affiliates are reasonable. Adoption of a preretail tax would be tantamount to importing those same problems into the domestic economy.

Exclusion of retail value added from the tax base would probably also have undesirable distributional consequences. Many goods and services characterized by high retail margins are consumed relatively more by high-income than by low-income households. These include many kinds of services and luxury consumer goods.

Accurate BTAs are also impossible under a preretail tax. For example, if transportation and advertising are commonly included in the price of manufactured goods, imports will have a competitive advantage over domestic products. The discrimination could, however, run in the opposite direction in particular instances.

Finally, any sales tax that does not extend to the retail stage is inherently hidden. By comparison, either a VAT or a retail sales tax can be made quite visible.

Turnover Taxes and Value-added Tax Compared

It may be worthwhile to examine briefly the difference between the VAT and the gross receipts or turnover taxes replaced by the VAT in Europe. A gross receipts tax is literally that, a tax levied on the receipts of a firm, with no allowance for taxes that have been paid on purchases of capital goods, intermediate goods, or other business inputs. Although the defects of gross receipts taxes are so obvious and so well known that such taxes should—and generally do—receive no serious consideration, taxes of this kind are occasionally proposed.[19] Moreover, understanding these defects will facilitate appreciation of the advantages of a VAT over a retail sales tax in eliminating tax on business inputs.

Table 17 will help clarify the distinction between the VAT, which is a tax only on net accretions of value, and the tax on gross receipts. It shows the total turnover tax liabilities that would be incurred by three hypothetical industries, each producing $1,000 of value added, if a cascade tax were levied on gross sales at a rate of 5 percent. Industry I is repeated from table 1 to provide a benchmark for comparison. Industry II is completely integrated, so that there is only one stage in the productive process. Finally, industry III has three stages, like industry I, but the split of value added by stages is quite different.

Because gross sales in the three stages of industry I total $2,000, the 5 percent turnover tax on gross sales yields the same total revenue as the 10 percent tax on value added, $100.[20] But sales of the vertically integrated industry II are entirely to ultimate consumers, so that gross sales equal the value added of $1,000. Thus in this industry a 5 percent turnover tax yields but half the revenue of the 10 percent tax on value added. Whereas either the VAT or the retail sales tax would impose the same percentage tax burden on the products of the two industries, the turnover tax discriminates in favor of vertically integrated industries and production processes.

Industry III has the same number of stages as industry I. But because more value is added earlier in the production process, more of it is subjected to the turnover tax repeatedly as it moves through later stages, and total sales at the various stages are greater than for industry I. Thus, if the tax rate is 5 percent, the industry bears a $135 total tax burden, rather than the $100 burden on industry I. As a rule the turnover tax discriminates against industries whose value added occurs early in the production process. Of course, it is impossible for consumers to know the amount of tax collected on a given item.

Suppose that the goods produced in the three industries were exported at stage C, instead of being sold to consumers. Ideally the exports would occur tax free under the destination principle. For industry II tax-free export would be achieved simply by exempting exports from the turnover tax. But for industries in which some value is added at earlier stages, taxes paid at prior stages would have to be rebated. Export rebates would, however, be virtually impossible to determine accurately, especially if goods had passed through several stages. Besides the direct exemption of exports from the tax, rebates would need to be made at different rates depending on the value of input purchases in industries I and III. In industry I a rebate of $50 of taxes on purchases of $700, or about 7 percent, would be required; in industry III a rebate of $85 on purchases of $900, or almost 9½ percent.

TABLE 17
THREE-INDUSTRY COMPARISON OF 10 PERCENT VAT,
10 PERCENT RETAIL SALES TAX,
14.3 PERCENT MANUFACTURING-STAGE VAT,
AND 5 PERCENT GROSS TURNOVER TAX
(dollars)

| | Stage of Production | | | |
	A	B	C	Total
Industry I (from table 1)				
Sales	300	700	1,000	2,000
Purchased inputs	—	300	700	1,000
Value added	300	400	300	1,000
Value-added tax	30	40	30	100
Retail sales tax	—	—	100	100
Gross turnover tax	15	35	50	100
Manufacturing-stage VAT	43	57	0	100
Industry II				
Sales	—	—	1,000	1,000
Purchased inputs	—	—	—	—
Value added	—	—	1,000	1,000
Value-added tax	—	—	100	100
Retail sales tax	—	—	100	100
Gross turnover tax	—	—	50	50
Manufacturing-stage VAT		—Unknowable—		
Industry III				
Sales	800	900	1,000	2,700
Purchased inputs	—	800	900	1,700
Value added	800	100	100	1,000
Value-added tax	80	10	10	100
Retail sales tax	—	—	100	100
Gross turnover tax	40	45	50	135
Manufacturing-stage VAT	114	14	0	128

Moreover, there is no obvious way to differentiate purchases leading to exports and those leading to production for domestic markets.

The situation is no better if export rebates are geared to the value of exports rather than to purchases of exporters. There is no way that rebates could be given automatically and accurately, as under the VAT. Ideally the rebate would be 5 percent, 0 percent, and 8.5 percent of exports, respectively, in the three industries. Although this kind of differentiation by industry might be possible, no such differentiation would be possible within industries. Rebates would of necessity be based on averages, which means that discrimination would inevitably occur between industries, methods of production, and firms. In particular, average rebate rates would create competitive disadvantages for unintegrated producers and favor integrated producers. This is one of the primary disadvantages of the turnover tax.

The situation is, of course, the same on the import side. Ideally, imports would be taxed at the same ad valorem rate as domestic goods at the same stage of production. But by stage C domestic output in the three industries is being taxed at rates varying from 5 to 13.5 percent. There is no one rate at which to levy a compensating tax on imports.[21]

Because of the distortions created in domestic economies by this non-neutral tax and the difficulties in calculating BTAs precisely, members of the European Economic Community replaced turnover taxes with the nondistorting tax on value added. Because of the discrimination inherent in it, the turnover tax is a decidedly inferior form of taxation and should not be considered for the United States.

Notes

1. This discussion draws heavily on arguments presented in Carl S. Shoup, "Experience with Value-added Tax in Denmark, and Prospects in Sweden," *Finanzarchiv* (March 1969), pp. 236–52; idem, "Factors Bearing on an Assumed Choice between Federal Retail Sales Tax and a Federal Value-added Tax," in Richard A. Musgrave, ed., *Broad-based Taxes: New Options and Sources* (Baltimore: Johns Hopkins University Press for the Committee for Economic Development, 1973), pp. 215–26; and John F. Due, "The Case for the Use of the Retail Form of Sales Tax in Preference to the Value-added Tax," in Musgrave, *Broad-based Taxes,* pp. 205–14. See also John F. Due, "The Choice between a Value-added Tax and a Retail Sales Tax" (1985 Conference Report, Report of Proceedings of the Thirty-seventh Tax Conference, Canadian Tax Foundation, 1986), chap. 16; Claudia Scott and Howard Davis, *The Gist of GST: A Briefing on the Goods and Services Tax* (Wellington, New Zealand: Victoria University Press, Institute of Policy Studies, 1985), chap. 4; and *Reform of the Australian Tax System*, Draft White Paper (Canberra: Australian Government Publishing Service, 1985), pp. 129–32.

2. The Sixth Directive of the EEC provides that where reduced rates are employed, they should not be so low that refunds of taxes paid at prior stages are common.

3. It has been estimated that in the United States the retail sales tax would apply to about 10 percent fewer firms than the VAT; see U.S. Department of the Treasury, *Tax Reform for Fairness, Simplicity, and Economic Growth* (Washington, D.C., 1984), vol. 3, p. 32.

4. For further discussion of this point, see Due, "The Choice." It is sometimes suggested that the VAT could be used to extract tax from those who do not pay the income tax. This deserves two comments. First, those who do not pay income tax are unlikely to comply with legal requirements to collect and remit VAT. Second, although those who evade the income tax will pay VAT when they spend their untaxed income on consumption, so will those who do pay income tax.

5. For a formal demonstration of the desirability of not taxing intermediate inputs, see Peter A, Diamond and James A. Mirlees, "Optimal Taxation and Public Production I: Production Efficiency," *American Economic Review* (March 1971), pp. 8–27. The limitations of that analysis are summarized in Anthony B. Atkinson and Joseph E. Stiglitz, *Lectures on Public Economics* (New York: McGraw-Hill, 1980), pp. 470–73.

6. Under the VAT there is, of course, the problem of credit's being taken for taxes on goods ostensibly purchased for business use but converted to consumption by the owner of the business. This problem seems to be comparable for the two taxes, although under a VAT this result requires a falsified tax return and under the retail sales tax only a lie to a vendor. Shoup, "Factors Bearing on Choice," has emphasized this point.

7. It is instructive to quote Due, "The Choice," on this issue (pp. 8–9):

> RST [retail sales tax] users . . . have made no serious attempt to avoid cascading by excluding business inputs. Because of the problems of doing so completely, most jurisdictions have limited the exclusion to sales for resale, materials and parts physically incorporated into the final products, and, in some instances, fuel, industrial machinery, and farm feed, seed, and fertilizer. Otherwise, inputs are taxed with no serious attempt to exclude them. In fact, many jurisdictions do not accept the principle that inputs should be excluded from tax. At least part of their reason is that it is politically unattractive to shift tax burden to individual consumers from business firms —even though such a shift is essential for optimality in production.

8. Shoup, "Factors Bearing on Choice," p. 243, has noted that professionals may be given the option of entering the VAT system.

9. See ibid.; and Due, "Case for Retail Form of Sales Tax." Due notes that it should be possible to implement a hybrid tax that, though essentially a retail sales tax, would allow business firms to buy inputs tax free, subject to audit, or receive credit for taxes paid on inputs. Carried to the extreme, this would be a credit system with suspension of tax on certain sales to business.

10. In the terminology of earlier chapters, the retail sales tax, though basically a destination-based levy, contains elements of an origin-based system.

11. See Charles E. McLure, Jr., "TVA and Fiscal Federalism," in *Proceedings of the 64th Annual Conference of the National Tax Association–Tax Institute of America* (Kansas City, Mo., 1971), pp. 279–91; and idem, "State-Federal Relations in the Taxation of the Value Added," *Journal of Corporation Law*, vol. 6 (Fall 1980), pp. 127–39. See also chapter 9.

12. It is sometimes suggested that a federal VAT would involve less intru-

sion into the sales tax area than a federal retail sales tax. This argument is based more on illusion than on reality. Since retail sales taxes and consumption-based VATs are essentially equivalent, a federal retail sales tax would involve no more intrusion into the general consumption tax field than a VAT.

13. This point is also mentioned in Due, "Case for Retail Form of Sales Tax."

14. Claudia Scott, "VAT and Tax Reform" (Paper presented at World Bank Conference on Value Added Taxation in Developing Countries, Washington, D.C., April 21–23, 1986), makes this point in the following terms:

Given the tradeoff between higher administrative and compliance costs of the GST over the RST and the slightly improved efficiency associated, the choice of RST vs. GST has centered on the issue of the tax rate. International tax advisers increase their support for use of GST the higher the tax rate to be imposed. Though there is no number that finds universal acceptance, tax rates in excess of 7 percent to 8 percent were often discussed by the NZ Treasury as points where serious attention should be given to a VAT, though Australian counterparts have suggested rates above 12 percent.

GST (for general sales tax) is the name given the VAT in the recent proposals of the government of New Zealand.

15. See Advisory Commission on Intergovernmental Relations, *Significant Features of Fiscal Federalism, 1985–86 Edition* (Washington, D.C., 1986), pp. 92, 99–100.

16. An early proposal for a tax on business transactions had this feature, as does the VAT proposed to finance the Superfund.

17. Due, "The Choice," offers the following succinct summary of the disadvantages of excluding the retail level from sales taxation (p. 1):

Lengthy experience in a number of countries, including Canada, Switzerland, Australia, and New Zealand, provides conclusive evidence that any sales tax that stops short of the retail level is basically unsatisfactory and a subject of endless controversy. As is well known, the basic difficulties center around the inevitable tendency of firms to push various activities beyond the point of impact of the tax, the inability to treat different distribution systems equally for tax purposes, the inability to tax imports and domestic goods equally, and the higher tax rate necessary for a given revenue.

U.S. Department of the Treasury, *Tax Reform*, vol. 1, pp. 217–18, includes single-stage taxes levied before the retail stage and VATs that exclude the retail stage along with the multiple-stage turnover taxes discussed in the last section of this chapter in a category of "sales taxes unworthy of consideration." See also ibid., vol. 3, pp. 33–35; and George N. Carlson and Charles E. McLure, Jr., "Pros and Cons of Alternative Approaches to the Taxation of Consumption," in *Proceedings of the 1984 Conference of the National Tax Association–Tax Institute of America* (Nashville, Tenn., 1984), pp. 147–54.

Many of these same problems would accompany any failure of a VAT to cover retail sales. But they would be pervasive if the tax systematically excluded the retail stage.

18. Another form of economic distortion has occurred under the Canadian

tax on manufacturers. Affluent persons contract with jewelers to produce jewelry on a consignment basis, using materials of the customer, to avoid the manufacturers' tax. Canada has been considering for several years the possibility of replacing its federal manufacturers' sales tax with either a retail sales tax or a VAT, to eliminate the distortions discussed in the text.

19. For example, the Deficit Reduction Act of 1984 directed the Treasury Department to conduct a study of a tax on gross income, and proposals for similar taxes have been amazingly common during the recent debates on tax reform. The proposal for a low-rate tax on financial transactions also has elements of a turnover tax.

20. This example is inaccurate in one respect. The tax at any stage would be incorporated in the price of the taxed good. Thus the tax at the next stage would be applied to the gross price, including taxes paid at earlier stages. This aspect of taxing previous taxes, sometimes called cascading, is much less important than the multiple taxation of value added as it moves through the production process.

21. Because of the necessity of using averages, BTAs were not exact under the European turnover taxes, as they are under the VAT, and it was generally agreed that Germany, in particular, undercompensated under the old turnover tax. Thus in shifting to the VAT and its perfect equalization, Germany gained a temporary trade advantage, although it was doing something that was perfectly legitimate under the rules of the General Agreement on Tariffs and Trade (GATT). To avoid adverse effects on international monetary stability, Germany initially allowed BTA at only half the rate of the domestic VAT, moving to full BTA when the deutsche mark was revalued.

8
Problem Industries and Activities

Much of the discussion to this point has been conducted in general terms, without reference to how particular industries or activities might be treated under the value-added tax. Certain industries and activities, however, for social, economic, political, or administrative reasons, are usually not accorded the standard textbook treatment. These include small business, farming, services, housing, used goods, the services of financial institutions, benefits in kind, and the activities and purchases of governments and nonprofit organizations.

This chapter briefly describes the problems that arise in these areas, how they might be handled, and how they are handled in Europe and elsewhere. Since many of these problems are complex and do not readily yield satisfactory solutions, it is not possible to do more than scratch the surface in a brief survey such as this.[1] For the most part the discussion is couched in terms of the credit method of implementing the VAT. But possible solutions under both the naive and the sophisticated versions of the subtraction method are also discussed. Particular attention is devoted to Senator William Roth's proposal for an extraordinarily high small-business exemption, since a large exemption would have even more adverse effects under a subtraction-method VAT such as Roth's business transfer tax (BTT) than under the credit method.

Small Business

Most countries allow special treatment for small businesses under the VAT.[2] To some extent this reflects political compromise and recognition of administrative reality.[3] It may not be feasible or fair to subject numerous small-scale businesses to the complex requirements of compliance with the VAT.[4] Some countries simply exempt small businesses, recognizing that under the credit method firms not in the system pay tax on their purchases, so that only their own value added escapes taxation.[5] Others attempt to employ ad hoc levies that approximate the amount that should be payable by the representative firm with the characteristics of the taxpayer.[6]

If the small business that is exempt or subject to the ad hoc substitute for the VAT operates at the retail stage, either of these approaches may be satisfactory. If, however, it operates earlier in the production-distribution process, exemption creates a break in the chain of credits that puts the small business at a competitive disadvantage, and an ad hoc substitute for the VAT that cannot be claimed as a credit by the customers of the small business may aggravate that problem.[7]

It appears that special treatment of small businesses would be largely unnecessary in the United States, since such businesses are required to file returns under the income tax. Although there is much to be said for this view as a general proposition, it must be qualified in at least two respects. First, it would not be desirable to include in the VAT system the many children who earn insignificant amounts of income from baby sitting, mowing lawns, and so on. Of course, they are not required to file income tax returns unless their income exceeds the filing requirement. Even for adults with small amounts of income from self-employment, the administrative costs of enforcing the VAT could easily outweigh the benefits in equity, neutrality, and revenue of including them in the VAT system. Most such persons probably file income tax returns primarily because they also have income from other sources.

Second, it would be desirable to prevent credits and refunds of VAT paid on purchases to those who would otherwise simply use taxes on personal expenses to offset—or more than offset—taxes on receipts from self-employment. An important example of this kind of abuse would be hobby losses of gentlemen farmers. Clearly if farming is entirely for personal pleasure and no sales are made, no refunds should be allowed for taxes paid on purchases. Even if some sales are made, it seems reasonable that no refunds be allowed if taxes paid on expenses of hobby farming exceed taxes due on receipts.

The first of these problems could probably be dealt with by requiring registration under the VAT only for those with either a permanent business establishment or a minimal level of receipts.[8] European experience suggests that an exemption of no more than about $25,000 in gross receipts might be appropriate.[9] The difficulties created by breaks in the chain of credits produced by exemption could be avoided by allowing those eligible for exemption the option of participating in the regular VAT system.[10]

This approach, however, does not deal with the second problem. Indeed, an unrestricted option to be in the VAT system might actually

116

accentuate the problem; those with minor amounts of business receipts might opt into the system to take improper credit for tax paid on purchases for consumption. For activities such as hobby farming, it might be possible to prohibit refunds in certain instances, for example, where there is presumed to be no expectation of profit. Of course, even this would not reach the consumption element of some such activities. In the extreme case such activities might be declared exempt; tax would not be collected on sales, but relief would not be allowed for taxes paid on purchases.

Small Business in the Business Transfer Tax

Senator Roth's proposal for a BTT would provide an "exemption for organizations with gross receipts below $10 million."[11] This exemption figure is far greater than any in use in other countries, as shown in table 18.[12] Thus it raises an important question: What are the advantages and disadvantages of such a high minimum? In what follows ⸱ address that question first in the context of an ordinary credit-method VAT and the sophisticated subtraction-method tax. I then assess the likely effects of including a large exemption in a naive subtraction-method tax of the kind proposed by Senator Roth.

Under a credit-method VAT an exemption is attractive only to firms selling directly to households. For business conducted before the retail stage, an exemption breaks the chain of credits and results in higher, not lower, taxes. The same can be said of the exemption equivalent under the sophisticated subtraction method. Many business groups would therefore strongly oppose a proposal for mandatory exemption of firms with gross receipts below $10 million under a credit-method tax or the sophisticated subtraction method. At the very least, optional registration, which implies eligibility for credits as well as liability for tax, would be economically desirable and politically probable. Most likely only quite unsophisticated businesses involved in preretail activities would be willing to pay the price of higher taxes and competitive disadvantage to gain the compliance benefits of exemption. In short, if only preretail activities under a credit-method VAT were at issue and optional registration were available, there might be no substantial objection to provision of a small-business exemption much higher than is commonly found in other countries.

Of course, exemption at the retail stage does free value added at the last stage in the production-distribution process from tax. This might be extremely important for sectors serving primarily a household clientele and characterized by both relatively small firms and a

TABLE 18

EXEMPTIONS OF SMALL FIRMS FROM SALES TAXES, BASED ON SALES VOLUME, VARIOUS COUNTRIES, 1975–1984

Country	Year	Firms Exempt with Annual Sales under	Exchange Rate May 1984	Exemption Expressed in U.S. Dollars	Treatment
Value-added taxes					
Belgium	1980	Bfr 2.5 million	55.8	44,803	exempt
		Bfr 2.5–4.5 million		44,803–80,646	equalization tax on supplier
		Bfr 4.5–15 million		80,646–268,817	forfait
Denmark	1975	kr 5,000	10.05	498	exempt
France	1980	fr 500,000	8.41	59,453	forfait[a]
Germany	1984	DM 20,000	2.735	7,312	exempt
		DM 20,000–60,000		7,312–21,938	digressive scale
Ireland	1980	£2,000 for 2 months if 90% sales exempt or 10% rate	0.8937	2,238	
		£1,000 for 2 months if rate above 10%		1,119	exempt
		£300 service and others		336	
Italy	1980	L 6 million[b]	1,687.5	3,557	forfait
Luxembourg	1977	Bfr 100,000	55.8	1,792	exempt
Sweden	1980	kr 10,000	8.08	1,238	exempt
United Kingdom	1980	£5,000	0.714	7,003	exempt

Bolivia	1977	B 200,000	196	1,020	exempt
Costa Rica	1977	C 800,000	41	19,410	exempt
Indonesia[c]	1984	R 24,000,000[d]	982	24,439	exempt
Manufacturer's sales tax					
Canada	1984	$C 50,000	1.22	40,983	exempt
Philippines	1983	P 2,400	11	218	exempt
Kenya	1977	Ks 100,000	14.4	6,944	exempt
Zambia	1982	K 10,000	1.35	7,407	exempt
Guyana	1982	G$10,000	3	3,333	exempt
Wholesale sales taxes					
Australia	1982	A$12,000[e]	1.113[f]	10,782	exempt
New Zealand	1982	NZ$5,000	1.54	3,246	exempt
Switzerland	1983	Sfr 35,000	2.26	15,486	exempt
Retail sales taxes					
Zimbabwe	1983	Z$20,000	1.05	19,047	exempt
Paraguay	1977	G 1,800,000	126	14,285	tax applies to purchase
States of India[g]	1983	R 10,000–50,000	10.22	978–4,892	exempt

(Table continues)

TABLE 18 (continued)

Country	Year	Firms Exempt with Annual Sales under	Exchange Rate May 1984	Exemption Expressed in U.S. Dollars	Treatment
		Exemption Based on Tax Liability			
France	1980	fr 1,350	8.41	161[f]	exempt
Equivalent sales figure		fr 7,670		912	
Netherlands	1980	G 2,050	3.08	665	exempt
Equivalent sales figure		G 11,388		3,697	
Australia, alternative	1982	A$250	1.113[f]	225[f]	exempt

a. Exempt if annual tax under fr 1,350.
b. And all retailers.
c. Tax limited to manufacturing sector.
d. Or R 100 million capital.
e. Or total tax liability under A$250. Exemption applies to manufacturers only.
f. Figures appearing in publication from which this table is reproduced have been corrected to eliminate errors.
g. Most are retail sales taxes; three are essentially wholesale taxes; one is dual point; four are cascade (turnover) taxes.
SOURCE: John F. Due, "The Exclusion of Small Firms from Sales and Related Taxes," *Public Finance*, vol. 34, no. 2 (1984), pp. 202–12.

high ratio of value added to gross receipts. Many services have exactly this characteristic; few other sectors do. Providing a high exemption based on gross receipts under the credit method would thus run precisely counter to the policy position stated later in this chapter that insofar as possible a VAT should be levied on services as well as on goods, to avoid economic distortions and horizontal inequities. Of course, retail firms would generally not avail themselves of an opportunity to opt out of exemption and pay VAT on sales.

In activities where exemption would be attractive, the use of a high ceiling to determine eligibility for exemption would create a notch, in which a small increase in sales from just below the threshold to just above it would produce a large tax liability. Suppose, for example, that value added constituted one-half of gross receipts. Eligibility for exemption under a $10 million ceiling would be worth up to $500,000 per year in tax savings if the VAT rate were 10 percent. Even if value added were only 10 percent of sales, the tax saving would be $100,000. The inequity of an exemption of this magnitude should be obvious. Moreover, a substantial incentive would exist for fragmentation of household-oriented businesses characterized by a high ratio of value added to receipts in order to take advantage of multiple exemptions.

A high exemption with optional registration would, moreover, undesirably distort choices of economic organization. Distribution through franchises or independent dealers who could benefit from the small-business exemption would be preferred to sales by manufacturers or large retailers. Firms with substantial transactions in both goods and services would have an incentive to split into separate legal entities. A separate entity conducting those portions of the business characterized by a high ratio of value added to gross receipts could then be exempt, provided its receipts fell below the statutory limit. The entity selling goods would be registered so that it could use tax credits. Of course, such jointly owned and operated businesses might very well be housed in the same building and share overhead activities. They would then need to apportion overhead costs among the taxable and exempt entities. Moreover, it would be surprising not to find manipulation of transfer pricing of services provided by the taxable entity to the tax-exempt affiliate or vice versa; purchases might be made by the taxable entity and transferred at below cost to the exempt affiliate or made by the exempt entity and transferred at above cost to the taxable entity to reduce taxable sales or inflate usable tax credits artificially.

Problems such as these might be handled through rigorously enforced rules for arm's-length pricing or carefully constructed requirements for consolidation of VAT returns. Besides adding another important layer of complication, such requirements would need to be consistent with rules for consolidation under the income tax.

The implications of a large exemption would be even more far reaching under a naive subtraction-method VAT of the kind proposed by Senator Roth than under the credit method or the sophisticated subtraction method.[13] Exemption under the naive subtraction-method VAT implies that value added at the exempt stage actually escapes tax, in contrast to the situation under a credit-method tax or the sophisticated subtraction-method tax. Under a credit-method tax, exemption brings about a loss of revenue and a competitive advantage for exempt firms only for sales to households. (Competitive disadvantage is avoided if preretail firms are allowed the option of registration.) But under the naive subtraction-method tax, exemption poses those same problems for all activities, including those occurring before the retail stage.

Exemption would favor not only activities provided primarily to households and characterized by a high ratio of value added to receipts, such as services, but any activity with a high ratio of value added to receipts conducted by a "small" business. The cost in lost revenues, inequities, and economic distortions would be considerable. Businesses would be induced to use outside providers of services rather than supply them in house.

Moreover, under the Roth proposal any activity housed in a separate legal entity with receipts below the ceiling for exemption would apparently qualify for exemption. If so, many firms would find it worthwhile to set up separate but affiliated entities to provide them with such services as accounting, legal services, cleaning, and maintenance. Even manufacturing processes might be fragmented to take account of the exemption. This kind of abuse could be arrested by carefully constructed requirements for mandatory consolidation, but the Roth proposal makes no mention of such requirements or the administrative costs and impediments to ordinary business dealings that they would involve.

The opportunities for manipulation of transfer prices under this system would also be enormous. For example, interposition of a "small business" between the seller and purchaser of a major piece of equipment could be quite lucrative. If the exempt conduit firm were affiliated with either the buyer or the seller or both, it would buy low and sell high, thereby isolating from tax the fictitous value added reflected in its artificially inflated profit margin.[14] Arm's-length pricing rules might effectively prevent affiliated firms from being parties to such transactions, but not without costs. These tendencies would be limited by the transactions costs involved. But the tax saving on a $10

122

million transaction would support a substantial and lucrative industry in tax-motivated intermediation of this kind.

The existence of a large exemption under the naive subtraction method creates questionable distributional effects, as well as economic distortions and administrative difficulties. It is relatively easy to show analytically, as well as intuitively obvious, that a tax is much more likely to be borne by consumers if it is levied on virtually all suppliers of a given good or service than if it is levied on only a small portion of supply.[15] If 99 percent of output were produced by taxable firms, we would expect prices to rise by roughly the amount of the tax. If only 1 percent of output were taxed and 99 percent were exempt, we would expect prices to rise by only a minuscule amount in response to the tax.

These results imply that if relatively few exempt suppliers operate under the tax umbrella in a generally taxable sector, they will either have higher profits or be less efficient and have higher costs than their tax-paying competitors. Taxable firms, however, will have great difficulty in competing in markets dominated by exempt entities. The implications seem appealing neither for efficiency nor for equity. These considerations argue against the use of a high exemption even more strongly under the naive subtraction method than under the credit method.

Farming

Throughout the world agriculture, which may include such activities as fishing and silvaculture, is accorded preferential treatment (or at least different treatment) under the VAT.[16] This is true for some combination of political, economic, and administrative reasons.

First, in many countries farmers are extremely numerous, have low incomes, are relatively uneducated, and may lack the sophistication needed to comply satisfactorily with the requirements for record keeping and filing under the VAT. In addition, if agricultural products are exported and hence zero rated or if domestic sales of food are zero rated, as in the United Kingdom, it is administratively inefficient to collect tax on sales by farmers and provide credits at the next stage in the production process; it may be simpler just to exempt all or most sales by farmers.

Moreover, in many countries farmers have enough political influence to be effective in demanding exemption, regardless of its merits on objective grounds. Of course, exemption of preretail sales is generally less favorable than zero rating, because producers whose sales are exempt are not allowed credit for taxes paid on purchased inputs. Thus ad hoc measures are sometimes taken to avoid or relieve the burden of VAT on farm inputs.

The case for according preferential treatment to farmers in the United States does not seem compelling.[17] Most American farmers do not make numerous small sales, as many small businesses in other sectors do; they typically engage in fewer larger transactions, selling to businesses that would want invoices showing tax eligible for credit. The primary exception appears to be sales to households, where there would be no need to issue invoices. Like other taxpayers, farmers are required to comply with the income tax laws. That they must maintain books of account for income tax purposes suggests that they could also comply with a VAT. Certainly this is true of a naive subtraction-method tax, and it is probably true of a tax levied under either the sophisticated subtraction method or the credit method. The smallest and most primitive agricultural operations would probably be handled satisfactorily by a generalized exemption for small business.[18] The strongest argument in favor of exemption or zero rating of farming is that substantial amounts of the output of U.S. agriculture are exported.[19]

The rest of this section describes in greater detail various kinds of preferential treatment that might be accorded to agriculture. It is provided to indicate the difficulties inherent in deviation from universal coverage, rather than to mark out the pathway to differential treatment. It is useful to distinguish between at least two potential reasons for differential treatment of agriculture: administrative simplicity and an explicit desire to reduce VAT on agriculture or its products.

Suppose first that it is thought desirable for distributional reasons to avoid collecting VAT on food sold for home consumption.[20] One theoretically attractive way to achieve this end under the credit method is to zero-rate only sales of food to households. Any tax collected before the retail stage would be allowed as a credit (and rebated, if necessary), so that all sales of food for home consumption would occur tax free.[21] (Whether sales of food to restaurants also occur tax free is irrelevant, since any tax collected on such sales would be allowed as a credit to the restaurant.) Although the logic of this process is unassailable, a substantial amount of paperwork, including payment and refund of tax in many instances, would be required to produce the desired result: no net revenue on the sales of food to households.

If food for home consumption is to be relieved of taxes, a simpler approach would be to zero-rate all sales of food from the farmer through the retail stage, as in the United Kingdom. No tax would be collected on food as it moved through the productive process, but credit would be allowed for any taxes paid on purchased inputs employed in growing or processing food.

Even this approach might be thought to entail too much record keeping by farmers. After all, it would still be necessary to keep farmers in the VAT system, so that they could qualify for credits and refunds of taxes paid on purchased inputs. The pervasive payment of refunds would be an open invitation to fraud, as well as the source of an overwhelming administrative burden. An alternative would be to exempt farmers while zero-rating sales of food at subsequent stages of the production-distribution process. Large farms would presumably be given the option of being in the VAT system.[22] The trouble with this solution is that foodstuffs would not be totally relieved of taxation, to the extent of tax paid on inputs purchased by exempt farmers. Moreover, any farmers who opted for exemption rather than zero rating—presumably the smaller ones—would be placed at a competitive disadvantage vis-à-vis those who chose zero rating, presumably the larger ones.

One way to reduce this problem substantially would be to exempt sales by farmers and zero-rate sales of a few items that are important agricultural inputs but constitute only an insignificant portion of household consumption.[23] (Zero-rating sales to nonagricultural business would pose no problem, since credits at the next stage would be smaller by the amount of the revenue lost through zero rating.) Obvious examples include feed for livestock, seed, fertilizer, and agricultural implements and equipment. Motor fuels, another important agricultural input, could not be zero rated, because of the risk of leakage into use by households. It should be fairly simple to relieve farmers of VAT paid on motor fuels by expanding the income tax credit now allowed for motor fuels purchased for off-highway use, but this approach can also be abused.

A different situation arises if food is not exempt but farmers are not required to register, for political or administrative reasons. (If farmers are required to register and pay tax, the calculation and payment of taxes net of credits proceeds as in the textbook example of chapter 3.) Exemption of farming would create a break in the chain of credits, place exempt farmers at a competitive disadvantage, and result in higher than average taxation of products incorporating significant amounts of agricultural output. This problem can be substantially ameliorated by zero-rating selected agricultural inputs. Of course, it is assumed that any farmer, like other businesses, would be allowed to opt into the system rather than required to choose exemption.

The same results could be achieved under the sophisticated version of the subtraction method. For example, receipts from sales of food could be excluded from taxable receipts; deduction would be allowed only for purchases on which tax had been paid at the previous stage. This would be equivalent to a full-fledged system of zero rating under the credit method. Alternatively, farmers might be excluded from the VAT system. The sales of excluded farmers would then contain a tax component, because of VAT collected on inputs. Again, sales of selected agricultural inputs might be excluded from taxable sales.

A very different situation can arise under the naive subtraction method. Under this method, if any slice of value added is not taxed at a particular stage, the lost tax is never recouped. If farmers were exempt, tax would be collected on their purchased inputs and on value added to agricultural output after the exempt stage. But value added in farming would remain free of tax. This illustrates the potential importance of this defect of the naive subtraction method. Not only would there be intense political pressure to eliminate tax on both farming and agricultural inputs; if efforts to gain exemption of agriculture were successful, substantial incentives would exist to expand the definition of exempt farming and to alter business organization so that as much value as possible would be added before products left the exempt stage.

Services

Both economic neutrality and equity demand that value-added taxation be applied to services as well as to goods.[24] Those arguments have two quite different aspects. First, failure to tax services provided to households creates an undesirable bias in favor of the consumption of services over goods that are taxed.[25] Moreover, if such services are not taxed, equity suffers—both horizontal equity, because not all households with a given income split their consumption in the same way between goods and services, and vertical equity, because upper-income families spend relatively greater amounts on services than those with lower incomes.[26]

The argument is quite different for services provided to business, such as advertising, computing, and legal services. Here the exemption of services would create a break in the chain of credits, since providers of services, being outside the system, could not claim credit for taxes paid on their business purchases. Thus exempting such services would create a bias against using them, against activities requiring substantial use of services, against acquiring services commercially rather than providing them internally, and against firms in service-intensive activities that are unable to provide their own services, perhaps because they are too small.[27] The case for according

126

regular tax treatment to services is strong indeed.

Some services are provided primarily to households (such as haircuts, medical and dental care, and funeral services), others primarily to businesses (such as accountancy and computing). But many of these and others (architectural services, interior design, legal services, cleaning and maintenance, gardening) are provided in substantial amounts to both households and businesses. Administrative and compliance considerations suggest that all services of a given kind should be treated the same way. Otherwise, a provider of service would be required to account separately for taxable and exempt receipts and allocate taxes on purchases between the two categories.[28] Moreover, any firm both providing exempt services and making taxable sales or vice versa would need to allocate receipts and purchases between the categories. Given the arguments stated above, all services should be included in the base of the VAT, to the extent practicable.

The primary argument against taxing services is administrative: the inability to enforce the tax on many small providers of services who keep inadequate books of account. There are several responses to this concern. First, such providers of services are not excused from paying income tax; there is no reason that they should not pay VAT. Second, most of the difficult cases would be covered by the small-business exemption; others should be in the VAT system. Third, even if most services were exempt for administrative reasons, those who provide services to business would need to be given the option of being in the system, to avoid putting them and firms using their services at a competitive disadvantage. Having said this, it must be recognized that enforcing VAT on the provision of many services to households is inevitably difficult.[29]

A further qualification to the economic argument for taxing all services is the incentive to engage in self-supply that doing so gives to households and other economic units (such as exempt businesses and perhaps government and nonprofit organizations) that are unable to recover tax on purchases. As a recent paper on the treatment of services under a VAT puts it:

> Because services are predominantly labour, "self supply" is more readily substitutable for a purchased supply than it is in most other sectors. Consumers will not usually be inclined to make their own steel, but cooking their own food or cleaning their own kitchen is a viable alternative to paying someone else to do so. . . . It is neither efficient nor equitable to have services provided by those who do not have a comparative advantage in their provision.[30]

It seems unlikely, however, that this would be a major source of either distortion or inequity.[31]

Housing

The tax treatment of housing under a VAT deserves special attention for several reasons. First, housing is the most important item of expenditure in the budgets of most households. Thus the treatment of housing—especially owner-occupied housing—is a politically sensitive issue. Second, the normal VAT cannot easily be applied to the imputed value of owner-occupied housing. Third, it is important to maintain approximate parity between the tax treatment of owner-occupied housing and of rental housing. Much rental housing is owned by persons who would not be in the VAT system unless receipts from residential rentals were subject to tax. Even then they might be excluded by a small-business exemption.

Fourth, the tax treatment of housing interacts with the tax treatment of other real estate, because it may be possible to use at least some parts of a given building for commercial purposes, residential rental, or owner-occupied housing or to convert from one use to another. Moreover, the tax treatment of housing has potentially important implications for the tax treatment of the construction industry, an area where tax evasion may be widespread and difficult to control. This section elaborates on these points and offers some possible ways of resolving the problems raised. But, as in many of the areas covered in this chapter, it makes few definitive recommendations.

A substantial majority of the value of housing services in the United States is provided to themselves by owner-occupants. The taxation of owner-occupied housing is difficult for several reasons. First, the provision of such services by owner-occupants creates imputed rental income rather than monetary income in the form of rental payments.

Second, the provision of housing services is extremely capital intensive. This need not pose a problem in itself. But the nature of housing as a capital asset, when combined with owner occupation, does create a particular kind of problem, as well as suggest a possible solution. (Imputed income also arises when a person washes his or her own car or cleans the house. But tax experts usually worry relatively little about this kind of imputed income, since taxing it is generally agreed to be impossible.) The consumption value of owner-occupied housing is prepaid at the time a home is bought, rather than purchased periodically through rental payments in market transactions.[32]

There are, in principle, two conceptually correct ways to tax the services from owner-occupied housing. One would be administratively infeasible, and both would be politically difficult.

First, all owner-occupants of housing could be registered and required to pay VAT on the imputed rental value of their homes.[33] Merely stating this proposition suggests how unlikely it is to be implemented for both political and administrative reasons.[34] Moreover, most owner-occupied housing would be eliminated from the tax base by a small-business exemption of as little as $10,000, in any event.

Alternatively, VAT could be charged on the purchase price of new housing. In theory this would be economically equivalent (in present-value terms) to taxing the imputed rental value of the home, since the present value of housing services should equal the purchase price.[35] Full taxation of the purchase price of new housing would not be politically popular. A less extreme approach would be to tax all materials used in the construction of housing but not the sale of houses to consumers. This approach would presumably be less unpopular because the value added by the builder would not be taxed and VAT on the house would not be quoted separately. Taxing sales of houses at a preferential rate would reduce the tax burden on housing but would not hide it.[36]

There is no difficulty in applying "regular" VAT treatment to commercial and industrial structures, considered by themselves. Under the credit method tax would be paid on the purchase of a building and then taken as a credit against liability on receipts.[37] Under the subtraction method the purchase of a building, like any other purchase, would be deducted from receipts in calculating taxable value added. Problems arise, however, if regular taxation is not also applied to housing.

Before continuing with the discussion of applying VAT to owner-occupied housing, I turn briefly to consideration of the tax treatment of rental housing and industrial and commercial real estate. In principle, regular VAT treatment could also be applied to rented residential real estate. In fact, however, there are important administrative reasons to consider treating residential rentals differently from other forms of business. A substantial amount of residential real estate is owned by taxpayers who have no other source of business income and who would not be part of the VAT system except for the application of VAT to value added in residential rentals. In the absence of an exclusion for small business, an unmanageable number of small-time owners of residential real estate would be swept into the VAT net. Allowing a small-business exclusion and applying it to residential real estate would alleviate this administrative problem, but at the cost of a substantial revenue loss and discrimination against apartment owners unable to qualify for the exclusion.[38]

These considerations suggest that it may be best to exempt all value added in rental residential real estate. Under this approach, tax would be applied to the sale of buildings to registered taxpayers but not to residential rents. Owners of rented residential real estate would not pay tax on their value added but, being out of the system, would not be allowed credits for taxes paid on purchased inputs (under the credit method) or deduction for such purchases in calculating taxable value added (under the sophisticated subtraction method).

Mandatory application of this same approach to commercial and industrial rental real estate would cause significant economic distortions, because of the break in the chain of credits. Moreover, complex rules would be required to achieve equity in the taxation of those who would otherwise resort to tax-motivated self-construction. This problem would only arise under the credit method or the sophisticated subtraction method; it would pose no problem under the naive subtraction method. It could be solved by allowing the owner of commercial or industrial real estate the option of being subject to the regular VAT regime. Although this would avoid a break in the chain of credits, it would raise the problem of allocation of credits (or deductions in the case of the sophisticated subtraction method) between exempt and nonexempt activities for buildings used for both exempt and taxable purposes. On balance this does not seem to be a major problem.

For owner-occupied housing the primary problem appears to be the political issue of whether to subject such housing to taxation. Both economic analysis and administrative reality suggest that such housing should be taxed in a way comparable to the taxation of rental housing. Suppose that sales of homes to owner-occupants were to be zero rated. Even if the VAT did not extend all the way to the rental stage but construction of rental units was taxed, substantial horizontal inequity between owner-occupants and renters would result. Moreover, this would accentuate the existing preferences under the income tax for overinvestment in owner-occupied housing.[39] These inequities and distortions would be even worse if rents on residential real estate were subject to the regular VAT.

If both rental residential real estate and owner-occupied housing were zero rated, the discrimination between forms of housing tenure would be eliminated, but discrimination in favor of housing over other forms of investment would be accentuated. Of course, the revenue implications of such an exclusion of all housing from the tax base would also be substantial. Excluding value added in housing from the tax base would reduce that base by more than 10 percent of consumption expenditures. Zero rating would reduce the base by a further 6 percent of consumption.

All things considered, the best solution to this complex problem may be to subject newly constructed buildings, including homes for owner occupancy, to tax at the first point of sale. Rentals of both residential and commercial and industrial real estate would be exempt unless the owner of real estate opted to participate in the regular VAT system, in which case rental receipts would be included in taxable receipts and credit would be allowed for tax on purchases or deduction for the purchases themselves under the subtraction method.[40] Any business registered for VAT could claim credit for taxes paid on purchases or could deduct purchases of buildings or claim credit or deduction for rentals from registered owners. The net result would be that the portion of residential rentals or imputed income on owner-occupied housing represented by the purchased residence itself would be subject to VAT but other elements of rent or imputed rent would escape tax.[41]

Most owners of commercial real estate would presumably exercise the option to be taxed under the regular VAT, to avoid a break in the chain of credits. Owners of residential real estate would presumably not register, so as to avoid tax on their value added. This approach avoids the difficulty of requiring numerous individuals with small amounts of rental income to comply with (or even know about) the requirements of the VAT, including the small-business exemption. Although some discrimination in favor of housing would remain, it would be relatively minor; certainly it would be less than exists under the income tax. It would, however, create unfortunate incentives for apartment owners to use employees to perform such services as maintenance and repair, which would not be subject to VAT, rather than purchase them from service companies, which would pay tax on their value added.

Remaining issues in this area concern the tax treatment of existing housing and of land. Strictly speaking, a VAT that is intended to tax all consumption should apply to the value or imputed rent of existing owner-occupied houses. Otherwise, substantial inequities would be created between those who own houses at the time the tax is imposed or announced and those who do not.[42] Opponents of this approach would characterize it as a capital levy on existing houses. Political opposition based in part on this characterization would probably be strong enough that this approach deserves little further discussion. Moreover, valuation of existing houses for this purpose would raise serious issues of tax administration.[43] Thus I do not further consider the possibility of applying VAT to existing houses.

Used Goods

Transactions in used goods pose interesting conceptual and practical problems. This issue is not important only for such obvious items as used cars; it arises for areas as disparate as pawn shops, art galleries, and dealers in scrap metal. Appreciated assets pose particular difficulties. For transactions in used goods between businesses all three methods (credit, sophisticated subtraction method, and naive subtraction method) would work equally well, provided the original sale was subject to tax. Sales of used business assets are thus not discussed further, except when application of special regimes to used goods causes problems in this area.

It would be administratively impractical and generally economically improper to collect VAT on ordinary and irregular household sales of used goods, as in occasional yard sales. Only if sales by households regularly exceeded the small-business exemption, as in the case of those involved in repeated garage sales or flea markets, or if there were no small-business exemption would the question normally even arise. Even one-time or irregular sales of used goods in excess of the small-business exemption would appropriately be exempt in many cases, the sale of greatly appreciated assets being the primary question mark.

The simplest case is one in which a durable consumer good is originally bought in a taxable transaction, depreciates in value as it provides economic benefits, and is sold directly to another household at a price that reflects both the value of services previously provided and the present value of expected future services. In other words, the difference between the original cost and the resale price simply reflects depletion of the potential supply of consumer services, with no extraordinary appreciation or depreciation. In this simple case no tax should be collected when the item is resold, since the tax collected when the good was new included the value of services to be provided after the resale of the used good.

A more complicated situation occurs if a secondhand dealer is interposed between the original owner and the purchaser of the used good. The margin of the secondhand dealer, which might include repairs as well as the services of intermediation, should ideally be subject to tax, but the underlying value of the used good (represented by the price paid by the secondhand dealer) should not be taxed. This result is achieved naturally under the naive subtraction method but not under a pure credit-method tax. Regardless of whether the price paid to the original owner includes an allowance for the VAT on the residual value of the asset, the dealer will not have a receipt verifying that tax has been paid and therefore can take no credit against tax liability on resale. Nor does the sophisticated subtraction method produce the correct answer; since the original purchaser is out of the system, he or she cannot provide the dealer in used goods with a tax-paid invoice. It might, however, be possible to provide an exception for dealers in used goods under a sophisticated subtraction-method tax, by applying the naive subtraction method to their purchases from households.

Similarly, it should be possible to handle this problem fairly easily under the credit method by allowing secondhand dealers to take imputed credits (calculated as the product of the purchase price and the tax rate on the used good) for the residual VAT presumed to be embodied in the price of used goods purchased from households.[44] For used goods purchased from registered businesses, the ordinary credit method would apply. It would be necessary to distinguish between goods bought from households (taxed under the subtraction method) and those bought from businesses (taxed under the credit method), but this does not seem to pose a major problem. Nor does it seem that insurmountable problems would arise in the case of dealers in both new and used goods. Exemptions and multiple rates could cause severe compliance problems, however, since the subtraction method cannot accommodate them. This problem would be especially grave if similar items were taxed differently.

Several potential problems with this approach (one of them transitory) need to be mentioned. First, it would be inappropriate to allow imputed credits for purchase of used goods not originally subject to VAT. Allowing such credits would cost revenues and give such used goods a competitive advantage over new ones. Moreover, there would be an incentive to export used goods and scrap (which would be zero rated) to get the credit. Second, there would be substantial opportunities for overstatement of purchase prices of used goods to inflate imputed credits. Of course, exactly the same incentives exist under the income tax and would exist under the subtraction method.

As an alternative, it might be feasible to allow subtraction-method treatment for secondhand dealers, even under a credit-method tax. The difficulty of doing so, however, seems overwhelming. First, it would be necessary to distinguish between purchases from businesses, which would be subject to tax, would carry a credit for tax, and would be handled under the credit method as usually applied, and purchases from households, which would not carry a credit and would be handled under the subtraction method. Thus it would be necessary for dealers handling both new and used goods to employ dual accounting systems.

Second, it would be necessary to allow credit-method taxpayers to take credit for the subtraction-method taxes of dealers in second-hand goods; otherwise, resale to business of goods bought from households would be subject to double taxation because no credit could be taken for tax paid by either the household or the dealer. Moreover, exports would not occur tax free, for similar reasons. For reasons such as these the members of the European Economic Community employ a modified credit system based on imputed credits.

Appreciated property poses special problems under the VAT. Ideally the amount of appreciation should be subject to VAT when the asset is sold.[45] But both the modified credit method based on imputed credits and the subtraction method would allow the increase in value to escape tax. This is especially unfortunate since assets that commonly appreciate (such as artwork, antiques, jewelry, stamps, coins, and rare books) absorb investment funds into unproductive uses. Moreover, they are especially likely to be bought by upper-income groups, so that the exclusion of appreciation increases the regressivity of the VAT.

Appreciated used goods can be handled in at least three ways. First, transactions in such goods could be subject to tax if the small-business exemption were exceeded. If applied across the board, this approach would create potentially unacceptable compliance problems for households that would not otherwise be subject to VAT. It might, however, be workable if coupled with an extraordinary small-business exemption for sales of such assets.

Second, it might be possible to allow no imputed credit (or deductions, in the case of the subtraction method) for purchases of such assets by dealers—or at least to limit the credit to VAT shown on invoices of the previous owner, if available. Allowing no credit would cause multiple taxation; allowing full credit for VAT paid by previous owners would unfairly neglect the value of consumption by the previous owner. Moreover, this approach necessitates the definition of appreciated assets.

The third approach is the one used in the EEC. It is to exempt sales of appreciated assets by households and allow the ordinary imputed credit to business purchasers.

Financial Institutions and Insurance

The primary service provided by financial institutions is intermediation, that is, bringing together the funds of depositors and making them available to borrowers, usually absorbing risks of default and delinquency in the process. Insurance companies provide to their policyholders the service of pooling risks of loss of life or property.[46] In addition, some insurance policies are important vehicles for saving; in those instances insurance companies provide financial intermediation similar to that provided by banks, savings and loan associations, and other financial institutions.

The value added in financial intermediation is appropriately measured by the spread between interest rates charged borrowers and rates paid on deposits, minus the cost of purchased inputs. Alternatively, it can be measured as the sum of factor payments (especially wages) and profits of the institution.[47] Value added in insurance is measured by the costs of underwriting, net of purchases of inputs—again the factor payments and profits of insurance companies. It does not include the portion of premiums that reflects transfers from policyholders that experience no loss to those who do experience losses (the transfer component).[48] Nor does it include the amounts saved through insurance or the earnings on such savings.

Whether services of financial institutions and insurance companies that are provided to households should be taxed is subject to controversy. If the services are provided to business, they should ideally be taxed; of course, the tax should be allowed as a credit under the credit method. It can be argued that at least some financial services provided to households should not be taxed, since they constitute costs of earning income. For the purpose of this discussion it is assumed that these services should be taxed.

The services of financial institutions and insurance companies are notoriously difficult to tax satisfactorily under a credit-method VAT.[49] The most important of these services are not the subject of explicit fees. Rather, charges for the core services of financial institutions are commonly implicit in the spread between the interest rates paid to depositors and those charged on loans to borrowers. In addition, charges for some secondary activities such as checking accounts have traditionally failed to cover the costs of servicing them, the difference being absorbed by below-market rates of interest on such accounts. Similarly, loan origination charges may not fully reflect the costs of processing loans; rather, excess costs may be reflected in higher interest rates on loans.

Much the same can be said of the insurance sector. Premiums do not distinguish between the administrative costs and profits of underwriting insurance, the premium that would be necessary in a world without transactions costs (the transfer component), and the saving element. Rather, all three costs (or at least two, in the case of insurance with no saving component) are commingled in one premium.

Zero-rating financial services and insurance would be relatively simple; no tax would be collected on zero-rated services, but credit would be allowed for tax on purchases by financial institutions and insurance companies. Business purchases of such services would carry no credit. Zero rating would avoid the many problems associated with efforts to tax these services that are described below. But it would distort choices in favor of this kind of consumption.[50]

It is difficult to subject the value added in financial intermediation and underwriting of insurance to taxation without running the risk of also taxing interest or insurance settlements.[51] But if the value added in these core activities is not taxed, in the extreme case the base for a VAT in the financial sector might be little more than fees for safe deposit boxes. Although deregulation of the financial sector has substantially increased the degree to which explicit charges are made for services provided, a significant amount remains to be achieved. Moreover, subjecting only explicit charges to VAT would almost certainly impede this process and perhaps reverse it. The problem, then, is to know how best to deal with this unusual industry. This entails both how and whether to tax services for which prices are not explicit and how to treat taxes on inputs purchased by financial institutions.

The most common treatment of financial institutions is to exempt certain services, as is done in all countries in the EEC. Exemption, however, causes a variety of problems in the context of a credit-method VAT, beyond the obvious distortion in favor of household use of the exempt services. First, exempt services provided to other businesses cause a break in the chain of credits and multiple taxation.[52] As always this implies that businesses have an incentive to acquire such services from taxpayers who are in the system or supply them internally, as far as possible, rather than acquire them from exempt suppliers. If that is impossible, they have an incentive to underuse the exempt services, with a consequent suboptimal level of financial intermediation and discrimination against activities that depend on intermediation.

The effects of exemption can be especially adverse for financial institutions and insurers operating in highly competitive international markets, since foreign countries commonly zero-rate at least this component of their financial sectors. Zero-rating only foreign transactions while exempting others would, of course, considerably complicate compliance and administration.

If only certain services provided by an institution are exempt and others are taxable, it is necessary to prorate the cost of purchased inputs between exempt and taxable activities. This inevitably creates administrative difficulties and disputes. Moreover, since no credit can be taken for taxes paid on purchased inputs, it is advantageous for exempt firms to perform many activities internally that might more economically and naturally be acquired commercially. For example, banks would have an incentive to operate their own computer centers and employ lawyers and financial analysts rather than acquire their services in taxable transactions. The same incentives apply to janitorial or guard services.

An alternative approach, which has been used in Israel, is to employ the addition method in taxing financial institutions and insurance companies.[53] Although this system avoids the failure to tax this component of household consumption, it also suffers from severe defects. First, profits of those two sectors are notoriously difficult to tax appropriately under the income tax; there is little reason to expect matters to be much better under the VAT, which requires calculation of profits. A practical compromise might be to tax only wages and salaries as a surrogate for value added.[54]

Second, using the addition method for financial institutions and insurance companies in the context of a general credit-method VAT would produce even worse multiple taxation of services provided to business than under outright exemption. Complaints of financial institutions and their customers about the lack of credits for either the addition-method tax on financial institutions or the tax on purchases of such institutions eventually led Israel to replace the addition-method VAT on financial institutions with a separate tax outside the VAT system.[55] (There would be no similar problem under the general subtraction method.)[56] Finally, an addition-based tax is inherently origin based, and it would be difficult to make accurate border tax adjustments or to convince our trading partners that the BTAs were both appropriate and accurate.[57]

It is commonly agreed that the recent Treasury Department proposal for the taxation of financial institutions is defective.[58] Applying the standard credit method to financial institutions, it would levy VAT on interest received on loans and allow a credit for VAT paid on interest payments to lenders (depositors, in the case of financial institutions). For transactions between registered taxpayers, this approach works satisfactorily. But in the case of deposits by households it results in taxation of interest income, contrary to the nature of a consumption-based VAT.[59]

There is, in short, no easy way out of the inherent difficulties in applying VAT to financial institutions and insurance companies. On balance it may be best to follow the common practice of exempting domestic provision of these services and zero-rating foreign provision. An alternative and more complex approach would be to exempt such services when supplied to households, to tax insurance provided to businesses, and to zero-rate financial services provided to businesses.[60]

Employee Benefits

Many businesses provide fringe benefits and other perquisites that employees might otherwise purchase for themselves out of their wage and salary income. These include subsidized meals, entertainment, club dues, the use of automobiles, and employee discounts. If fringe benefits are not treated properly under the VAT, substantial inequities and distortions will occur. Compare the tax consequences of employers' provision of cafeteria meals with employees' purchase of such meals, which are assumed to be taxable. If the employer reduced wages and salaries by the value of cafeteria meals and provided those meals directly, a deduction or a credit for tax paid would be allowed for food and other nonlabor inputs to cafeteria meals as a purchased input, and taxable value added would be reduced by the value of the meals.[61]

Clearly this preferential treatment of fringe benefits would encourage uneconomical decisions to pay wages and salaries in forms that can benefit from this treatment and thereby encourage overconsumption of such goods and services.[62] Of course, it would be unfair, since not all employees or employers are likely to have equal access to opportunities to receive or pay benefits in this form.

The conceptually correct solution to this problem is to collect tax from the employer on the imputed value of benefits in kind provided to employees.[63] To avoid the valuation problems inherent in this approach, it might be necessary to adopt a fallback position in which deduction for purchases employed to provide benefits in kind to employees or credit for taxes paid on such purchases is disallowed. Although this approach fails to tax the value added by the employer in providing benefits in kind, it would generally be substantially simpler than the conceptually correct approach.[64]

Even this approach could not be applied widely to all benefits in kind provided to employees. While cafeteria meals are a relatively straightforward example,[65] it would clearly be impossible to extend this treatment to general amenities of the workplace, including, for example, office furnishings or a scenic view. All that can be done is to pick out the most important and most easily handled cases.[66]

Governmental Activities

Goods and services provided by governments range from commercial activities in which goods and services are provided in exchange for fees or other consideration, perhaps in competition with private firms, to services provided free of charge and financed through taxes for which there is no explicit quid pro quo. It is necessary to decide how the sale of services, other receipts, and purchases of governments should be treated under a federal VAT. While the discussion that follows may appear to be most relevant for state and local activities, most of it is equally applicable to activities of the federal government.

If commercial services provided by governments are financed by charges and user fees, such fees and charges should be included in the base of the VAT. Otherwise publicly provided goods and services will enjoy an artificial advantage over both similar and different goods and services produced in the private sector and subject to VAT. Under this view tax would be levied on the sale of such services by governments, and governments would claim credit for taxes paid on purchased inputs used in providing the services or pay tax on the difference between charges and purchases under the subtraction method. Businesses paying such fees would be allowed to deduct them from sales under the subtraction method or claim credit for taxes paid on such charges against tax liability on sales under the credit method.

At the other end of the spectrum are public services financed by broad-based taxes such as income, sales, and property taxes. For these it is difficult to claim a sufficiently direct link between taxes paid and benefits received to justify treating the taxes in the same way as user charges.[67] Moreover, the possibility that VAT could ever be applied to income, property, and sales taxes seems quite remote, if only for political reasons.[68]

If preference is not to be accorded tax-financed goods and services provided publicly by federal, state, and local governments, it seems necessary to treat the noncommercial activities of governments as those of exempt entities for purposes of the VAT.[69] That is, it is appropriate to collect tax on sales to governments but not to allow such governments a credit or refund of tax under the credit method or to allow the purchases themselves as a deduction under the subtraction method, except to the extent that purchases are employed in

139

providing goods and services that are financed through taxable user charges.

This approach raises several obvious objections. First, it would involve a net transfer from state and local governments to the federal government. This could be avoided by a system of grants that returned revenue from VAT on government purchases to state and local governments. Even if this approach were politically acceptable, constitutional issues would exist.

As always, the presence of both tax-exempt and taxable activities implies troublesome problems of prorating the costs of purchases. Moreover, although this treatment has the advantage of avoiding substantial discrimination in favor of public provision of goods and services to households, it has the disadvantage of breaking the chain of credits in the case of benefits supplied to business that are clearly related to the business taxes used to finance them.[70] Finally, state and local government taxes on business must be higher to raise enough revenue to pay VAT on purchases of governmental entities.

Taxing the purchases of state and local governments but not value added by governments would, of course, create incentives to rely on self-supply rather than purchase of goods and services.[71] Moreover, governments would probably rely more heavily on fees and charges, a change in policy that would be attractive for other reasons.[72]

If it were decided that purchases of governments should not be taxed, the administratively simplest way to achieve this would probably be to collect taxes on sales to governments and have the governments file for credits and refunds, except in the case of large contracts, which might be zero rated. This would save merchants and other suppliers the need to segregate sales to governments from other sales. Moreover, it would avoid the need for governments to differentiate between creditable purchases of inputs to commercial activities and nontaxable purchases, on which credit would not be allowed.

Nonprofit Organizations

Nonprofit organizations are commonly accorded preferential treatment under the income tax, presumably because they provide goods and services having some element of "publicness" that might otherwise be provided through government. Under a VAT the question naturally arises whether and how such organizations should be accorded preferential treatment on either their purchases or their receipts.

For expositional purposes it may be worthwhile to consider three prototypal activities of nonprofit organizations. The first are those provided free of charge to nonmembers as well as members, presumably because of their public content. At the other end of the spectrum are commercial activities that closely resemble and often compete with similar goods and services provided in the profit-making private sector. Closely related to those are goods and services provided only to members, for example, in exchange for membership fees or subscriptions.

Between these two extremes are activities for which charges are made that do not cover the full cost of the goods and services provided, including such important activities as education and medical care. They resemble and may compete with similar goods and services provided by governments. They may also compete with goods and services provided in the profit-making private sector. In addition to fees received for goods and services provided, nonprofit organizations commonly receive some combination of membership fees, donations, and governmental grants. The question, then, is how to treat these various receipts and purchases or taxes paid on purchases of inputs employed by nonprofit organizations in providing goods and services.

The proper tax treatment of regular commercial activities of nonprofit organizations seems to be clear: they should be subject to the regular VAT. That is, tax should be collected on sales, and credit should be allowed for taxes paid on purchases; under the subtraction method purchases should be deducted from sales. Meshing this approach with zero rating of free provision of goods and services poses no administrative problems.

In the case of goods and services provided free of charge to nonmembers as well as to members, the only practical issue is whether to eliminate tax on purchases.[73] The answer to this question seems to depend on one's philosophical view of such activities. To someone with little sympathy for such activities, nonprofit organizations should be treated like households, that is, exempted. Since such organizations would be out of the system, they would pay tax on purchases, with no relief. If some activities of the organization were either fully taxed or zero rated, exemption of other activities would create problems of prorating purchases or taxes paid on them. Prorating could not, of course, be based on the proportion of exempt and taxable receipts, because there would be no receipts from the activities discussed in this paragraph.

If such activities were thought to be more deserving of public support, they would be zero rated, so that the organizations providing them could obtain refunds of taxes paid on their purchases. A distinctly inferior approach would be to allow such organizations to make purchases tax free. Except for large items, employment of a registration system for such purchases, rather than simply relying on the normal credit and refund procedures under the VAT, seems to be distinctly inferior. Zero rating of some activities can, of course, coexist quite easily with taxation of others.

Many activities provided free of charge are financed, at least in part, through donations from households and businesses. The most reasonable approach—and the one most likely to be adopted—would be to exclude such receipts from the tax base of nonprofit organizations. If, however, such donations are included in taxable receipts, the purchases they finance should be allowed as a deduction, or tax paid on purchases should be creditable.

The most difficult problems arise in the intermediate cases of goods and services that compete with those provided by governments and private firms and are provided at less than cost. The treatment of such goods and services poses a basic policy question: Should these services be subject to tax, or should they be excluded from the tax base? Further, if they are excluded, should this be through exemption or zero rating? The same answer should, of course, be chosen for both state and local governments and tax-exempt organizations providing a given service.

Exemption creates the usual problems of a given entity's making both exempt and zero-rated sales. Purchases must be prorated between the two. Moreover, substantial distortion of the decision making of nonprofit organizations such as universities and hospitals may occur. Under exemption tax is paid on purchases from external vendors but not on the value of services provided by the organization's own employees. Thus there could be substantial incentives for self-supply of such services as laundry, food preparation, and repairs and maintenance.

Zero rating is totally appropriate if it is thought desirable to eliminate VAT entirely on the activities of nonprofit organizations. Moreover, it avoids the compliance problems of combining exemption and taxation in the same entity. But some may object to payment of refunds, which would be necessary if such organizations were zero rated. It should be noted, however, that allowing credit only up to the amount of taxes paid on sales (or paying no refunds on negative taxable value added under the subtraction method) would create undesirable incentives for nonprofit organizations to acquire commercial activities so as to take full advantage of credits or deductions on purchases.

Notes

1. For further discussion, see U.S. Department of the Treasury, *Tax Reform for Fairness, Simplicity, and Economic Growth* (Washington, D.C., 1984), vol. 3, chap. 6.

2. For a recent survey of practice in this area, see John F. Due, "The Tax Treatment of Farmers and Small Firms under Value Added Taxes" (Paper presented at World Bank Conference on Value Added Taxation in Developing Countries, Washington, D.C., April 21–23, 1986).

3. Considerations of revenue may also play a part in such decisions, since preretail exemptions imply more revenues, not less.

4. Cedric Sandford and Michael Godwin, "Administrative and Compliance Problems Unique to VAT: The Rebate System, Invoicing Issues, and Related Problems" (Paper presented at World Bank Conference on Value Added Taxation in Developing Countries, Washington, D.C., April 21–23, 1986), have estimated on the basis of incomplete survey data for the United Kingdom that compliance costs relative to tax liability of small firms (those with sales below £20,000) may be thirty times as high as those of firms with sales greater than £1 million.

5. Due, in "Tax Treatment of Farmers," notes that seven European countries (West Germany, Denmark, the United Kingdom, Ireland, Luxembourg, Sweden, and Norway) follow this approach. Exemption levels range from the equivalent (at early 1986 exchange rates) of $1,100 (in Denmark) to $28,700 (in Ireland).

6. Five European countries, including France, Belgium, and Austria, use this approach, commonly called the *forfait* system. Such schemes are inherently capricious, unfair, and subject to corruption. Due describes three other systems that are used to some extent in Europe to deal with small business (ibid.): (1) France and the Netherlands allow firms with tax liability below a very small figure ($176 and $738, respectively) to invoice customers for tax paid on purchases (thereby providing the customer with the invoice required to take credit for the tax), rather than charging and remitting tax on sales. (2) Germany allows firms of intermediate size (sales under about $41,000) to calculate tax paid on purchases by applying a percentage markup to sales. Italy applies a similar but more complicated system to even smaller firms. Belgium reverses the system, basing tax liability on sales on purchases of the firm. (3) Luxembourg, Germany, France, and the Netherlands allow small firms to remit as tax payments less than has been collected from customers to compensate for their higher compliance costs.

Due offers the following assessment of these efforts to deal with the problem posed by small business (ibid.):

> Outright exemption is the simplest system but creates the problem of the breaking of the chain; the attempt of two countries to eliminate this effect by allowing the small firms to invoice the tax paid on their purchases lessens the effectiveness of the system in mitigating the

problems of the small firms. Allowing small firms to simplify the calculation of the tax has merit but introduces an arbitrary element into the operation of the tax, since actual markups of most firms are not identical with the standard markups provided. *Forfait* assessment simplifies the tasks of the firms, but is certain to deviate from the appropriate tax liability in most instances and is an invitation to corruption. Similarly, features that reduce the tax liability on the small firms but not the amount they invoice to their customers only very roughly compensate for the higher compliance costs.

7. For a demonstration of this proposition, see the second section of chapter 6.

8. An exemption based on value added would be more attractive from a conceptual viewpoint than one based on receipts. But the need to calculate value added to determine eligibility for exemption would defeat one of the primary purposes of small-business exceptions—simplification.

9. U.S. Department of the Treasury, *Tax Reform*, notes (vol. 3, p. 58) that in 1979–1980 a $25,000 exemption would have removed 70 percent of nonfarm proprietorships and almost half of nonfarm partnerships but only 7 percent of sales of such firms. For an exemption of $10,000 the three percentages are 53, 33, and 2.5, respectively.

Since most services provided by children are to consumers rather than to businesses, it might be possible to formulate an exclusion based on a dollar limit on receipts "exclusively" from households. An alternative would be to have a dual limit—that is, separate limits based on the dollar amount of receipts only from households and from all sources.

10. Due, in "Tax Treatment of Farmers," notes that the disadvantage of exemption creates an incentive for firms near the borderline of the exemption requirement to register to claim credit for taxes paid on purchases. He notes, however, that although firms are allowed to opt into the VAT systems of most countries, few in fact do so.

11. William V. T. Roth, "The Roth Reforms" (Speech to the National Press Club, Washington, D.C., February 20, 1986, and supporting documents).

12. Although the figures in table 18 are several years out of date, they indicate clearly that exemption levels in other countries are far below the $10 million figure proposed by Senator Roth. Ireland's exemption of $28,700 is the highest in any European country.

13. Much of the following discussion is also applicable to the VAT proposed for finance of the Superfund. But the Superfund tax would be levied at an extremely low rate (0.08 percent) and only on manufacturing.

14. It really makes no difference whether the conduit is affiliated with the seller or with the purchaser. It can buy at below the market price from the affiliated seller and resell at the market price to the unaffiliated purchaser. Alternatively, it can buy at the market price from the unrelated seller and resell at an inflated price to the affiliated purchaser. Of course, this suggests an even more attractive form of manipulation: interposition of a conduit firm between two related entities, buying at artificially depressed prices from one and selling at inflated prices to the other, thereby removing substantial pieces

of the value added of the group of affiliated firms from the tax base.

15. See Charles E. McLure, Jr., "Market Dominance and the Exporting of State Taxes," *National Tax Journal*, vol. 34 (December 1981), pp. 483–85.

16. For a survey of practice in this area, see Due, "Tax Treatment of Farmers."

17. For the most part farmers are treated like other taxpayers in Denmark, the United Kingdom, Sweden, and Norway. See ibid.

18. U.S. Department of the Treasury, *Tax Reform*, notes (vol. 3, p. 62) that during 1979–1981 some 2.2 million of the 3.2 million farmers in the United States had gross receipts of less than $25,000 per year.

19. Ibid., vol. 3, p. 62, indicates that 30 percent of farm output is exported. The figures for major crops range from 27 percent for corn to 64 percent for wheat.

20. Chapter 4 has argued, however, that this would not be the appropriate way to attack the potential regressivity of the VAT.

21. Under the naive subtraction method it would be necessary to exempt the sale of food at each stage in the production-distribution process. This would entail apportioning expenses of firms selling both taxable and exempt products.

22. Alternatively, any farmer who chose not to claim allowable credits under a system of zero rating of food could, in effect, opt out of the system and thereby become exempt de facto. Such farmers would, however, still be in the VAT system from the legal point of view.

23. Due, "Tax Treatment of Farmers," notes that one option would be to exempt farmers and zero-rate all sales to them. This approach is not discussed in the text because, as Due says, "It requires identification of sales to farmers and opens the way to escape from tax of some sales for consumption use."

Exempting both farmers and sales to farmers seems even more troublesome. The same problems of identification would arise, and multiple taxation of farm inputs would not be eliminated. Zero rating of selected farm inputs seems far more satisfactory.

Several European countries (including West Germany, Italy, and Austria) apply tax to purchases of farmers and allow farmers to apply and invoice a tax rate on their sales that is intended, on the average, to equal the tax paid by the farmer but is not remitted to the government. See ibid.

In Ireland and the Netherlands the problem of multiple taxation caused by exempting farmers is handled by allowing purchasers of agricultural outputs to take a credit based on those purchases, which is intended to approximate the VAT paid on purchases by the farmer. Although such a system is relatively simple, its results are highly arbitrary. Ireland also exempts major farm inputs and allows farmers to claim credits for VAT paid on major purchases, such as buildings and the drainage and reclamation of land; see ibid.

24. For a careful discussion of the treatment of services under a VAT, see J. A. Kay and E. H. Davis, "The VAT and Services" (Paper presented at World Bank Conference on Value Added Taxation in Developing Countries, Washington, D.C., April 21–23, 1986). In addition to the neutrality and equity arguments stressed here, Kay and Davis also discuss the possibility of bias in

economic development resulting from differential taxation of services.

25. In contemplating the pros and cons of taxing services, it is instructive to recall the furor that arose because the U.S. Treasury Department's tax reform proposals to President Reagan (1984) would have shifted the burden of taxes from services to manufacturing. This shift was said to be detrimental to international competitiveness. Given this attitude, it is anomalous that services are taxed so lightly under state sales taxes.

26. Kay and Davis, "The VAT and Services," conclude from the examination of survey data on the pattern of consumption in the United Kingdom that "consumption of services rises as a proportion of spending as spending itself rises. . . . This is true of all household types, and the sample overall." Kay and Davis also note that in the United Kingdom horizontal differences are muted by the fact that two of the greatest potential sources of horizontal differences, health and education, are provided primarily by the state.

27. Under the naive subtraction-method VAT the exemption of business services would create just the opposite distortions, because it implies under-taxation.

28. If it were thought desirable to exclude some services to households from the tax base for social reasons, zero rating would be preferable to exemption. All sales would be tax free, and credit would be available for all taxes paid on purchases. The biases of business decisions listed in the text would not exist. Although economic choices of consumers would be distorted somewhat more by such a policy than by exemption, the difference would probably be small, given the large ratio of value added to receipts in most service sectors. Moreover, if there is a justification for preferential tax treatment of consumption, it would presumably imply zero rating, not exemption.

29. Part of the conventional wisdom in this area is that in Europe two prices exist for such services as house painting, depending on whether the customer insists on paying VAT.

30. See Kay and Davis, "The VAT and Services." Incentives for self-supply are discussed further in the sections of this chapter dealing with housing and the activities and purchases of state and local governments and nonprofit organizations.

31. Kay and Davis suggest that distortion is likely to be greatest against commercial food preparation and restaurant meals (ibid.). Factors such as inadequate expertise, economies of scale and scope, and complementarity or substitution of taxed inputs (such as automobiles and washing machines) for household labor prevent substitution of untaxed self-supply for taxed commercial supply in most other areas.

32. The terminology is from U.S. Department of the Treasury, *Blueprints for Basic Tax Reform* (Washington, D.C., 1977). This way of viewing the problem follows Robert F. Conrad, "The Value Added Tax and Real Estate" (Paper presented at World Bank Conference on Value Added Taxation in Developing Countries, Washington, D.C., April 21–23, 1986).

33. It may be worthwhile to note that inclusion of imputed income from owner-occupied housing has long had a place on the agenda of income tax reform.

34. Henry J. Aaron, *Shelter and Subsidies: Who Benefits from Federal Housing Policies?* (Washington, D.C.: Brookings Institution, 1972), argues, however (p. 71), "Though such a remedy [taxation of imputed income from owner-occupied housing under the income tax] may be politically unthinkable, it is workable despite significant administrative problems."

35. See also Conrad, "Value Added Tax and Real Estate." Strictly speaking, this analysis applies only to the value of housing services attributable to the capital value of the house itself; it does not apply to value created by the addition of the owner-occupant's labor.

36. The VAT proposed by Representative Al Ullman in 1979 would have taxed housing at only 5 percent, rather than at the 10 percent rate applied to all other consumption. The 1980 revision of the Ullman bill would have totally exempted housing.

37. Consideration might be given to establishing some sort of "suspension" system under which sales of commercial and industrial buildings and perhaps other large investment expenditures would, in effect, be zero rated to avoid the cash-flow problems that sometimes arise when tax liabilities must be discharged before credits and refunds are available. Of course, if a purchaser of capital goods eligible for suspension of tax made both exempt and either taxable or zero-rated sales, the apportionment problems described in chapter 6 would complicate matters, because suspension would not be allowed for expenditures related to exempt sales. Moreover, zero-rating such sales would only push the cash-flow problem one step earlier in the production-distribution process.

Another problem with such an approach is that it carries the risk that exempt persons will inappropriately benefit from the zero rating of their purchases. This should not be a major problem, however, as long as a fairly high floor is placed under expenditures eligible for suspension treatment and such treatment is accorded only to sales of selected items to registered taxpayers.

38. The widespread use of the partnership form in the real estate industry raises a crucial issue in the application of the small-business exemption: Should the exemption be applied to the partnership or to each partner? For administrative reasons and to prevent abuse, the exemption presumably must be applied to the entity.

39. If residential real estate were exempted (by exempting the rental stage but taxing all inputs, including the purchase of the building) rather than taxed under the regular VAT, a further administrative difficulty would arise. Zero-rated housing could be purchased for owner occupancy and then converted to rental use without payment of tax. Attempting to police such conversions, which also commonly occur for nontax reasons, would be administratively burdensome and would probably raise public outcry.

40. This appears to be roughly the method introduced in New Zealand in October 1986. Although generalization is difficult, this seems also to be broadly consistent with practice in most European countries. See also Conrad, "Value Added Tax and Real Estate."

41. Thus the services of the house, commercially provided repairs and

improvements, and materials used by the owner in maintenance and repairs would be taxed, but the value of labor of the owner would not be taxed.

42. If the VAT did not extend to existing houses, one would expect the value of existing houses to rise in relation to the value of new (post-VAT) houses, with the likelihood of passage of the VAT. Note that application of VAT to existing housing would have no effect on resource allocation, except to the extent that it reduced the tax rate required to raise a given amount of revenue.

43. Conrad, "Value Added Tax and Real Estate," presents an imaginative scheme that would involve application of VAT to the existing stock of housing. Conrad would avoid the valuation problem by applying the VAT only to sales occurring after introduction of a VAT.

44. This approach is endorsed in U.S. Department of the Treasury, *Tax Reform*, vol. 3, p. 79.

45. In principle, appreciation should be defined as the excess of the selling price over the inflation-adjusted depreciated basis of the asset. This point is important for the discussion of the second option described below. Even this definition avoids the question of the proper depreciated basis to assign to an asset that appreciates in value.

46. The purchase of an annuity is economically equivalent to the selling of insurance by the annuitant. Thus the taxation of annuities under a VAT is not considered separately. As with insurance, the objective should be to tax the value added in administering annuities but not the transfer component. Since annuities are bought almost exclusively by households, exemption or use of the addition method should involve only a minor amount of multiple taxation of the kind discussed below.

47. As defined, value added is income generated in the financial sector, rather than consumption of financial services.

48. The value added in insurance can be seen by noting that the actuarial value of insurance is less than its cost by the amount of the costs of administering the pooling of risks, plus profits. The concept of value added in insurance is most easily understood in the context of "pure insurance," in which there is no saving component and all premiums in excess of the "load" for administrative costs and profits received in a given period are paid out during the same period to policyholders who experience losses. Property and casualty insurance and term life insurance are the best examples of this, but even they typically contain a small saving element.

49. Thus Malcolm Gillis, "The VAT and Financial Institutions" (Paper presented at World Bank Conference on Value Added Taxation in Developing Countries, Washington, D.C., April 21–23, 1986), states, "After 25 years of experience with value-added taxation in Europe, it is now clear that truly satisfactory solutions to problems of taxing financial institutions under a value-added tax (VAT) have yet to be devised, much less implemented." Though concerned primarily with the taxation of financial institutions in developing countries, Gillis provides a useful survey of problems in this area and of efforts to solve them in Europe and elsewhere.

50. Gillis (ibid.) favors zero-rating financial services in the context of tax policy for developing countries. His concern with not inhibiting the development of financial intermediation is probably less relevant for a developed country such as the United States. Concern about international competitiveness may, however, be even more relevant than in developing countries.

51. Thus, for example, a tax on gross insurance premiums would clearly reach the transfer component of insurance as well as the value added, even for property and casualty insurance.

52. Gerard Brannon, "VAT and Financial Institutions" (Xeroxed, April 12, 1985) estimates that some 20 to 30 percent of the loading in the financial sector reflects purchases from other firms. It would be extremely cumbersome to zero-rate only transactions with business firms. Of course, under a subtraction-method tax the multiple taxation of such services would not be a problem.

53. The experience in Israel is discussed further in Gillis, "VAT and Financial Institutions."

54. This has the advantage that under certain circumstances a consumption-based VAT is equivalent to a tax on labor income. See Carl S. Shoup, *Public Finance* (Chicago: Aldine Publishing Co., 1969), pp. 266–69.

55. See Gillis, "VAT and Financial Institutions."

56. Appropriate taxation of financial institutions is one advantage of the subtraction-method business transfer tax being considered in Canada.

57. Our trading partners might reasonably argue that an addition-based tax, being levied on the sum of factor payments and profits, does not qualify as an indirect tax for which BTAs are allowed under the GATT.

58. U.S. Department of the Treasury, *Tax Reform*, vol. 3, pp. 49–53.

59. It would be possible to avoid this problem by applying VAT to the entire cash flow of a bank. Deposits and repayments of loans would be subject to tax, and withdrawals and loans would carry a tax credit or refund. On balance only the spread of financial institutions would be taxed, as would be appropriate. Despite the conceptual attraction of this approach, it is not considered further because it seems to suffer from insurmountable problems of adverse perception.

A similar cash-flow approach could be applied to insurance, with all premiums (including the part used to settle claims and to build reserves, as well as administrative costs) being treated as taxable sales and all payments (including settlement of claims, return of investment, and return on investment) being treated as purchases carrying credit for VAT. Like the counterpart for financial institutions, it is not considered further.

60. Gillis, "VAT and Financial Institutions," has proposed a similar scheme for developing countries. He would exempt life insurance and subject other insurance to tax.

61. Consider the following simple subtraction-method example in which a manufacturer and a cafeteria that serves only employees of the manufacturer are operated either as separate entities (the base case) or as a unit providing VAT-free meals in exchange for lower wages (the benefits case).

	Manufacturer	Cafeteria	Total	
			Base case	Benefits case
Sales	2,000	40	2,040	2,000
Purchases	1,200	20	1,220	1,220
Value added	800	20	820	780

Taxable value added is lower in the benefits case by the amount of the value of cafeteria meals provided as a fringe benefit.

62. Like all problems in the fringe-benefit area, the cost of providing tax-preferred benefits can be expected to exceed the value placed on benefits by employees, who, in effect, receive them free of explicit charge.

63. In the example of note 61 this implies that taxable sales of the manufacturer would include the $40 worth of cafeteria meals provided to employees, replicating the results in the base case.

64. Thus, in the example of note 61, taxable sales would be $2,000, but deductible purchases would be only $1,200. Taxable value added would be $800, more than in the benefits case but less than in the conceptually correct base case. This approach would result in some taxation of fringe benefits if the provision of the benefits required expenditures on purchased inputs that would otherwise carry tax credits.

65. Even here, there would be troublesome problems of apportioning expenses—especially those of capital—between deductible (or creditable) and nondeductible categories. This fallback position is tantamount to treating the provision of benefits in kind as exempt.

66. France allows no credit for taxes on automobiles, motor fuels, business entertainment, gifts, or housing provided for executives.

67. Moreover, income taxes pose a particular problem. Even if we accept the argument that corporate income taxes should be deductible under the subtraction method as a kind of cost of public services, we are left in a quandary about what to do with taxes paid on the business income of partnerships and proprietorships. (Note that the analogous treatment under the credit method —levying of VAT on income tax liabilities—appears to be politically impossible or at least highly improbable. It would require that receipts for state corporate income taxes indicate an amount, the product of income tax and the VAT rate, to be claimed as credit in calculating the business taxpayer's net VAT.) On the one hand, it can be argued that those taxes are as likely to be related to benefits as the corporate income tax. On the other hand, it is hard to justify allowing a deduction for personal income taxes paid on business income if comparable relief is not provided for individual income taxes paid on labor income.

68. The New Zealand proposal for a VAT does, however, provide for the taxation of receipts from the property tax as though they were sales proceeds.

69. It may be thought unnecessary or even ridiculous to subject purchases of the federal government to the federal VAT. That this is not the case is easily shown. Suppose that the cost of gasoline net of tax is $1 per gallon and that the tax on gasoline (including the VAT) is $0.25 per gallon. If purchases of

gasoline by the federal government are subject to the same tax as private purchases, the representative taxpayer (through the budgetary process) properly considers the true relative cost of private and public consumption of gasoline. If, however, only private purchases of gasoline are subject to the tax, public consumption will appear artificially cheap, and gasoline will be uneconomically diverted to public use.

70. Whether it would be possible to allow state and local governments to opt to be in the system as far as their broad-based taxes are concerned deserves further consideration. Of course, governments could, in effect, avoid this problem by adjusting the relative taxation of businesses and households.

71. This problem could be avoided by subjecting the payrolls of state and local governments to VAT. The Hall-Rabushka tax would do so.

72. See, for example, Dick Netzer, *Local Alternatives to the Property Tax: User Charges and Nonproperty Taxes,* Working Paper no. 4, Tax Analysis Series (Washington, D.C.: Academy for State and Local Government, 1983).

73. From a theoretical point of view, the addition method could be used to tax the value added in the nonprofit sector where there are no sales. This seems sufficiently unlikely to receive serious legislative consideration that it is not discussed here. Note, however, that the Hall-Rabushka tax would have this effect.

9

Intergovernmental Issues

The American debate on the value-added tax is complicated by an issue that was virtually absent from the European discussion of the VAT in the early 1960s. Although the United States has a federal system of government, five of the six original members of the European Economic Community have unitary governments; that is, except in West Germany, no government comparable to the American states is interposed between the national and local governments.

The existence of state governments raises at least two kinds of intergovernmental issues. First, a decision must be made about whether to tax the purchases and the commercial activities of subnational governments. These issues are discussed in chapter 8. Second, and more important, since the states and their localities have historically had exclusive access to the general sales tax base, the possibility of the federal government's introducing a VAT or retail sales tax raises fundamental issues of intergovernmental fiscal relations.[1] These are the topics of this chapter.[2]

The question most commonly asked is whether federal entry into this area would preempt the sales tax base, making it more difficult for state and local governments to tap that traditional revenue source. In addition, there are important issues of coordinating a federal sales tax—whether a VAT or a retail sales tax—with the sales taxes levied by the states. These include concern for compliance problems of business, questions of the coordination of collection techniques (VAT versus retail sales tax) used by the two levels of government, and harmonization of state and federal efforts. Understanding of these more technical issues is necessary to flesh out concern about federal preemption.

Setting the Stage

A few preliminary remarks, including a statement of criteria of appraisal, are in order. First, the entire discussion of this chapter is predicated on the assumption that state and local governments will want to continue to rely heavily on sales taxes, even though under the recently enacted federal tax reform those taxes will no longer be allowed as itemized deductions in calculating the federal income tax liability of individuals. Since deductibility has been eliminated only for sales taxes, states and local governments will have an incentive to shift away from sales taxation and toward greater reliance on property and income taxation.[3] Eliminating the deduction for state sales taxes but not for state income and property taxes constitutes a partial usurpation or a de facto preemption of the state sales tax base by the federal government.

The primary advantages of a VAT over a retail sales tax are the complete elimination of tax on purchases of capital goods, intermediate products, and other business inputs; accurate border tax adjustments; and the administrative advantages of collecting tax as a good or service moves through the production-distribution process rather than entirely at the retail stage. The higher the total state and federal tax rate being contemplated, the more important all these considerations are. The chief advantages of the retail sales tax are its relative simplicity and its familiarity in the American context. These considerations must constantly be kept in mind in evaluating the prospects for harmonizing state and federal sales taxation.

Federal adoption of a sales tax would probably create strong pressures for reducing the diversity of tax bases, and perhaps rates, now found in state sales taxes. One of the strong economic arguments for fiscal federalism is the diversity a federal system makes possible. Rather than being confined to providing the public goods and services that can be financed with a standard tax structure, the states can provide different amounts of goods and services, depending on the preferences of their residents, as indicated by their willingness to pay different rates of tax. For this reason, it is important to retain state sovereignty over tax rates, at the very least.

Opinions differ about whether the case for fiscal sovereignty extends to the definition of the tax base. Arguments in favor of diversity must be weighed against the possibility that state tax bases may be defined in ways that lack rationality. A rationally defined uniform base would clearly be preferable to the diversity now found in state tax systems. A uniform system, for example, might tax services and achieve greater success in excluding business purchases from taxation. The present diverse system might clearly be preferable, however, to a uniform but badly defined tax base.

I have repeatedly noted that the retail sales tax is a destination-based levy; it applies to imports but exempts exports. The same can be said about the taxation of interstate trade, for the most part; goods shipped to out-of-state purchasers are commonly exempt from state sales taxes, and consumer purchases are commonly subject to the tax of the state of residence of consumers, with one important exception. In *National Belas Hess*, a case decided in 1967, the Supreme Court decided that mail-order houses cannot be required to collect and remit sales and use taxes to the state of residence of a customer unless they have a business presence in that state.[4]

This ruling is unfortunate: it gives out-of-state mail-order houses a competitive advantage over in-state merchants subject to the sales tax of the states in which they do business; it undermines the revenues of states whose residents resort to shopping by mail order; and it produces a patently unfair result. An important goal of public policy should be to subject sales of mail-order houses to the sales and use taxes of the states of residence of their customers. Some approaches to the coordination of state and federal sales taxes either solve this problem directly or create conditions conducive to its solution, while others do not.

Options for Coordination

In principle, state and federal sales taxes could be combined in four generic ways using the VAT and retail sales tax alternatives. Under two of them both levels of government would employ the same kind of sales tax; under the other two one level of government would use the VAT and the other the retail sales tax. In fact, however, neither of the last two, in which the two levels of government employ different sales tax techniques, should be considered seriously, because each suffers from serious difficulties. First, independent state imposition of a VAT in the context of a federal retail sales tax would face insurmountable technical difficulties, as well as being an unlikely candidate for serious consideration for political reasons.[5]

Continued state use of retail sales taxes in the face of a federal credit-method VAT would create substantial compliance problems for business. Two independent systems of registration and exemption would exist; tax liabilities would be calculated in two quite different ways; and a particular business and its sales personnel would probably be faced with different lists of taxable and nontaxable items under the federal VAT and the applicable state retail sales tax. Moreover, this approach would provide no progress toward satisfactory resolution of the *National Belas Hess* problem. In short, this alternative should probably also be removed from serious consideration.

It might appear at first glance that a subtraction-method federal

154

VAT could more easily be combined with the continuation of independently imposed state retail sales taxes, since it would not be necessary to quote the VAT separately, as under a credit-method tax. Indeed, this consideration appears to explain much of the apparent preference of the Canadian government for a federal subtraction-method VAT.[6] In fact, the subtraction method offers little promise as a means of severing the Gordian knot of intergovernmental relations in the sales tax area.

Chapter 6 argues that the subtraction method is distinctly inferior to the credit method unless a single rate is applied to all consumption. The potential vulnerability of a subtraction-method VAT to multiple rates is enough to disqualify it. Moreover, the potential advantages of the subtraction method in coordinating a federal VAT and state retail sales taxes could be fully realized only in the unlikely event that the VAT applied to all goods and services, without exception or differential rates. Once there is a retreat from such a pure system, especially if it is to a sophisticated subtraction-method tax, the combination of a federal subtraction-method VAT with a state retail sales tax suffers from the same debilitating problems as a combination based on a federal credit-method VAT.

Imposition of retail sales taxes by both the state and the federal governments has the substantial advantage that American business is generally familiar with retail sales taxation. Moreover, the retail sales tax is somewhat simpler than the VAT. But such an approach suffers from several potential problems, aside from the difficulties of dealing appropriately with business purchases and making accurate border tax adjustments.

First, the vulnerability of a single-stage tax to evasion would be accentuated if combined state and federal retail sales taxes reached 10 percent or more, as would be likely in many states.[7] Moreover, such an approach would really function satisfactorily only with substantial harmonization of registration requirements and tax bases of the state and federal taxes. Otherwise, differences in registration requirements, tax bases, and other administrative details would make compliance by taxpayers burdensome. Coordination could take either of two forms: independent state administration of a sales tax basically identical with the federal tax or federal collection of a state tax piggybacked on the federal tax and collected by the federal government.[8]

The second approach has the obvious advantage of requiring less effort and expense in tax administration and compliance. It also deals automatically with the *National Belas Hess* problem. It is sobering to note, however, that since its enactment in 1972 not a single state has taken advantage of a federal law that provides for federal collection of state income taxes patterned after the federal tax.[9] Moreover, whether the total harmonization of state and federal tax regimes inherent in this approach is an advantage or a disadvantage depends on whether the tax base chosen by the federal government is sensible. Of course, this approach entails substantial loss of state fiscal sovereignty; the only sovereignty remaining in the sales tax area would be the choice of rate (or rates, if there were also local supplements).

A less extreme version of this approach would entail independent state imposition of a sales tax patterned after the federal tax. Minor deviations in the definition of taxable sales could probably be tolerated without undue burden on business, but substantial deviations would produce the kind of chaotic lack of coordination that could doom the proposal. (Of course, the chaos would be felt primarily in states that deviated significantly from the federal tax provisions.) This approach maintains at least limited state sovereignty with regard to the tax base, as well as the tax rate, but does not offer a solution to the *National Belas Hess* problem.

It would be extremely difficult (not merely inefficient) for the states to implement independently imposed VATs, even if the federal government also introduced a VAT. For this reason, the only form of reliance on the VAT by both state and federal governments that deserves attention would be a system in which the federal government collected VAT for the states and then remitted it to the states of destination.[10] Such a system would obviously eliminate state sales tax administration and state fiscal sovereignty in the determination of the tax base. But there is no reason in principle why tax rates could not vary from state to state.[11]

This approach has the substantial advantages of the value-added technique: proper treatment of business purchases, exact border tax adjustments, and the administrative safeguards of a tax collected at multiple stages in the production-distribution process. Moreover, it would inherently solve the *National Belas Hess* problem. Its primary disadvantage would be the substantial loss of fiscal sovereignty by the states.

A more extreme solution to the issue of intergovernmental relations would be tax sharing, under which a fraction of receipts from the federal sales tax (a VAT or a retail sales tax) would be shared with the states on the basis of a formula.[12] In return, the states would vacate the sales tax area, leaving it exclusively to the federal government.[13] Such an approach would involve complete loss of state fiscal sovereignty in the sales tax area. It would eliminate the latitude of individual states to adjust sales tax collections to reflect the attitudes of their citizens toward publicly provided goods and services.[14] All things considered, this does not seem to be an appropriate or politically viable solution to the issues of intergovernmental relations discussed here.

Whether the federal government should introduce a sales tax depends heavily on how relationships between the state and federal sales taxes would be handled. Virtually any administratively satisfactory solution to the problems that would arise would entail substantial loss of state fiscal sovereignty. It is perhaps in this way that the preemption issue is best understood. States have more room to maneuver in the sales tax area if they do not need to be concerned with how their taxes interact with those of the federal government. Total state autonomy in choosing the sales tax base—which is a mixed blessing—is difficult to achieve in a system in which compliance is not overcomplicated. But techniques that maintain state autonomy in setting sales tax rates—the really important issue—should be quite feasible. Even some autonomy in determining the tax base might be feasible if both levels of government employed similar retail sales taxes.

If states are willing to forgo autonomy in determining their sales tax base and to employ a uniform base, the preferred approach is for the federal government to collect tax for the states as part of its administration of the VAT. This approach maintains state autonomy over rates and solves the *National Belas Hess* problem. More important, it achieves the advantage of the VAT collection technique. Federal collection of a retail sales tax with a uniform base (but not uniform rates) seems to be somewhat inferior, despite the greater familiarity of the tax, at total state and federal tax rates of 10 percent or more. If, however, states are adamant about retaining some autonomy over the sales tax base as well as rates, there seems to be no alternative to use of the retail sales tax by both levels of government. Substantial diversity in the tax base and other features could render such an approach unworkable from the point of view of compliance and administration.

Notes

1. At many points in this chapter I refer to states or to state governments purely for expositional facility, even though reference to both states and localities or to their governments would be more appropriate. Usually the proper connotation is clear from context.

2. The issues covered in this chapter are also discussed in Charles E. McLure, Jr., "State and Local Implications of a Federal Value Added Tax" (Prepared for the Academy for State and Local Government, Washington, D.C., 1986). For more technical discussions of tax coordination under the VAT, see Charles E. McLure, Jr., "TVA and Fiscal Federalism," in *Proceedings*

of the 64th Annual Conference of the National Tax Association–Tax Institute of America (Kansas City, Mo., 1971), pp. 279–91, and "State-Federal Relations in the Taxation of the Value Added," *Journal of Corporation Law*, vol. 6 (Fall 1980), pp. 127–39.

3. It would have been better to eliminate the same portion of the deduction for all state and local taxes, since such a policy would not distort state choices of tax instruments.

4. For a more complete analysis of the *National Belas Hess* case, see Advisory Commission on Intergovernmental Relations, *State and Local Taxation of Out-of-State Mail Order Sales* (Washington, D.C., 1986).

5. For a discussion of the technical difficulties involved in independent state imposition of a credit-method VAT in the absence of a federal VAT on which to piggyback, see McLure, "State-Federal Relations." State use of the addition method also suffers from serious problems, but this is not the place to discuss them. See, however, McLure, "State and Local Implications."

6. On July 18 the Canadian Ministry of Finance announced that it would consider the role of a business transfer tax (a subtraction-method VAT) in a comprehensive reform of the Canadian tax system, rather than proposing enactment of such a tax, as had been expected.

7. As noted in chapter 4, it does not seem sensible to adopt a federal sales tax at a rate of less than 5 percent. State tax rates are at least 5 percent in twenty-two states, and at least thirty-five states have combined state and local rates of at least 5 percent in major cities. See Advisory Commission on Intergovernmental Relations, *Significant Features of Fiscal Federalism, 1985–86 Edition* (Washington, D.C., 1986), pp. 91–92, 99–100. Note, however, that several Canadian provinces and several foreign countries levy retail sales taxes greater than 10 percent, with apparent success. See John F. Due, "The Choice between a Value-added Tax and a Retail Sales Tax" (1985 Conference Report, Report of Proceedings of the Thirty-seventh Tax Conference, Canadian Tax Foundation, 1986), chap. 16.

8. It has sometimes been suggested that the states could collect a federal supplement to their sales taxes. Such an approach would, of course, be quite unacceptable, since states do not levy sales taxes on a nationally uniform base. Moreover, states would have a substantial economic interest in the deterioration of both the base and the administration of their sales taxes, to reduce their relative support of the federal government through the supplement. (In the extreme case of states with no sales tax, there could be no federal supplement.) States concerned about revenue loss could levy a legally distinct tax with a base equivalent to retail sales, worded in such a way as not to attract the federal supplement. Federal regulation to prevent such a scheme from unfolding would be tantamount to implementing a federal tax with state supplements in a clumsy and inefficient way.

9. See Daniel G. Smith, "Benefits and Disadvantages of Federal Collection of State Individual Income Taxes," in Charles H. Gustafson, ed., *Federal Income Tax Simplification* (American Law Institute, 1979).

10. Such an approach is described in Satya Poddar, "Value-added Tax at the State Level" (Paper presented at World Bank Conference on Value Added

Taxation in Developing Countries, Washington, D.C., April 21–23, 1986). Alternative approaches suggested by Sijbren Cnossen, "Interjurisdictional Coordination of Sales Taxes" (Paper presented at World Bank Conference on Value Added Taxation in Developing Countries, Washington, D.C., April 21–23, 1986), seem less promising in the U.S. context. It is assumed that the destination principle would continue to be chosen for state and local sales taxes.

11. Note, however, that variations of tax rates among localities would be much harder to handle under the federal clearinghouse arrangements anticipated here.

12. The federal government of West Germany shares revenues from its VAT with its states; for a description, see Ewald Nowotny, "Tax Assignment and Revenue Sharing in the Federal Republic of Germany and Switzerland," in Charles E. McLure, Jr., ed., *Tax Assignment in Federal Countries* (Canberra, Australia: Centre for Research on Federal Financial Relations, 1983), pp. 260–86.

13. One means of implementing such an approach that would not require advance cooperation between the federal and state governments would be for the federal government to allow credit against liability for the federal tax for state sales taxes patterned after the federal levy and collected by the federal government. Such an approach would probably be effective in inducing states to vacate the sales tax field. It could be employed far more easily under a federal retail sales tax than under a VAT.

14. The only remaining latitude would be to try to influence the jointly determined level of shared taxes and the formula used to set state shares.

10
Conclusions

The value-added tax is essentially an administrative technique for implementing a sales tax. Rather than collecting tax only at the retail stage, as under the sales taxes levied by most states, the VAT technique allows tax to be collected as goods and services move through the production-distribution process and value is added to them. The VAT and the retail sales tax have similar economic effects if their tax bases are comparable.

The United States is one of only a few major developed countries of the free world that do not have national sales taxes. Over the next few years interest in introducing a VAT or some other form of national sales tax will probably increase substantially as the Gramm-Rudman-Hollings targets for deficit reduction become increasingly difficult to meet. Already several proposals for federal VATs have been advanced, though not in the context of deficit reduction. These include the proposal by Senator William Roth of Delaware for a business transfer tax (BTT), the low-rate manufacturing-stage VAT proposed as a method of financing the Superfund, and the personal-exemption VAT proposed by Robert Hall and Alvin Rabushka in the context of income tax reform. Notably, none of these proposals would employ the credit method of implementing the VAT that is—for very good reasons—used in virtually all countries (currently almost forty) that levy VATs.

Under the credit method a registered taxpayer calculates tax liability by applying the tax rate to sales and then taking credit for taxes paid on purchased inputs. Under the subtraction method envisaged in the three proposals described, the taxpayer would apply the tax rate to value added, which is calculated by subtracting purchased inputs from sales. The mechanics of implementing a VAT in these two ways are described in chapter 3.

If tax is levied at a single rate on all goods and services (that is, with no exceptions or differential rates), the credit and subtraction methods produce identical results, and the subtraction method may be somewhat preferable from the standpoint of taxpayers' compliance and administration. If, however, coverage is not universal or differential rates are employed, the subtraction method has severe drawbacks. It distorts economic decision making more than the credit method. Moreover, accurate border tax adjustments (the rebate of VAT on exports and collection of VAT on imports, for which VAT is noted) are generally impossible. These defects of the subtraction method are particularly troublesome since the method itself would create considerable political pressure for exceptions and preferential rates. The credit method is more or less immune from these problems.

This dependence of the viability of the subtraction method on a single-rate tax and universal coverage can be seen as either an advantage or a disadvantage. An optimist might advocate adoption of the subtraction method, arguing that the difficulties caused by exceptions and differential rates would force adoption of a "pure" single-rate tax applied to all transactions. But such a strategy entails considerable risk that a highly defective multiple-rate tax might emerge from the political process. A more realistic attitude would recognize that, for both administrative and political reasons, imposition of a single-rate tax with universal coverage is highly unlikely; it would therefore be extremely unwise to introduce a subtraction-method VAT rather than use the credit method. These arguments are spelled out in chapter 6.

Many goods and services would probably be excluded from the base of a VAT, for either administrative or political reasons. Chapter 8 describes some of the problems commonly encountered in applying the VAT in such areas as housing, financial intermediation and insurance, farming, and small business. Food, medicine, and a few other items might be excluded as a matter of social policy. Relatively limited exclusions would reduce the base of the VAT to about 80 percent of total consumption. More liberal exclusions might reduce the base to less than half of total consumption. Thus at 1988 levels of income, each percentage point of the VAT rate would yield some $14 to $25 billion, depending on the exclusions allowed. The likely base of a VAT is discussed further in chapter 3.

The economic effects of a VAT (discussed in chapter 4) are not very dramatic; in most cases they are similar to those of a retail sales tax. Unless shot through with exceptions and differential rates, the VAT would not greatly distort economic decision making. Nor would it favor present consumption over saving, as the income tax does. The relative neutrality of the VAT is one of its primary attractions, in comparison with taxes that cause substantial economic distortions, such as the income tax.

Introduction of a VAT would probably cause a one-time increase in prices, but it need not cause inflation to accelerate. It would not in itself improve the competitive position of the United States, aside from any effect of deficit reduction, because the export rebates and collection of VAT on imports merely compensate for VAT levied on domestic output. The same result occurs, though somewhat less completely, under the retail sales tax. Substituting the VAT for part of the corporate income tax might, however, have a beneficial effect on U.S. trade. The longstanding view that introducing a national sales tax would lead to the expansion of federal spending by providing the Congress with a relatively painless "money machine" has recently been challenged, but not convincingly.

Probably the primary economic disadvantage of the VAT is its regressivity. As a tax on consumption, the VAT would constitute a smaller fraction of higher incomes than of lower ones. Perhaps more important, it would impose a significant burden on low-income families. Even though that burden would be reduced or eliminated by the indexation of many transfer payments, including social security, the coverage of indexing is not complete, and a substantial number of low-income households would bear the burden of a VAT.

Burdens on low-income families and regressivity can be reduced or even eliminated by exempting food, medicine, and a few other necessities from the tax base and applying increased rates to items that appear predominantly in the market basket of high-income families. This is, however, an extremely expensive, complicated, and blunt instrument to use in the attempt to avoid regressivity, and the weight of expert opinion is that it should be avoided.

A much more efficient means of avoiding burdens on low-income families and regressivity is a system of low-income allowances, such as an expanded credit patterned after the earned-income credit or a negative income tax. Such a policy deserves to be considered on its merits rather than adopted without due consideration as an adjunct to a VAT. Finally, the personal exemption allowed under the Hall-Rabushka version of the VAT would provide substantial relief for low-income recipients of labor income, though not for those who receive income from capital.

Many of the economic effects of the VAT are roughly the same as those of the retail sales tax employed by most states. At low rates of tax, the United States might be well advised to choose the more familiar and simpler retail sales tax over the VAT, if a decision is made to introduce a federal sales tax. The VAT has the advantage of more easily eliminating tax on capital investment and other business inputs and on exports and collecting comparable taxes on imports. Moreover, it is somewhat less vulnerable to evasion than the retail sales tax. At higher rates of tax (say, at rates greater than 10 percent) these economic and administrative benefits of the VAT probably outweigh the greater familiarity and relative simplicity of the retail sales tax. These differences are discussed in chapter 7, along with the defects of several alternative forms of sales taxation.

Federal revenues can be increased, of course, in other ways if that is thought desirable. Income tax rates could be increased; the base of the income tax could and should be broadened further than in the recently enacted tax reform; or taxes could be imposed on various forms of energy, as has recently been proposed. Chapter 5 considers taxation of imported oil, all oil, all sources of energy, and motor fuels, as well as an increase in all excise taxes. All these sources of taxation are distinctly inferior to a VAT or other form of broad-based sales tax, especially if substantial revenue must be raised. Further reform of the income tax would be preferable to introduction of a federal sales tax, but it seems highly unlikely that the Congress will soon return to tax reform for this purpose. Application of higher tax rates on income, as defined by the tax reform bill, might be preferable to introducing a national sales tax, but again this outcome seems unlikely.

The proposal for a BTT offered by Senator Roth is severely flawed in at least three respects (described in detail in chapters 6 and 8). First and most fundamentally, the Roth proposal is based on the subtraction method rather than the credit method. As explained in chapter 6, the subtraction method is quite unworkable except in the unlikely situation of a single rate applied universally.

Second, the $10 million "small business" exemption in the Roth bill would create difficulties even under the credit method. Under the subtraction method an exemption of this size would create substantial inequities, administrative difficulties, and economic distortions.

Finally, the proposal to allow the BTT to be taken as a credit against the payroll taxes used to finance social security (the FICA offset) would constitute a thinly veiled attempt to subsidize American exports and protect domestic producers from foreign competition. It would not be legal under the General Agreement on Tariffs and Trade and would be vigorously opposed by our trading partners.

Of course, neither the exceptionally high small-business exemption nor the FICA offset is an inherent component of a subtraction-method VAT such as the BTT. Even so, the potential defects of the subtraction method (arising from its vulnerability to multiple rates and gaps in coverage) warrant rejection of the proposal for a BTT. If the United States is to introduce a VAT, it should use the standard credit method.

The original members of the European Economic Community adopted the VAT for reasons that are largely irrelevant for the United States. Most of them already imposed gross receipts or turnover taxes, a form of sales tax that is inferior to either the retail sales tax or the VAT (for reasons explained in chapter 7). That being the case, substitution of the VAT was clearly an improvement. The United States has no defective federal sales tax to replace. The VAT would either be a source of new revenue or replace part of the existing revenue system; either of these options is more difficult to appraise than the choice facing the EEC. The Europeans chose the VAT over the retail sales tax for several other reasons that are also less relevant in the U.S. context (see chapter 4).

American consideration of the VAT occurs in a context that differs in another important respect from that in most countries that have adopted it. Most state governments and many local governments employ sales taxes and would consider federal adoption of a VAT or other form of sales tax an unwelcome intrusion into a fiscal realm that has traditionally been reserved for them.

More important, imposition of sales taxes by both state and federal governments could be achieved without substantial problems of compliance and administration only if there were far-reaching cooperation between the two levels of government. Greater cooperation would have the potential advantage of providing both greater uniformity among states and a solution to the problem of tax-free sales by mail-order houses across state borders. But it would entail considerable loss of state fiscal sovereignty and restrain options in the sales tax field (these issues are discussed in chapter 9). This consideration should, and almost certainly will, condition any discussion of whether the United States should adopt a national sales tax and whether such a tax should be a VAT or a retail sales tax.

Commentary

Mark A. Bloomfield

Charles McLure's monograph is an excellent discussion of the advantages and disadvantages of a value-added tax (VAT), a business transfer tax (BTT), a retail sales tax, and specific excise taxes such as energy taxes. It also provides a thorough treatment of the technical aspects of implementing a consumption tax. The monograph is timely, needed, and certain to be widely and usefully read by tax policy experts and academicians.

Politicians and economists will sooner or later put the consumption tax on the nation's agenda. This brief commentary on McLure's detailed treatment of the subject makes the political and economic case for a consumption tax in our fiscal structure and responds to common criticisms of a VAT or retail sales tax.

The Political Case for a VAT

It may be peculiar or at least lonely to argue with conviction for a consumption tax to replace part of the individual and corporate income tax or as an additional tax to reduce the deficit. McLure, however, makes the case well that "many Americans concerned about fiscal affairs seem to be increasingly convinced that a new source of federal revenue must be found."[1] Of course, as McLure notes, there is no reason why we cannot raise income tax rates, but doing so, he rightly says, would undermine one of the primary reasons for the current round of tax reform.[2] The monumental Tax Reform Act of 1986 trades off lower individual and corporate income tax rates for some of

Mark A. Bloomfield is president of the American Council for Capital Formation and its education and research affiliate, the American Council for Capital Formation Center for Policy Research. The views expressed are not necessarily those of either organization. The author is greatly indebted to Dr. Margo Thorning, chief economist of the American Council for Capital Formation, for her help in developing the theme of this commentary, her invaluable research, and her wisdom on matters economic and political.

165

the preferences enacted for social and economic objectives over the past several decades. The American people want and deserve reduced tax rates, and lower marginal rates make economic sense. As McLure observes, however, proposals to tax all real economic income uniformly can be objected to on the ground that "the choice of income, rather than consumption, constitutes an important form of interference with market forces: preference for present versus future consumption."[3]

Furthermore, there is cause for concern about how lower income tax rates are paid for, from the point of view of capital formation. Although lower rates are at first blush attractive, the seeds of discord are present in what will be a unique tax structure. Except for Hong Kong, no economic power relies on an income tax structure with such low rates. Few other major industrial countries have tax structures as pro-consumption or as anti-investment. Moreover, as McLure points out, the Tax Reform Act of 1986, allegedly revenue neutral, does not address the foremost economic issue of the day, large structural deficits stretching indefinitely into the future.

More and more political observers (including in private some key administration officials) are convinced that, once the dust settles on the Tax Reform Act of 1986, this country will soon be looking hard at consumption taxes. There are several reasons.

First, the tax reform legislation of 1986 plays Russian roulette with capital formation through the tax code. The repeal of the investment tax credit and the increase in tax rates on capital gains could have negative economic consequences that may manifest themselves in renewed interest in consumption taxes for purposes of tax policy and deficit reduction. Consider the political history of the now repealed investment tax credit, which has been on and off six times since 1962 as capital spending ebbed and flowed. If, as some political pundits predict, international competitiveness becomes a major political issue, a consumption tax might become the revenue alternative for financing a procompetitive tax policy. Analyses of the economic effects of the Tax Reform Act of 1986 by Data Resources, Wharton Econometrics, Chase Econometrics, and L. H. Meyer & Associates all conclude that investment will decine in 1987 and beyond.[4] Declining investment may force policy makers to turn their attention to consumption taxes to pay for improved capital formation incentives.

Second, the federal deficit is structural and will not automatically go away; most people believe some tax increase is needed for effective control. Since the Tax Reform Act of 1986 may lock in lower marginal rates and will use up the last "easy" revenue raiser in the code (the investment tax credit), the consumption tax alternative will have to be strongly considered for reducing the deficit in the years ahead. An additional impetus arises because state governments are no longer running the surpluses that helped offset federal deficits in recent years.

Third, our foreign competitors either rely heavily on consumption taxes (see table 1) or are considering them (Canada and Japan).

Finally, the public prefers consumption taxes to income taxes. A survey by the Advisory Commission on Intergovernmental Relations in 1985 found that 38 percent of the public believe the federal income tax is the worst or least fair of all taxes while only 16 percent believe the state sales tax is least fair.[5] Surveys also show that the public consistently prefers a consumption tax to higher individual income taxes if additional tax revenue is needed for deficit reduction.[6] With the right campaign a popular president could sell consumption taxes to the American people as a means of cutting the federal deficit. True, the new low-rate, broad-based income tax might prove to be more popular, but the evidence is lacking.[7]

McLure very perceptively catalogs the concerns of both liberals and conservatives about a consumption tax but observes that those concerns might forge an "unholy alliance" in support of consumption taxes. The alliance might consist of supply-siders who favor lower income tax rates, conservatives who fear deficits, liberals who worry about further holes in the social safety net, and Americans who are concerned about defense. Consider, for example, a political deal between President Reagan and conservatives who favor a higher defense budget but worry about tax increases and members of Con-

TABLE 1

MAJOR SOURCES OF TAX REVENUE, 1983

(percentage of total taxes)

Country	Taxes on Income				Taxes on Goods and Services
	Individual	Corporate	Payroll	Total	
Canada	35.6	7.5	13.1	56.2	32.7
France	13.4	4.3	43.9	61.6	29.0
Japan	25.6	19.6	30.0	75.1	15.2
United Kingdom	27.7	10.8	17.7	56.2	29.8
United States	37.1	5.5	28.7	71.4	18.0
West Germany	28.3	5.1	35.7	69.1	27.5

SOURCE: Organization for Economic Cooperation and Development, *Revenue Statistics of OECD Member Countries: 1965–1984*, Paris.

gress willing to hold military spending hostage to avoid cuts in the domestic safety net and more deficit spending.

The macroeconomic question to be answered is, What happens when the anti-saving and anti-investment provisions of the Tax Reform Act of 1986 work their way through the economy and when deficit reduction puts pressure on the federal tax system? One can sympathize with McLure's belated conviction that continuation of large deficits is a greater problem than the possibility that a VAT or a federal sales tax will become a "money machine" in the hands of Congress.[8] Given the projected large budget deficits, Congress might restore higher marginal tax rates while leaving the U.S. tax system denuded of its current allowances and deductions. As David Hale, chief economist of Kemper Financial Services, says, "Under such circumstances, the tax reform program could prove to be a Trojan horse for significantly increasing the overall progressivity of the U.S. tax system, with adverse consequences for capital formation, growth and inflation."[9]

The Economic Case for a VAT

Policy makers are attracted to a broad-based consumption tax such as a VAT instead of an income tax for one of three reasons. First, they think that, if substituted for income taxes, it would encourage higher saving and investment. Second, they believe it would have beneficial effects on the U.S. trade balance, again if used as a replacement for income taxes. Third, and perhaps most important, a broad-based consumption tax is a powerful revenue raiser and thus an attractive option for deficit reduction.

Saving and Consumption Taxes. Harvard's Lawrence H. Summers observes in a recent study:

> The allocation of resources between present and future consumption or savings is, perhaps, the most fundamental choice facing any economy. Just as an economy faces a choice between guns and butter today, it faces a choice between consumption today and consumption in the future. The stakes involved in this choice are extremely large. The rate of savings determines the rate of economic growth a country can enjoy—it can also have an important influence on a nation's competitiveness in international markets.[10]

Other analysts, including Summers's colleague at Harvard Benjamin M. Friedman, observe that since the late 1960s U.S. net capital formation has fallen by almost any measure. The United States de-

TABLE 2

SAVING AND INVESTMENT AS PERCENTAGE
OF GROSS DOMESTIC PRODUCT, 1964–1982

| | Saving | | Investment | |
| | | | Gross nonresidential fixed capital formation | Gross fixed capital formation |
Country	Net saving[a]	Gross saving[b]		
Canada	10.2	21.6	17.5	22.5
France	11.7	22.6	n.a.	22.3
Japan	19.9	33.4	25.0	32.1
United Kingdom	7.2	18.3	14.6	17.7
United States	6.9	18.8	14.0	18.2
West Germany	12.8	23.8	15.8	22.4

n.a. = not available.
a. The main components of the OECD definition of net saving are personal saving, business saving (undistributed corporate profits), and government saving (or dissaving). The OECD definition of net saving differs from that used in the National Income and Product Accounts published by the Department of Commerce primarily because of the treatment of government capital formation.
b. Net saving plus consumption of fixed capital. The main components of the OECD definition of consumption of fixed capital are the capital consumption allowances (depreciation charges) for both the private and the government sectors.
SOURCE: Derived from Organization for Economic Cooperation and Development, *National Accounts*, vol. 2, various issues.

voted an average of 8.3 percent of its net national product (after subtraction of depreciation allowances) to increasing its nonresidential fixed capital during the 1960s but only 7.7 percent during the 1970s and less than 4.0 percent during the early 1980s. Economists agree that investment, or specifically the amount of machinery and equipment that each worker uses, is a critical determinant of productivity growth. During the 1960s the amount of capital per worker grew by an annual average of 3.2 percent. Because of declining capital formation rates and an unusually large growth of the labor force, capital per worker grew by only 1.3 percent per year during the 1970s.[11]

Net saving averaged only 6.9 percent of gross domestic product (GDP) in the United States over the 1964–1982 period, considerably less than the 12.8 percent in West Germany and 19.9 percent in Japan (see table 2). Total saving (private and government saving plus depreciation charges) was only 18.8 percent of GDP in the United States during the 1964–1982 period, substantially below Canada's 21.6 percent and Japan's 33.4 percent.

169

Recent research by Michael J. Boskin and John M. Roberts, using alternative measures of national and private saving, suggests that the actual gap between the U.S. and Japanese saving rates is less than that shown in the table.[12] Nonetheless, they conclude that the disparity is still substantial.

A good case can be made for a cause-and-effect relationship between this country's lower saving rate and its comparatively slow rate of growth in per capita income. GDP per capita grew at an average annual rate of only 1.8 percent over the 1964–1982 period in the United States; the comparable figures were 3.2 percent in France and 5.3 percent in Japan (see table 3). Over the 1972–1982 period, the U.S. record was even worse; average U.S. per capita income growth was 1.1 percent, while the figures for France and Japan were 2.2 percent and 3.2 percent, respectively.

As Summers notes in a recent article:

> It's no accident that Germany and France, with national savings rates twice that of the United States, have had twice as rapid productivity growth, while the Japanese, with a savings rate three times ours, have enjoyed three times as great a productivity growth rate over the last 15 years. Of the major developed nations, only the British have had a savings rate as low as ours, and only they have had as bad a record of productivity growth.[13]

Economic Growth and Consumption Taxes. Analysis by tax policy experts including Don Fullerton, John Shoven, John Whalley, Dale Jorgenson, and Kun-Young Yun suggests that U.S. saving and eco-

TABLE 3

GROSS DOMESTIC PRODUCT PER CAPITA,
AVERAGE ANNUAL PERCENT CHANGE, 1964–1982

Country	1964–1982	1972–1982
Canada	2.6	1.6
France	3.2	2.2
Japan	5.3	3.2
United Kingdom	1.7	1.4
United States	1.8	1.1
West Germany	2.6	2.0

NOTE: Compound rates.
SOURCE: U.S. Department of Labor, Bureau of Labor Statistics, Office of Productivity and Technology, unpublished data, May 1985.

nomic growth would increase if the United States relied more on consumption taxes and less on income taxes. Major factors that would contribute to faster growth are (1) the reduced bias against saving and (2) efficiency gains as capital was reallocated from low-return to high-return projects. Research by Don Fullerton of the U.S. Treasury Department, John Whalley of the University of Western Ontario, and John Shoven of Stanford suggests that replacing the current U.S. income tax with a personal consumption tax integrated with corporate income taxes would bring about increased personal saving and faster economic growth.[14] Shoven believes that the effects of such a policy shift would probably include increased saving, a higher capital-to-labor ratio, and higher real wage rates.

A similar conclusion about the welfare gains from shifting toward a consumption tax system was reached by Dale Jorgenson and Kun-Young Yun of Harvard.[15] They find that replacing taxes on income from capital with a consumption tax would produce dramatic gains in social welfare in the United States. A revenue-neutral consumption tax that permitted expensing of investment would have increased the value of U.S. private national wealth by about 26 percent during the 1980–1985 period, because the capital stock would be larger and capital assets would be worth more when taxed at a lower rate.

The success of Japan may in part be due to its having a tax structure with many of the characteristics of a consumption-based system. A recent study by John Shoven notes that Japan allows four types of tax-free savings accounts for individuals: postal savings accounts; small savings tax-exemption accounts (bank deposits, mutual funds); tax-free central and local government bonds; and pension and home equity savings accounts.[16] A family of four can legally accumulate $244,000 in these accounts, and there is evidence that many families have more accounts than are legally allowed.

The Japanese tax code includes other saving incentives for the individual: the taxation of dividend income separately from other income at a rate of 35 percent (the maximum on ordinary income is 70 percent); a 10 percent tax credit on dividends received applied against personal tax liability; eligibility of interest income on ordinary deposits, which is not sheltered in tax-free accounts, for a separate tax rate of 20 percent; exclusion of capital gains on securities from tax; and nondeductibility of consumer interest expenditures from taxable income. Another factor that encourages personal saving is that the purchase of a house requires a 30–40 percent down payment (and houses cost more in Japan than in the United States).

In addition to the individual saving incentives and consumption disincentives, the corporate income tax in Japan is lower for income paid out as dividends. Intercorporate dividends are completely excluded from tax, and debt capital is deductible at the corporate level and very lightly taxed at the personal level. Shoven's study shows that the combined individual and corporate tax provisions mean that Japan is, in effect, on a consumed income tax system that gives it a lower effective tax rate on new investment (22 percent in 1985) than that of the United States (31 percent).

Consumption Taxes and Deficit Reduction. Although reduced spending may be preferable to increased taxes to meet the goal of shrinking federal deficits, a consumption tax such as a VAT or sales tax is preferable to higher income taxes. As McLure notes, "That the economic effects of the VAT are rather bland—we might call it a vanilla tax—is one of its chief advantages. After all, the primary purpose of taxation . . . should be to raise revenue, not to change economic behavior.[17] Income taxes, in contrast, "distort choices of methods of finance (especially debt-equity ratios and dividend payout rates . . .), choices of business organization (corporate versus noncorporate forms of organization), choices of production technology (capital- versus labor-intensive methods of production), and consumption decisions (corporate versus noncorporate products)."[18]

Consumption Tax Alternatives. McLure clearly describes the similarities and differences among the major consumption taxes being discussed today. These include the VAT, a federal retail sales tax, Senator Roth's business transfer tax, the Hall-Rabushka variation on a VAT, and energy taxes.

Politically, a federal retail sales tax would probably have the greatest chance of enactment, followed by a BTT and a VAT, particularly if the goal is deficit reduction. As McLure reports, the 1984 survey by the Advisory Commission on Intergovernmental Relations found that if taxes must be raised substantially, a national sales tax (with exemption for food and similar necessities) was preferred over an increase in income taxes by a substantial margin.[19] The public's familiarity with state and local sales taxes also makes a federal sales tax more palatable. McLure offers sharp criticism of Senator Roth's BTT, particularly of its use of the subtraction method, offset for FICA taxes, small-business exemption, and multiple exclusions. In all fairness, Senator Roth's proposal is a well-intentioned attempt to make the VAT politically viable.

The Hall-Rabushka VAT is an elegant tax reform proposal. Because it would reduce the bias toward consumption in the tax code, it would stimulate more rapid economic growth. Politically, its time may have passed, since the Tax Reform Act of 1986 has co-opted its desirable goal of lower tax rates but ignored its much improved tax base.

McLure's discussion of energy tax options clearly points out the inequities and anticompetitive effects of such taxes. Higher energy prices would hinder the efforts of U.S. manufacturers to compete both at home and abroad. As politicians become more sensitive to trade issues, they may be less inclined to favor energy taxes to reduce the deficit.

International Trade and Consumption Taxes. Why do most industrialized countries have a VAT? It makes sense. Our largest trading partner, Canada, is now seriously considering the addition of a VAT to its fiscal arsenal.

U.S. politicians of all stripes eagerly embrace policies that they believe will increase exports and reduce imports. The reason for this seemingly irrational behavior (irrational because it means fewer goods for domestic consumption) is their desire to retain high-paying manufacturing jobs for their constituents. Because a VAT or retail sales tax would be rebated on exports and imposed on imports, politicians instinctively believe that it would make U.S. exports more attractive in world markets than higher corporate income taxes.

In his excellent review of the literature on the incidence of the corporate income tax, McLure appears to offer support for the politicians' instinctive belief that a VAT would help U.S. international competitiveness if it were substituted for the corporate income tax. The corporate income tax, he notes,

> is likely to produce a shift in the relative prices of corporate and noncorporate output and a reallocation of capital from the corporate to the noncorporate sector. This drives down the return to noncorporate investors and partially restores the return to corporate investment. As a result the tax is borne by all owners of capital, not just by shareholders. Moreover, it induces a shift in the relative prices of corporate and noncorporate output, making the former relatively more expensive. Second, by depressing capital formation, the tax reduces the productivity of labor and thus is borne in part by workers.[20]

Thus, McLure concludes, reducing the corporate income tax should help American industrial competitiveness.[21]

McLure's analysis of the possible beneficial consequences of replacing part of the corporate income tax with a consumption tax leads to the conclusion that if taxes must be raised for deficit reduction, a

173

VAT or a retail sales tax would be less detrimental than higher income taxes.

Myths and Realities about Consumption Taxes

Consumption taxes such as a VAT have come under attack in the media and in political circles for being unfair and unworkable.

- Liberals oppose the VAT on the grounds of regressivity.
- Conservatives fear the VAT as a "money machine."
- Both liberals and conservatives worry that a VAT would be inflationary.
- State and local officials are concerned about a VAT's intrusion into their traditional preserve for raising revenue.
- Both federal and state officials fear that the VAT would be an administrative nightmare.

Myth No. 1: A Consumption Tax Is Inevitably Regressive. Historically, commentators have shared the view that because most saving is done by middle- and upper-income persons, a consumption tax is regressive. The commentators base their conclusion on tax incidence studies that rely on annual rather than lifetime income, because government data on income and consumption are annual.[22] As Edgar Browning and William Johnson explain, using annual data imparts a systematic bias to consumption-income statistics because many people in the lowest income class are there for only a brief period. In addition, factors such as unemployment or illness may temporarily cause a person to fall into a lower income class. Browning and Johnson conclude that the relation between consumption and income for longer periods than a year should be used in tax incidence studies.[23]

Recent research by James Davies, France St. Hilaire, and John Whalley on the distributional effects of taxes over the lifetime of Canadian taxpayers has come to different conclusions from those of analysts using annual data.[24] The variation in ratios of consumption to income among income classes is smaller for lifetime calculations than for annual calculations, a result that is consistent with numerous other studies on the life cycle of saving and consumption. The implication of this result is that the lifetime measure of the distributional effect of consumption-based taxes that are assumed to be passed forward to consumers is substantially less regressive than the annual measure.

The estimated distributional effects of Canadian sales and excise taxes under both annual and lifetime incidence assumptions are shown in table 4. When tax burdens are computed at a single time, taxpayers in the lowest income class (decile 1) paid 27.2 percent of their income in sales and excise taxes while high-income taxpayers (decile 10) paid only 8.5 percent. In contrast, when tax burdens are computed over the taxpayers' lifetime, low-income taxpayers paid 15.0 percent of their income in sales and excise taxes, and high-income recipients paid 12.4 percent. Comparable estimates for the United States could be expected to produce the same distributional results. The annual and lifetime effects are strikingly different, the annual estimates showing much greater regressivity of consumption taxes than the lifetime estimates, which are only mildly regressive.[25]

The lifetime incidence argument is an important one that should be introduced into the debate on any taxes, particularly the VAT, because the annual and lifetime incidence measurements would be so greatly different. The fact that consumption patterns, or ratios of income to consumption, do not vary greatly over a lifetime among wealthy, middle-class, and lower-income individuals, if better understood by policy makers, would help remove one of the stumbling blocks to a constructive dialogue on consumption taxes.

Furthermore, proponents of a consumption tax are not calling for the replacement of the U.S. income tax with a VAT or retail sales tax. They advocate a consumption tax as an addition to our federal fiscal structure for reasons of deficit reduction and tax policy.

TABLE 4

SALES AND EXCISE TAXES AS PERCENTAGE OF ANNUAL AND
LIFETIME INCOME, CANADIAN HOUSEHOLDS, BY INCOME DECILE

Decile	Annual Incidence	Lifetime Incidence
1	27.2	15.0
2	20.3	14.3
3	15.8	14.1
4	14.6	13.9
5	14.0	13.8
6	13.4	13.5
7	13.5	13.6
8	13.2	13.3
9	12.8	13.2
10	8.5	12.4

NOTE: Decile 1 is lowest income class, decile 10 highest.
SOURCE: Davies, Hilaire, and Whalley, "Some Calculations of Lifetime Tax Incidence," p. 643.

There are, as McLure describes, several ways to offset the regressivity of a consumption tax. Among the most politically attractive are differential rates for necessities such as food and health care, zero rating (rather than exemption) for necessities, and refundable tax credits for low-income individuals. Refundable tax credits are used by several states, including New Mexico, Hawaii, Idaho, Vermont, Wyoming, and South Dakota, to help residents offset the payment of state sales taxes. Refundability means that residents need not have any state tax liability to receive a cash refund. State tax officials report that refundable tax credits seem not to have significantly increased administrative costs even though residents who would not have filed tax returns have been drawn into the system to claim refunds.[26]

Myth No. 2: The VAT Is a "Money Machine." Conservatives fear that instituting a VAT or a retail sales tax would be as risky as turning over the wine cellar key to an alcoholic. They worry that the federal government might go on a spending spree because of the VAT's great revenue potential.

Although some critics, such as Henry Aaron, give credence to this fear, other scholars, such as Jacob Stockfisch, suggest otherwise. Stockfisch's examination of the data shows that while government spending has increased noticeably more in the VAT countries than in the non-VAT countries, the VAT countries also had greater reductions in surpluses and greater increases in deficits than the non-VAT countries. That is, the greater increased government spending on the part of VAT countries was financed by reduced government surpluses or increased deficits to a greater extent than in non-VAT countries. VAT countries were big government spenders when they introduced the VAT. They have continued to be so, in part through increased reliance on deficit spending.[27] An additional way to ensure that a VAT does not provide a honey pot for federal spending would be to adopt a constitutional amendment to limit increases in the original rate.

Myth No. 3: The VAT Is Highly Inflationary. The European experience with the introduction of a VAT, as McLure so thoroughly documents, suggests an effect on prices, although it need not be large. There may very well be a price increase when a VAT is introduced, but it is only a one-time occurrence. If a VAT were used to replace part of the individual and corporate income tax, the effect on prices would probably be small, especially if the rate were only 2 or 3 percent. Added to the current system, a low-rate VAT would have only a one-time effect on prices if the transition were properly handled.

176

Myth No. 4: The Consumption Tax Is the Traditional Preserve of State and Local Governments. The sales tax area is often considered the special revenue preserve of state and local governments. If a VAT or a national sales tax were levied at the retail stage, state and local governments might very well complain that it was an invasion of their fiscal turf. With the Reagan era cutbacks in federal categorical and general revenue sharing, local and state governments are more than ever concerned about their own tax bases.

There are, however, ways to accommodate the needs of the state and local governments if a VAT or national sales tax is imposed. First, some of the additional tax receipts might be allocated to the states. Second, the Tax Reform Act of 1986, with its broadened tax base on which state and local governments can piggyback, will be a boon to their fiscal situation. With the expected increase in revenues, state government officials might feel less constrained today than in the past if a low-rate VAT or retail sales tax became part of the picture. From a political standpoint, a VAT may seem less intrusive to state and local officials than a national sales tax.

Myth No. 5: The VAT Is an Administrative Nightmare. Critics charge that a new consumption tax would be costly to implement and administer. McLure cites the Treasury Department's estimate that a VAT would require 20,000 additional employees and cost about $700 million per year and that implementation would take about eighteen months.[28]

Aaron notes that the degree of compliance with the European VAT and the cost of administering it seem to depend both on whether businesses are accustomed to keeping good written records and on the share of GNP generated by small businesses.[29] Experience in the United States and abroad suggests that with careful planning, particularly a minimum of exclusions and exemptions, the consumption tax need not become an unmanageable burden. Given that the VAT has been in use in the European Economic Community for about twenty years and that Japan and Canada are considering adopting it, the United States would presumably not find administrative problems insurmountable.

Conclusion

In conclusion, the yet to be unleashed politics of the Tax Reform Act of 1986, combined with the economics of an increasingly competitive world marketplace, may very well make the VAT or a broad-based consumption tax the next frontier of U.S. economic policy.

Notes

1. See chap. 2 in this volume.
2. Ibid.
3. See chap. 4.
4. See Roger Brinner and Jesse Abraham of Data Resources, "Tax Reform Requires Gramm-Rudman-Hollings" (Testimony before Joint Economic Committee, September 15, 1986); Wharton Econometrics, "Economic Impact of the Tax Reform Act of 1986," October 1986; Lawrence Chimerine of Chase Econometrics, statement before Joint Economic Committee, September 12, 1986; and Joel L. Prakken of L. H. Meyer & Associates, "The Macroeconomics of Tax Reform" (Paper prepared for "The Consumption Tax: A Better Alternative?" a conference sponsored by the American Council for Capital Formation Center for Policy Research, September 1986).
5. Advisory Commission on Intergovernmental Relations, *Changing Public Attitudes on Government and Taxes*, 1985.
6. A 1984 survey conducted by ACIR showed that sales taxes were preferred to income taxes by 32 percent of the public; only 7 percent preferred higher income taxes. A private survey also found that Americans prefer sales taxes to income taxes by a substantial margin if additional tax revenue is needed. The poll, which consisted of 2,500 telephone interviews with a cross section of the voting-age population, asked, "If the federal government had to raise taxes substantially, should a new national sales tax be instituted, or should federal income taxes be raised?" By a margin of more than two to one, respondents preferred a sales tax (Market Opinion Research, *U.S. National Survey: The Federal Deficit and Tax Policy*, August 1984).
7. In fact, recent analysis suggests that the American public's support of tax reform is only lukewarm. As William Schneider notes: "Tax reform did not get through Congress on a wave of popular pressure, the public had to be brought along. Even now, it gives only wary approval to what Congress has done" ("Americans Still Wary on Tax Reform," *National Journal*, July 12, 1986, p. 1740–44). Kevin Phillips observes: "Poll evidence continues to mount that the tax bill just passed by the Senate amounts to an elite bandwagon without a grassroots cheering section" (*American Political Report*, June 27, 1986, p. 4).
8. See chap. 5.
9. *Bureau of National Affairs Daily Tax Report*, May 21, 1986, p. LL-1.
10. Lawrence H. Summers, "Issues in National Savings Policy," in F. Gerard Adams and Susan M. Wachter, eds., *Savings and Capital Formation: The Policy Options* (Lexington, Mass.: Lexington Books, D.C. Heath, 1986), p. 65.
11. Benjamin M. Friedman, "Managing the U.S. Government Deficit in the 1980s," in Michael L. Wachter and Susan M. Wachter, eds., *Removing Obstacles to Economic Growth* (Philadelphia: University of Pennsylvania Press, 1984), p. 266.
12. Michael J. Boskin and John M. Roberts, "A Closer Look at Saving Rates in the United States and Japan," American Enterprise Institute, Working Paper no. 9, June 1986.

13. Lawrence H. Summers, "IRA's Really Do Spark New Savings," *New York Times*, May 25, 1986.

14. Don Fullerton, John B. Shoven, and John Whalley, "Replacing the U.S. Income Tax with a Progressive Consumption Tax: A Sequenced General Equilibrium Approach," *Journal of Public Economics*, vol. 20 (February 1983).

15. Dale W. Jorgenson and Kun-Young Yun, "Tax Policy and Capital Allocation," Harvard Institute of Economic Research Discussion Paper no. 1107, November 1984.

16. John B. Shoven, "A Comparison of the Taxation of Capital Income in the United States and Japan" (Prepared for the Coalition for Jobs, Growth, and International Competitiveness, September 1985).

17. See chap. 4.

18. Ibid.

19. See chap. 5.

20. See chap. 4.

21. Ibid.

22. Edgar K. Browning and William R. Johnson, *The Distribution of the Tax Burden* (Washington, D.C.: American Enterprise Institute, 1979), p. 25.

23. Ibid.

24. James Davies, France St. Hilaire, and John Whalley, "Some Calculations of Lifetime Tax Incidence," *American Economic Review* (September 1984).

25. Policy Economics Group (formerly de Seve Economics Associates), "Distributional Impact of a Business Transfer Tax," February 1986, p. 14.

26. Based on research by John Due and John L. Mikesell and telephone interviews with state tax officials conducted by Margo Thorning, chief economist, American Council for Capital Formation. See John F. Due and John L. Mikesell, *Sales Taxation* (Baltimore: Johns Hopkins University Press, 1983), chap. 3.

27. Jacob A. Stockfisch, "Value-added Taxes and the Size of Government: Some Theory and Some Evidence" (Paper prepared for "The Consumption Tax: A Better Alternative?" a conference sponsored by the American Council for Capital Formation Center for Policy Research, September 1986).

28. U.S. Department of the Treasury, *Tax Reform for Fairness, Simplicity, and Economic Growth*, vol. 3, *Value Added Tax* (November 1984), p. 113.

29. Henry Aaron, ed., *The Value-added Tax: Lessons from Europe* (Washington, D.C.: Brookings Institution, 1981), p. 8.

Index

Addition method, 5, 8 n.6, 16, 92, 94–96, 137
Administrative costs and feasibility, 60
  energy tax, 63
  excise taxes, 65
  exemption and zero rating, 72–75
  food sales tax, 124
  motor fuels tax, 64
  preretail taxes, 108
  services tax, 127
  VAT, 23, 48, 66, 71, 177
Advisory Commission on Inter-governmental Relations, 66, 167, 172
Africa, 119
Agriculture. *See* Farming
Annuities, 148 n.46. *See also* Insurance services
Appreciated property, 132, 134
Australia, 119
Austria, 44

Balance of payments, 40
Belgium, 44, 46
Border tax adjustments (BTAs), 31, 39, 47
  addition method, 96
  business transfer tax, 6, 86–88
  differential rates, 83–84
  energy tax, 63
  Hall-Rabushka personal-exemption VAT, 91
  preretail taxes, 108
  retail sales tax, 106
  subtraction-method VAT, 79–81, 83–84, 161
  turnover taxes, 111, 114 n.21
  VAT mechanism, 17–20
Budget deficit
  concern over, 10–11, 168
  revenue sources to reduce, 3–4, 11–12, 166–67, 172
Business transfer tax (BTT), 1, 5, 71, 115, 160
  assessment, 67–69, 81, 86, 163, 172
  FICA offset, 6–7, 69, 86–88

  mechanism, 6–7, 16, 117–23
  tax base, 32

Canada, 113 n.18, 119, 155, 167, 169, 170, 173
Capital goods, 91–94, 104–5, 162
Children's clothing, 44
Children's services, 116
Clubs and fraternal organizations, 22
Competitiveness. *See* International competitiveness
Construction industry, 128
Consumption-based tax, 11, 18, 31. *See also* Value-added tax
Corporate income tax, 39
  incidence, 48–50
  VAT substitution for part of, 2, 28, 30, 41–42, 162, 173–74
Credit method, 4, 5, 71, 72
  business transfer tax, 117–22
  differential rates, 81–82, 84
  exemption and zero rating, 72–75
  financial services tax, 135–38
  food sales, 124–25
  income-based VAT, 92
  mechanism, 16–17, 160
  real estate VAT, 129
  used goods VAT, 133–34

Debtor status of United States, 10
Deficit Reduction Act of 1984, 114 n.19
Denmark, 44, 46
Destination-principle tax, 7, 18, 31, 91
Differential rates, 5
  subtraction-method VAT, 81–85
Distributional equity, 60
  Hall-Rabushka personal-exemption VAT, 38
  motor fuels tax, 64–65
  oil import fee, 61–62
  oil tax, 63
  preretail taxes, 108
  services tax, 126

181

American Enterprise Institute for Public Policy Research

SELECTED AEI PUBLICATIONS

Who Should Pay for Collecting Taxes? Financing the IRS, C. Eugene Steuerle (1986, 75 pp., cloth $15.75, paper $6.00)

Exchange Rate Targets: Desirable or Disastrous? John H. Makin, ed. (1986, 59 pp., $6.00)

U.S. Fiscal Policy—Its Effects at Home and Abroad, John H. Makin (1986, 54 pp., $7.00)

Essays in Contemporary Economic Problems: The Impact of the Reagan Program, Phillip Cagan, ed. (1986, 362 pp., cloth $24.50, paper $13.50)

Crisis in the Budget Process: Exercising Political Choice, Allen Schick, with papers by David Stockman, Rudolph Penner, Trent Lott, Leon Panetta, and Norman Ornstein (1986, 88 pp., $7.00)

Protectionism: Trade Policy in Democratic Societies, Jan Tumlir (1985, 72 pp., $7.00)

Real Tax Reform: Replacing the Income Tax, John H. Makin, ed. (1985, 42 pp., $5.00)

- **For books,** *mail orders to:* AMERICAN ENTERPRISE INSTITUTE, 4720 Boston Way, Lanham, MD 20706 ● Or call (301) 459-3366. Make checks payable to UPA.

AEI PERIODICALS

Public Opinion, Seymour Martin Lipset and Ben J. Wattenberg, co-editors, is a bimonthly magazine that explores public opinion on a broad range of social and public policy questions. It combines feature articles with a special twenty-page roundup of data from major polling organizations.

$5.00 per issue/$26.00 for one year/$48.00 for two

The AEI Economist, a monthly newsletter, edited and often written by Herbert Stein, provides clear and objective analysis of a wide range of economic issues and an evaluation of future trends. *The AEI Economist* is designed to appeal to the economic expert and to the layman.

$2.50 per issue/$24.00 for one year/$44.00 for two

- **For periodicals,** *mail orders to:* AMERICAN ENTERPRISE INSTITUTE, 1150 Seventeenth Street, N.W., Washington, D.C. 20036. Make checks payable to AEI.